W9-BVE-151

ANGEL COURAGE

Also by Terry Lynn Taylor
Messengers of the Light
Guardians of Hope
Answers from the Angels
Creating with the Angels
The Alchemy of Prayer
Angel Days
The Angel Experience

By Mary Beth Crain
The Tao of Negotiation (with Joel Edelman)
The Best of L.A.

By Terry Lynn Taylor and Mary Beth Crain
Angel Wisdom

ANGEL
Courage

365 MEDITATIONS AND INSIGHTS
TO GET US THROUGH HARD TIMES

Terry Lynn Taylor
& Mary Beth Crain

HarperSanFrancisco
A Division of HarperCollinsPublishers

ANGEL COURAGE: *365 Meditations and Insights to Get Us Through Hard Times.* Copyright © 1999 by TERRY LYNN TAYLOR & MARY BETH CRAIN. All rights reserved. Printed in the United States of America. No part of this book may be used or reproduced in any manner whatsoever without written permission except in the case of brief quotations embodied in critical articles and reviews. For information address HarperCollins Publishers, 10 East 53rd Street, New York, NY 10022.

HarperCollins books may be purchased for educational, business, or sales promotional use. For information please write: Special Markets Department, HarperCollins Publishers, 10 East 53rd Street, New York, NY 10022.

HarperCollins Web Site: http://www.harpercollins.com

HarperCollins®, ■®, and HarperSanFrancisco™ are trademarks of HarperCollins Publishers, Inc.

FIRST EDITION

Designed by Laura Lindgren

Library of Congress Cataloging-in-Publication Data

Taylor, Terry Lynn
　　Angel courage : 365 meditations and insights to get us through hard times / Terry Lynn Taylor & Mary Beth Crain.
　　　　p.　cm.
　　Includes index.
　　ISBN 0-06-251583-7 (pbk.)
　　　1. Angels—Meditations.　2. Devotional calendars.　I. Crain, Mary Beth.　II. Title.
BL477.T36　1999
291.4' 32—dc21　　　　　　　　　　　　　　　　　　　　　　　98–55301

　　01　02　03　HADD　10　9　8　7　6　5　4　3

ACKNOWLEDGMENTS

The greatest blessing about coauthoring with Mary Beth is that she is one of the best friends anyone could have. We have been through a lot together in the last eleven years, and we agree that to approach life with angel consciousness brings infinite blessings and takes a special kind of courage and, most important for us, humor! Shared laughter and an eccentric take on life rule our friendship and in turn make life much more palatable.

The following friends came to my rescue when ideas were running thin, my sense of humor was in jeopardy, and my emotions were taking on a life of their own during the writing of this book. I am so blessed to have the following ultra-fun and creative people in my life. Thank you for all the great ideas and champion-ship: Jai Italiaander, Shannon Mroczkowski, Lisa Rome, Ellen Blake, Janet Harris, Holly Phillips, Peter Sterling, Michael Bennett, Geoffrey Menin, Ken Kalb, Tony Gwilliam, and Ed Wortz.

TERRY LYNN TAYLOR

— ❋ —

I would like to thank Sant Kaur Khalsa, Joanna Rice, and Steven Vance for providing inspirations for some of the meditations I wrote. I would also like to thank a few of my angelic helpers, among them Adam, George, and Arthur, for giving me fresh daily insights and awarenesses. Another thanks to our editor, Karen Levine, for having an angelically broad perspective on the concept of time when it came to manuscript deadlines and for her unwavering encouragement. And I'd like to thank Terry Lynn for being, as usual, a wonderful collaborator and friend.

MARY BETH CRAIN

We often discover the angels when we are in pain and when we have been faced with loss. The majority of those who have found comfort in our previous books are looking for a way to make sense of a painful situation and to stay closer to God in the process. *Angel Courage* takes a new approach to the idea of misfortune. It devotes an entire year's worth of daily meditations to concepts that are ordinarily defined as painful, uncomfortable, or tragic, offering a fresh and hopeful perspective intended to help you discern the deeper meaning behind pain and a "way out" that is, at the same time, a way in.

Angel Courage is really a greeting card from the angels. We look at the word *greet* as a means of being open to whatever comes our way. The Jungians use the word *greet* in its creative context, as embracing the whole picture, not simply getting locked into one aspect of it. Traditionally we have been taught that trials are something either to get through as quickly as possible, to suffer with if they can't be "cured," or to avoid altogether. But when we greet our trials instead of fighting them, running from them, or simply enduring them, we learn to communicate with and learn from our pain. When we greet something, we are recognizing it, responding to it, welcoming it. So, here we stand with ourselves, on the ground with the angels, our fears, and our humanness, willing to welcome and learn from whatever is in front of us. In the process, a greeting can change the chemistry of a situation, transforming pain into challenge, fear into courage, despair into hope.

We hope that *Angel Courage* will help you stay grounded in the midst of turmoil and stand your ground instead of trying to avoid, escape, or deny what is happening to you. It is a book about the way of humility, for the word *humility* comes from *humus,* or ground. It is only when we are totally down that we can go up. It is only when we are broken that we can be mended and healed. Instead of treating the angels as beings from above, *Angel Courage* explores the idea of meeting the angels where we are—especially when we are thrown to the ground, feeling as though we might never be able to get up again. This is when we connect with the humus—the earth, our roots, our humility. This is where we discover that when we surrender to our humanness, we are suddenly connected to our creativity. There is usually a positive side to seemingly negative events. Through these meditations, we hope that you will discover how loss can give you the freedom needed to find out who you really are and how you can create your own blessings by making use of your many interior resources.

Angel Courage does not try to give absolute answers, new age formulas for success, explanations, or false hope. Rather, we want to give you a means of staying awake in the midst of pain and of overcoming any fears that may be paralyzing you. By reading the book each day, you can download an ounce of courage into your psyche, so that when and if the day comes that you are there in the fire, facing a particularly challenging situation, you can instantly pull up your "courage file" and aim it in the best direction.

Above all, *Angel Courage* stresses the fact that the angels can't always change a situation or relieve us of pain. They cannot bring back something that has been lost forever. But they can provide the comfort and insight that sustain us in our loss and lead us to new awareness and, eventually, to the space of joy once more.

ANGEL COURAGE

ANGEL WARRIORS

An Angel Reminder: **And the truth shall make you free.**

The angel warrior is the embodiment of integrity. His or her mission is to reveal and uphold the truth, not as an act of virtue but as a way of life. It's often uncomfortable to confront the truth, let alone uphold it, which is why angel warriors are rare beings. The reason most of us have not yet become angel warriors is because we fear rejection or confrontation or just plain loss. Sometimes upholding the truth can cost us a lot, in terms of relationships, jobs, even our freedom. It seems so much easier not to make waves, to stifle our integrity in favor of maintaining the comfortable status quo. But in reality, when we are not true to ourselves we lose our freedom, condemning ourselves to the prison of fear. Any of us can become an angel warrior, if we're willing to let go of our fear of what might happen if we stick up for our principles and our true feelings. The angels are always ready to give us the courage to know ourselves and, even more important, to love ourselves, no matter what mistakes we might have made. Angel warriors are not perfect; they are just honest. They know that true strength comes from love and true power from the willingness to accept one's true self and to reveal that self to the world without fear.

Can you say that you are living with integrity? Are your actions and your lifestyle in alignment with your beliefs and values? Or are there times when you are afraid to stick up for the truth? If you feel that there are areas of your life in which you're not honoring the truth, realize that you may have been mistaking avoidance for safety.

An Angelic Reflection: **I know that confrontation is not the head-on collision of opposing forces but rather the acknowledgment of responsibility in the service of truth.**

IT'S MY PARTY

An Angel Reminder: "It's my party and I'll cry
if I want to . . . cry if I want to . . . cry if I want to. . . ."

Leslie Gore, "It's My Party"

If you're over forty you certainly remember the above hit of the early sixties. In this song, the "heroine" throws a tantrum at her own birthday
party when her boyfriend, Johnny, goes off with her rival, Judy. This little
soap opera soared to the top of the charts, and you can still hear it on
oldies stations all the time, which means that it's become a true fixture in
the mass unconsciousness. Of course there had to be a sequel, which was
the triumphant "Judy's Turn to Cry," in which our protagonist gleefully
proclaims, "Well now it's Judy's turn to cry . . . Judy's turn to cry . . . 'cause
Johnny's come back to me!" What do you suppose the angels are thinking
when such small-minded sagas become the melodies by which we live our
lives? They undoubtedly would say, yes, it certainly is your party and you
can certainly cry if you want to. But pity parties usually end up with only
one guest. The angels hope that we'd think enough of ourselves to
demand real loyalty in love. They assure us that if we want to be crybabies
we can go right ahead—but they won't be coming to our party.

*What do you think of crybabies? What do you think of people who gloat when someone else is
doing the crying? The next time you're tempted to be a crybaby over something you've created
for yourself, imagine the angels standing there watching you. If the situation starts to seem so
ridiculous it's embarrassing, there's a good chance that's because it is.*

An Angelic Reflection: I would rather laugh than cry about my life.

IF IT FEELS GOOD

An Angel Reminder: **If it feels like God, do it.**

There used to be a saying in the late sixties and early seventies: "If it feels good, do it." We have spent a good part of this century indulging in what makes us feel good, and we have had more than a few of these indulgences backfire and cause a lot of grief. We need a new view, one that comes from the angels. They offer us a look at human life that comes from above, yet they ask us to ground our experience in the Earth. Our senses are the way we interact with the world around us and with the Earth. It is time for many of us to be more sensible, more grounded in our common sense. Then we can see what it means to be a human beyond the notion of feeling good or simply seeking pleasure.

Although pleasure seeking can be fun, there is usually a price to pay if we go too far with it. But there is a way to be attuned to our senses and to the angels at the same time: we can have sensual interactions in a spiritual way. Turn your senses toward a spiritual source, and you will have a heightened perception of beauty and joy. In those ecstatic moments you can feel God awakening each of your senses with a love that washes all the dross away.

An Angelic Reflection: **I will open my senses to the spiritual sustenance of the angels.**

IMPOSSIBLE STANDARDS

An Angel Reminder: Sometimes the impossible *is* impossible.

Part of being a happy person is knowing your limits and not getting bent out of shape over what you can't do. This also tends to make those around you happy, too. When we set impossible standards for ourselves we tend to set them for others as well, making the world an exhausting and unrewarding place for everybody. God and the angels don't set impossible standards for us—what would be the point? Unlike insecure humans, they are not control freaks who have to either do or demand the impossible in order to feel okay. Instead, they love us for who we are and where we're at, and they would be very pleased if we would do the same.

Do you set impossible standards for yourself, like unreasonable or unreachable deadlines or achievements that are simply beyond your capabilities? If so, what do you think you're accomplishing? Are these impossible standards really yours, or were they instilled in you at an early age by parents or other authority figures? When we set the bar too high, we force ourselves to fall. Do you think you might be setting yourself and others up for failure? Ask the angels to help you appreciate your strengths and to understand that there is no shame in having limits.

An Angelic Reflection: I know and accept my limits and am learning how to work effectively within them.

BROKEN RULES

An Angel Reminder: **Rules are made to be broken.**

Rules, according to the dictionary, are an authoritative direction for conduct or procedure, a regulation, and a statement that describes what is true in most or all cases. But rules can become a problem pretty quickly, and some of them are made to be broken. When we assign rules for love, for instance, we are calling in the tricksters. If you or your company makes a rule that you cannot date someone you work with, most likely you will want to date one of your colleagues! What if you are working with your true love, but your rules say you cannot be in love with that person or even go out with them? A book on rules and love that came out a few years ago caused quite an uproar. In this book you found step-by-step "authoritative direction" for *getting* married or for *getting* a lover. But when we're focused only on getting, we're likely to be mired in manipulating others. Manipulation is another reason humans make rules. The angels find that rules interfere in their loving guidance of humans.

It is good to remember that rules are different from natural or spiritual laws. Rules are human inventions, while natural laws come from what is real. If you want to be real and authentic, then look to God for self-governing wisdom. A rule, just by existing, may give energy to the opposite of what it is stating. If you are attracted to someone you work with, ask yourself, Am I truly interested in loving that person? Or is it the danger and risk of breaking a rule that attracts me? How far do rules interfere, guide, or challenge my everyday life?

An Angelic Reflection: **The angels want us to question authority, then follow love.**

MAKING IT DIFFICULT

An Angel Reminder: Life is tough enough without making it any harder.

Have you ever had the experience of making something more difficult than it needs to be? A lot of times we expect something to be difficult, and so we make it difficult. This is because we feel overwhelmed by it. The difficult thing becomes bigger than we are, and we cower in its shadow. The larger it looms, the farther from it we retreat, until it seems we have no recourse except to run or be swallowed whole. Once we begin to understand that it is our own mind that is projecting this monster onto the screen of our life, we can stop and begin to think of how to make what seems so difficult easy, just by changing our perception of it. If, for instance, we have an activity we're not looking forward to, like doing our taxes or going on a diet, we can adopt an attitude of positive expectation rather than dread. We can say, "I'm going to make my taxes interesting. I'm going to enjoy going through receipts and recalling the events and people associated with them." Or we can say, "I'm going to make losing weight a game of finding foods I can eat that I can really look forward to, and I'm going to feel nourished rather than deprived." The angels know that life isn't always easy—why make it harder when we don't have to?

In what ways do you make things more difficult than they should be? Do you adopt negative and self-defeating attitudes that automatically predispose you to failure? Do you fail to realize your strengths? Do you tend toward worry instead of trust? If there's something you have to do that you have been making difficult, the angels say, just start doing it. Day by day, bit by bit it will get done, as long as you don't put up obstacles in your path.

An Angelic Reflection: I don't go out of my way to look for problems.

HONEST MISERY

An Angel Reminder: "Honest misery if far more energizing than perky dishonesty born of defending something that wants to die."
Caroline Casey

One of the first things we may think of when we hear the word *misery* is that old saying "Misery loves company." It's easy to wallow in misery, and most of us do it from time to time. Think of the last time you were miserable. What did you do? Maybe the weather was hot and irritable so you called up a friend and you both shared how miserable you were. One reason we want to share our misery is to seek validation when we are suffering. Sharing misery can be a way of getting close to someone, but if it becomes the only point of connection more misery will be created. Misery is agony, suffering, physical pain, and discomfort—not the most desirable things in life. However, as the quote above says, it is better to be honest about our misery than to cover it over with a facade.

Sometimes just acknowledging our misery can help to change its chemistry. If we need to share misery, remember that the angels don't seek its company. However, they do want us to express ourselves and to do it with the intention of moving out of misery, perhaps even laughing at ourselves. Next time you are miserable, really play it up, and then let the angels transmute it.

An Angelic Reflection: I will be honest about the misery in my life and consciously avoid wallowing in it.

ANIMAL COURAGE

An Angel Reminder: **Animals possess the instinctive courage to live precisely as who they are.**

Animals have many virtues that humans tend to neglect. They live simply and do not take more than they need from the Earth in order to survive. They will sacrifice themselves for their young and many times, if they are domesticated, for their owners. They are not concerned about their looks or status, and they present themselves to the world without pretense. The angels suggest that we take a closer look at our animal friends and that we begin to learn from them. Native American culture believes that each animal has a different "medicine" for the problems and ills that beset human life and that we can ask them to give us doses of courage, resourcefulness, patience, and any other qualities we need in order to overcome obstacles and live balanced lives.

Think about which animals you are drawn to and why. What qualities do they have that might reflect your own strengths or desires? The next time an animal crosses your path, stop and try to connect with it, not as something separate from and inferior to you but as an equal before God. Note what the animal is and what qualities it possesses. See if it is telling you something. If you have a pet, try listening to it rather than telling it what to do. What messages do you get that might be relevant to your life at this time?

An Angelic Reflection: **I revere the uniqueness of all life forms, and I give thanks for being accepted as a member of the earthly family.**

WEARINESS

An Angel Reminder: "I am weary with my groaning; all the night make I my bed to swim; I water my couch with my tears."

Psalm 6:6 KJV

Weariness is different from tiredness. When we're tired we are physically exhausted, in need of a rest to restore us to balance. But when we're weary, we often feel oppressed by circumstances, to the point where we can't just go too sleep and wake up refreshed. Life may feel like a burden that seems too difficult to bear. But the angels don't necessarily regard weariness as negative. Rather, weariness may be God's way of bringing us closer to home, that is, to God. Many of the psalms speak of weariness, when the soul, not the body, just can't take another step. It is then that the psalmist really turns to God for a hand up. When we're weary, it is a signal to stop and take some time out for communion with our spirit, to ask it to show us the way home, toward not death but life.

If you are feeling weary, ask yourself what has to change in your life. What do you need to do differently in order to feel renewed strength and energy? Have you been working too hard? Are certain relationships getting you down? Have you been oppressed with worry? One definition of weary is "exhausted of tolerance and patience." You might want to ask the angels to airlift you a supply of these two invaluable virtues, which can do wonders to calm and center you.

An Angelic Reflection: I will use the opportunity of weariness to reevaluate my life and respond to the needs of my spirit.

THE MISSING PIECE

An Angel Reminder: **We are already whole,
even though we might not know it.**

Sometimes life feels incomplete, as though a vital piece of it is missing.
We are lonely, dissatisfied, frustrated. At these trying moments we are
easily conned into believing that if the missing piece could only be
found, the whole picture would fall into place and we would finally be
happy. If that perfect partner could just appear. If our spouse would just
stop drinking. If we could just win the lottery. . . . The interesting thing
about the missing piece is that it is always predicated on the word *if*—a
word that is dependent on the future, not the present. But God and the
angels are residents of the now, not the when. Unbeknownst to us, they
are the missing piece, and once we reconnect to them we discover that we
can live happily—not ever after, but in the moment.

*Are there pieces missing from your life? Do you believe that there's something or someone out
there who could make you feel complete and whole? How would that happen? What would
happen if that something or someone were taken away? Try calling on the angels to give you
help in completing the picture of your life and making yourself happy and fulfilled.*

An Angelic Reflection: **The more I tune in to divine wisdom, the more
complete I become.**

QUARRELS

An Angel Reminder: "A man has no time
to spend half his life in quarrels."
Abraham Lincoln

Quarrels are like tumors: they can be either benign or malignant. Sometimes quarreling is a useful pastime that helps to define positions or clarify issues. Debates are healthy, even productive, forms of quarreling. A
friendly quarrel over who's going to pay the bill at dinner certainly won't
disturb life on Earth as we know it. But when quarrels are deep and hos-
tile, they tend to spread like cancers, eating away at our lives and the lives
of those around us. The quarrelers are so attached to their own egos that
they lose all sense of compassion and perspective. Being right is more
important than being a loving, caring human being. Parents who are
always quarreling usually have a devastating effect on their children.
Nations that quarrel can have a devastating effect on the world. The
angels keep reminding us that what we do and say is a community affair,
whose repercussions are felt far beyond our limited individual sphere.
They urge us not to waste our precious time on resentment and hatred,
and they are waiting to give us the courage to view our issues with the
intention of keeping the torch of peace rather than the fires of war burning brightly.

*Do you have a quarrel with anyone? If so, is it long-standing? What do you have at stake
that causes you to cling to the quarrel rather than come to a negotiated peace? If the other
person is too intractable to be reasoned with, you can still end the quarrel by refusing to
participate.*

An Angelic Reflection: I prefer to put my energy into productive, not
destructive, activities.

BYGONES

An Angel Reminder: **Let bygones be bygones.**

A bygone is something belonging to the past. This means we don't own it anymore, unless we are living in the past. If we live in the past, we are missing the angels, for they are with us here and now. The angels will help us transform our connection with the past if we are willing to change and create something new. Many things are bygones. Look into your life here and now and take stock of *what is.* If you are holding onto the hopes and wishes of a bygone relationship, realize that right now that person is not in the room with you. If you are stuck in the endless loop of a bygone victimization, realize that right now you can choose to put the victimization behind you. As soon as the angels are alerted to a change you have made within, they bless you with more light and love, to guide your way into a new future.

Let past offenses stay where they belong—in the past. To help them stay in the past, we need to put some energy into forgiving past offenses. What bygones should you leave behind? Forgive them and move on.

An Angelic Reflection: **I ask the angels to open my heart and let forgiveness come in.**

OUT OF CONTROL

An Angel Reminder: **"The best way to control people is to encourage them to be mischievous."**
Shunryu Suzuki

It is awfully tempting to try to control others. We do it all the time, in subtle and not-so-subtle ways. We give advice on what to do and how to do it. We criticize and condemn. We use power and money as means of getting others to do what we want. Or, we may be more passive-aggressive in our methods, manipulating through complaining or guilt-tripping, or overwhelming someone with kindness in an unconscious—or conscious—attempt to make them feel obligated to us. But ironically, the more we let go of something, the more in control of it we are. When the Zen teacher Shunryu Suzuki talks of allowing people to be mischievous, he is saying, let others explore their own lives at their own pace. Let them make their own mistakes and their own discoveries. Just watch them; observe the process. In so doing we will come to realize that we cannot control anyone. All we can control is our need to be in control. When we let go of that need—when we allow ourselves to get out of the illusory mindset of control—then we are at last on the way of being in control of our mind, our most powerful ally.

Do you ever try to control others? If so, how and why? How do they respond? How do you feel when others try to control you? Try gradually letting go of the idea of having to have things a certain way in order for you to feel comfortable and secure. Begin to enjoy the sense of freedom that comes with not having to be in control.

An Angelic Reflection: **I seek to understand, not to control.**

Testing, Testing . . .

An Angel Reminder: **There is an entrance exam
to the school of higher consciousness.**

We've all taken tests. When we're prepared we do well on them. When we haven't done our homework our score nose-dives accordingly. If only the tests God gives us could be so predictably handled! Unfortunately, the greatest teacher of them all usually prefers to give surprise exams. In fact, they're such a surprise that half the time we don't even know we're taking them. The only preparation we can make for such little cosmic pop quizzes is to be living in as centered and conscious a way as possible. If our spiritual foundation is shaky or if we are taking direction from our egos rather than our souls, our scores will most likely suffer. But when we are strong in courage, faith, compassion, and ingenuity, we can pass any test God springs on us.

What tests has God given you lately? Have you responded with self-pity and despair? Or have you hauled out your arsenal of spiritual skills and met the tests with courage and hope? Remember, God's tests are neither power plays nor exercises in sadistic pleasure; they are given in the spirit of love.

An Angelic Reflection: **I welcome God's tests as a chance to sharpen my spiritual skills.**

THE PRIVILEGE OF GIVING

An Angel Reminder: **"It is in giving that we receive."**
The Peace Prayer

There's a charming Zen story about a rich merchant who decided to donate a large sum of money to a Zen master who needed a larger school. The master accepted the money without a thank-you, almost as if he were doing the merchant a favor. This irritated the merchant, who informed the master in no uncertain terms that he was giving him a very generous gift.

"Do you want me to thank you for it?" asked the master.

"You certainly should," replied the merchant.

"Why?" countered the master. "The giver should be thankful."

The angels love this story, for they are total givers whose thanks come in the form of our joy and newfound wisdom. They want us to give in the same spirit—not expecting thanks but being grateful for the chance to exercise the virtue of generosity and to witness the joy we bring to others.

When you give, do you expect thanks? Acknowledging a gift is the decent and mannerly thing to do, of course, but our Zen master was not being boorish; he was testing the merchant to see in what spirit his gift was given. The next time you give something, detach yourself from the need to receive thanks, and give thanks instead for the opportunity to return to the universe a fraction of what it has given to you.

An Angelic Reflection: **I delight in the process of giving.**

COLORLESS

**An Angel Reminder: The spirit expresses itself
through a colorful life.**

Sometimes life seems colorless, like an overcast day. Where's the excitement, the energy? Where's the sun or the rainbow? On colorless days we can do several things. We can crawl under the covers and not emerge until the sun comes out again. We can sit back and appreciate the grayness. Or, we can try to create our own color, using the paints of our own warmth and light. The angels want us to remember that color is relative and that overcast days can be a welcome respite from blaring brightness and too much activity. When things seem colorless and depressing, the angels encourage us to let the grayness do its own magic, giving us time to reflect upon things. When we become clearer about what's making us feel bored, blah, or just plain sad, we can start adding splashes of color to the day in small, courageously creative ways.

Whenever life seems colorless, think of it as a canvas waiting for colors to be added. You're the artist. Begin adding, one by one, colors that represent different aspects of your being. Each color is said to have psychological and spiritual significance; red, for instance, is symbolic of fire, passion, and creativity; yellow represents intellect as well as faith and joy; green signifies healing and a connection to the natural environment, and so on. It is interesting to observe what colors you are particularly attracted to, for they can indicate the needs and strengths of your soul and spirit.

An Angelic Reflection: I allow color into my life.

ROADBLOCKS

An Angel Reminder: **A block in the road often turns out to be a not-unfriendly visit from the unexpected.**

When you come to a block in the road, you have several alternatives. If it's a temporary block, one that will hold you up for a brief period, you can get frustrated and force your blood pressure up a few notches. Or, you can use the time to do things you haven't had time for, like going over your checkbook, listening to music, writing a journal entry, even just closing your eyes and sneaking in a little relaxation. If it's the kind of roadblock that requires a detour, you must take a new path, changing your plans. Or, if the road is completely impassable, you may just have to turn around and retrace your steps. All of us encounter blocks on our life road. Sometimes they force us to reel ourselves in, calm down, and reflect upon the situation. Sometimes they require us to be open enough to take a new course or approach. And sometimes we simply have to go back to the beginning and do it all over again. The angels know that these obstacles have been put in our path for reasons we often can't fathom. When we refuse to be paralyzed by roadblocks but instead allow the angels to guide us, we can rest assured in the knowledge that we'll always be moving ahead.

When you come to a block in your life road, see the angels waiting there to direct you. Ask them what sort of block it is and why it has been put there. Find out if you should wait it out, take another route, or turn back and face your problem anew.

An Angelic Reflection: **If there is a block on my life road, I look at the reason it has been put there and trust the angels to escort me through.**

MAKING WAVES

An Angel Reminder: "Agitate! Agitate! Agitate!"
Frederick Douglass

In our ordered, structured, and busy lives, it is often a great temptation not to make waves or rock the boat. Such disruptive action is usually considered detrimental to the smooth functioning of the well-oiled machine of society. But while a placid body of water can be a source of calmness and serenity, it can also become a stagnant pool if it is not periodically shaken up. When waves crash against the shore, disrupting the repose, the sea becomes a source of renewed energy—sometimes violent, sometimes exhilarating, but always necessary. If we take our cue from nature, it becomes evident that waves are as integral as stillness. Everything needs to be renewed once in a while—debris cleared out, energy shifted, the environment challenged and cleansed. This is part of the natural law.

When we have the courage to go against public apathy or denial and make waves, we are doing our part to keep our environment healthy and balanced. Are there areas in your life where you're afraid to make waves? Do you feel you need to make waves in your family, workplace, or community or that you wish to fight for clarity and change on a larger platform? Know that as long as we are committed to calling attention to injustice and fighting for changes that will uplift human consciousness, the angels will heartily support us.

An Angelic Reflection: **I am not a slave to the status quo.**

WHY ME?

An Angel Reminder: **Why not?**

Do you ever feel as though you've been personally singled out by the universe to receive an extra helping of misfortune? If so, take heart because that means you must be awfully important. Imagine one little human being meriting all that attention from the cosmos! Can't you just see God, checking her daily to-do list and saying, "Now let's see. There's been a 9.0 earthquake in the Philippines. India's ready to drop the bomb. All of Africa is starving . . . but that can wait. I have to deal with Miss Mary Jane Doe over here, who's got more trouble than anybody." The angels know that life often isn't easy and that sometimes it seems as though it couldn't get any worse. They also know that all of us have our share of tough times, our specific challenges designed to speed up our personal growth by testing our faith and making us stronger and more compassionate human beings. The angels find it particularly interesting that so often it seems to be those who have endured the most pain and sorrow who complain the least, inspiring everyone else with their courage and optimism.

Have you gotten what seem like some bad breaks that you don't deserve? If so, take some time out to look around and see how they compare to the bad breaks others have experienced. Now, make a list of both the bad and good breaks in your life at present. Are there any good breaks that started out as bad ones? Do things seem to balance out?

An Angelic Reflection: **I meet life's challenges with courage, not resentment.**

LETDOWNS

An Angel Reminder: **When you're down,
you can't go anyplace but up.**

Being alive means having to experience, at some time or another, let-downs. A job prospect falls through. A proposal is rejected. Someone falls short of our expectations. A dream is shattered. When we have a letdown it's a good chance to examine the conditions that led to it. Did we pin our hopes on an unrealistic goal? Did we put all our eggs in one basket? Did we project qualities onto another person that he or she simply didn't possess? Or perhaps we were justified in our hopes but the timing just wasn't right, or circumstances beyond our control intervened. The angels remind us that letdowns, however painful, are always temporary. More often than not, something better is in store for us if we allow events to unfold instead of trying to predict or control outcomes. When we have a letdown, we can explore the dream or goal that we had and decide whether it was realistic or in our best interest. If the answer is yes, we can then formulate alternative strategies to help us reach our goal.

Have you suffered any letdowns lately? How did you react? Did you let the letdowns get you down, or did you pick yourself up and move on from them? Have you let anyone down, including yourself? If so, why do you think it happened, and how can you restore your confidence in yourself and others' confidence in you?

An Angelic Reflection: **I try to make my expectations and goals as realistic as possible, and I try not to depend on any one thing for my happiness.**

LIFE IMITATING A COUNTRY SONG

An Angel Reminder: **"If you're gonna play the jukebox would you kindly keep it country / 'Cause I'm feelin' so lonely tonight."**
Vince Gill, "The Key"

If you find yourself in a sticky situation in life and you want a theme song to go with it, your local country music station has plenty of songs to choose from. Country music was once perceived as unsophisticated and banal, but today it is alive and well, and many so-called sophisticated people are singing along. Most country songs are about matters of the heart, and these matters are pretty darn universal. We often find ourselves playing out similar scenarios in our own lives. Our hearts get stomped on, our lovers leave us, and everything bad that could go wrong often does. When our lives resemble a country song, the angels encourage us to sing along. With the angels on lead vocals, we can harmonize our way into better circumstances.

Does your life seem like a bad country song? Next time you feel like your heart has been stepped on, try singing along. Ask the angels to take over the mike, and hear a different harmony developing.

An Angelic Reflection: **The angels bring a new song to my life.**

IMPOSSIBLE SITUATIONS

An Angel Reminder: **All things are possible to one who lets go.**

Sometimes we're faced with what seems like an impossible situation. Nothing we do or say makes it any better, and every time we think about it we only get angrier and more frustrated. When such an impasse presents itself to us, the angels have two remedies. One, let it be. And two, give it over to the universe. Back in the 1920s, the famous metaphysician Emmet Fox wrote a potent little pamphlet called *The Golden Key*, in which he suggested that whenever we're overwhelmed by a crisis we "golden key" it by giving the person or situation over to God to deal with. Fox had many seeming-miracle stories of debts that got paid, errant husbands returning to the family fold, a new job suddenly appearing to someone who'd lost theirs—all occurring soon after the sufferer simply visualized handing over the problem to God and then relaxed. Why would this simple little procedure work? Because when we release a burden, we also let go of its attendant stress and anguish. We become lighter, freer, easier to be around. Our energy becomes clearer and begins to attract what is positive toward us. Because we are less preoccupied with our problem, solutions are better able to get our attention, and they look more obvious. People gravitate to us—people who can help us. The angels know that this unseen energy is no mystery and that when we choose to harness it, we can turn misfortunes into miracles.

If there are any impossible situations in your life, the angels invite you to "golden key" them right now. Hand them over to God with a prayer of thanks and release, and know that even as you say these words the angels are already working on a solution to your difficulty.

An Angelic Reflection: **I accept the help of a higher power when I feel overwhelmed.**

A GRACE ACCOUNT

An Angel Reminder: "To manifest the positive things in our lives, we need to store up high-voltage energy."

Caroline Myss

Medical intuitive Caroline Myss teaches that when we fear, blame, or manipulate we put ourselves in "energetic debt," which can potentially undermine us. To build up a "grace account," she teaches that we can offer prayers, maintain our integrity, and experience gratitude. When we build a grace account we have spiritual abundance to draw from to invest where we need it most, whether it be our health, work, or relationships. Each day we have many choices to make. Our choices will either drain our grace account or allow us to build strength and spiritual conviction. Fear can be met with prayer. Blame and manipulation are turned to spiritual capital through telling the truth and through giving thanks for life's blessings. The red ink of energetic debt is transformed easily into the black ink of the grace account when we turn to the angels for help.

What "energetic debts" have you stored up through lack of courage or gratitude? Remember how easy it is to change anything and give to the grace account with a simple prayer or an expression of gratitude. Next time you have a fear, stop and say a prayer. Don't worry about how you sound; just be honest and do it. The angels run the grace savings and loan, and they are only a password away!

An Angelic Reflection: I am accruing grace each time I choose love.

THE BLESSING OF IMPERFECTION

An Angel Reminder:

**Since everything is but an apparition, perfect in being what it is,
Having nothing to do with good or bad, acceptance or rejection,
One may well burst out in laughter.**

Long Chen-Pa

The great irony and paradox is that perfection doesn't—and does—exist. It doesn't exist in the form into which many religions and moral codes have perverted it: an ideal of behavior that we must attain if we want to achieve sainthood or eternal reward. It doesn't exist as a media-hyped unholy grail based on the superficial desire to look like the anorexic models on magazine covers or win the lottery or find Mr. or Ms. Right. But it does exist, as the Buddhist mystic Long Chen-Pa understood, in everything already, because God, who is the only perfect one, created the world with all of its warts and nose hairs, and anything that comes from God must somehow be perfect, even in its imperfection. The angels know that God speaks to us most directly through our imperfections, through the failures and disappointments that lead to awareness and change. If we were perfect, after all, we wouldn't need one another; we wouldn't even need God.

If you are a perfectionist or are searching for the perfect this or that, try accepting your imperfections and the imperfections of those around you. You might be surprised at how much freer you feel to love without fear of rejection, to explore without fear of disappointment, to create without fear of failure.

An Angelic Reflection: **I gratefully accept the inescapable fact of my humanness.**

THE DEVIL'S PLAYGROUND

An Angel Reminder: "The devil is an angel, too."
Miguel de Unamuno

We're probably all familiar with the old saying, "Idle hands are the devil's playground." But how many of us have stopped to ponder what this really means? Where is the devil's playground? What does it look like? What play equipment does it have? And idle hands don't necessarily mean that their owner is bored, lazy, and ripe for sinning. Idle hands may indicate that one is resting or thinking or meditating or even having visions. The ever-vigilant Puritans thought that humans should be kept busy at all times, engaged in "worthy" activities that kept them out of trouble, that is, kept them from having too good a time. In strict religious dogma, the devil is often a metaphor for our wilder side, that curious, creative, rebellious part of our nature that refuses to be cooped up in the tight spaces that narrow minds and guardians of the public morals have carved out to keep people in line. The angels don't want us to be inactive due to boredom, apathy, depression, or other life-draining states. Neither do they advocate keeping busy at the expense of enjoying life or being creative or simply making time for stillness and reflection. In fact, they aren't averse to the idea of paying a visit to the devil's playground every once in a while, just to see if it's still in working order.

The next time your hands are idle, imagine the devil inviting you to visit his playground. What does it looks like? Draw a picture or write down the images that come to you. Does it have swings, slides, and other instruments of abandon? Is it a place of temptation? What sort of games would you play there? Who else might you run into?

An Angelic Reflection: **I enjoy the creative and spiritual benefits of idleness.**

INFINITE GEAR

An Angel Reminder: **The territory of the imagination is ever changing, ever changeable.**

Most of us reside in a world of self-imposed limits created by a limiting belief system. We have a great idea and let it evaporate into thin air because we don't have the confidence to make it a reality. We think we can't do this or that, and so we don't. We are afraid to dream because our dreams might not come true; we are afraid to try because we might fail. We live, essentially, in finite gear. But the angels operate in infinite gear, and with their help and guidance we can do the same. Our imaginations know no bounds; they can be expanded or contracted simply by adjusting our attitudes and expectations. Once we shift from finite to infinite gear we discover that material reality changes accordingly. Doors begin to open, barriers begin to dissolve, dreams begin to come true.

What limits have you put on your dream power? What boundaries have you drawn around your "image-nation"? Think about why. Then, just for today, erase those limits and begin to shift from finite to infinite gear. Get into the feeling of being or doing something you've always dreamed of. What images, desires, or emotions come up?

An Angelic Reflection: **I take advantage of new perceptions and new possibilities.**

CONNECTIONS

An Angel Reminder: "I like the idea of the angel as connector. The tradition is that some connect in terms of knowledge and guiding, some in terms of healing, some in terms of defending, some in terms of inspiring."

Matthew Fox

Think about how long it takes to get to know someone. You may think it takes a long time, but with the right attitude, an ability to actively listen, and *awareness,* you can get to know someone better over a single lunch than you would working next to that person for a year. When we realize that depth of connection is the key to a conscious relationship, we will look at our lives much differently. We can be in a long-term relationship with someone and feel no real connection. Or, through awareness, we can have a deep connection with someone we talk with only once a week on the phone, feeling closer to them than we do to the people we see each day.

It is up to us to look into our life and make it vital and connected. We stay connected to the life force by staying awake and aware. Ask the angels to help you feel connected to people, places, and life itself. Think about the friends in your life, and examine how connected you feel. If you want to deepen the connection, think about how you might go about doing that.

An Angelic Reflection: I have connections in the highest places.

OVERINDULGENCE

An Angel Reminder: It's over.

Once in a while it happens, sometimes overnight. You oversleep, because you have overindulged. You overindulged because you were overextending yourself, or maybe the stress of what you overheard overtook your better senses. Or perhaps your generosity overflowed until it was overstepped, by the overstay of something that should have been over before it started. We can overcome the sense that we have gone overboard when we remember to go over things with the angels.

Before you find yourself overwrought and overwhelmed by life, ask the angels for an overview of the things in your life that you need to get over. Then have a good laugh over all of it.

An Angelic Reflection: Over night, over day, the angels' light is over me.

KNOWING BETTER

An Angel Reminder: **Even in stupidity we can act with wisdom.**

Have you ever done something dumb, all the while knowing better? One wonders what the motivation is behind these lapses of sensibility. Do we really want to sabotage ourselves? Are we secretly into the thrill of danger? Or are we just not listening to trusty intuition? Whatever the reason, the angels remind us that there is a reason. We may be seeking momentary comfort, like eating a chocolate bar when we're supposedly dieting. We may think we "just can't help it," like when we pursue someone we're crazy about who unfortunately doesn't love us, hoping against hope that they'll come to their senses. We may be punishing ourselves for something, either consciously or unconsciously. The angels suggest that the next time we choose to take a course that we know isn't the wisest, we stop and ask ourselves just why we're doing this. Once we're clearer about our motivation, we can choose whether or not to go ahead with our plans. If we still end up doing something and knowing better, well, who knows? Maybe we're supposed to learn from the experience.

What have you done lately that you knew wasn't too smart? Why do you think you did it? Make a list of some of your "I knew better" experiences, and see if you can discern a pattern. Do you make poor choices because you don't trust your better judgment? Do you feel compelled to do things almost against your will? Above all, have you learned from these experiences, or do you tend to repeat the same mistakes?

An Angelic Reflection: **The more I care about myself, the better able I am to listen to my better judgment.**

FORSAKEN

An Angel Reminder: "And about the ninth hour Jesus cried out with a loud voice, saying, 'Eli, Eli, Lama Sabachthani?' that is, 'My God, my God, Why hast thou forsaken me?'"

Matthew 27:46

To forsake means "to give up, desert, renounce, withdraw support from, and abandon." In the Bible it says that at the ninth hour Jesus felt that God had forsaken him. What happened in the tenth hour? Nine is the number of endings and of finishing up a cycle. There are times in our own lives when it feels like we have been forsaken, and it is often at the death of something. When we find ourselves at the ninth hour abandoned and deserted by love, it feels as though we will be lost in a nightmare forever. At these times we may cry out to God in anger. Anger stems from fear of abandonment; it is a real feeling, and God can handle it. When we are in the ninth hour, it is okay to flail and wail, because the tenth hour will come, and we will feel cleansed and ready to start anew.

Sometimes we need to forsake a former way of life or withdraw for a while. When we do this, what kind of trail is left behind? Are we important enough in someone else's life that this person would feel forsaken if we withdrew or left? The angels want to remind us that God may not seem near sometimes, just as the sun seems far away when it is shining on the other hemisphere, but the sun still shines and God is always love. We may forsake ourselves and others, but the angels and God will always be with us in one form or another.

An Angelic Reflection: I trust that the hour of renewal will come.

JUDGMENT DAY

An Angel Reminder: "Only our concept of time makes it possible for us to speak of the Day of Judgment by that name; in reality it is a summary court in perpetual session."

Franz Kafka

Judgment is a tricky business; as sentencing scandals fill the news, it's obvious that there are too many judges out there who don't even belong on a park bench, let alone a judicial one. We would all do well to stop every once in a while and ask ourselves what the real purpose of a judge is and how many of us are truly qualified to hold the title. The next time you're tempted to pass judgment, on someone else or on yourself, or the next time you catch somebody trying to pass judgment on you, remember that good judges are motivated by a concern for justice, not an investment in being right or having power. Ideal judges are wise, fair, impartial, severe in their compassion, and compassionate in their severity. They know that they are not saints judging sinners but human beings trying to be just to other human beings.

Imagine that Judgment Day has come and that you are your own judge and jury. How will you treat yourself? What will you find fault with? Will you give yourself compassion and understanding? What kind of sentence will you pass on yourself? You might want to recall this scenario the next time you are tempted to pass judgment on someone else.

An Angelic Reflection: I refrain from judging others, and I judge myself with honesty and compassion.

BAD SERVICE

An Angel Reminder: If we don't do it, who will?

It's been said that people serving the public today do not know what constitutes proper service, because caring about others and being conscientious about doing a job are becoming less and less a part of our moral upbringing. How many of us are all too familiar with waitresses and waiters who ignore us, store clerks who look at us blankly when we ask for help, or endless lines at the bank or post office with only two windows out of ten open? And is there one person reading this who hasn't been put on hold so long the only recourse is to hang up in despair? The reason bad service runs rampant in our society is because most of us feel it's futile to take the time and effort to call the culprits to account. The angels ask us to stand up for good service whenever we can—to make people aware when they are not treating others with kindness and respect, and to remember to dispense those qualities ourselves in our own interactions. The restoration of the human values our society so sorely needs inevitably begins with us.

Have you had bad service lately? If so, what was the situation, and what did you do about it? Have you given anyone bad service? If so, why? Are personal problems an excuse for bad service? The next time you encounter bad service, try to correct the problem. Speak to the serviceperson and to the supervisor. Write a letter to the CEO. Be proactive. If you get results, great. If you don't, you'll still know that you did your part to restore decency to the planet.

An Angelic Reflection: I know that if I don't address the problem, I become part of the problem.

PHILOSOPHER'S STONE

An Angel Reminder: **Symbols are portals into the deep mysteries that surround us and weave magic through our lives.**

In days past, every alchemist searched for the philosopher's stone, the "touchstone" or catalyst for transmuting metals into gold. Alchemists believed in change as the most basic process of life and in the ability of elements to be transformed into something else. Alchemy can also be seen as a symbolic process of spiritual transformation. Spiritual alchemy takes the base metal of our undeveloped divine self, the primal stuff we were born with, and transforms it into gold. Gold symbolizes inner purity and the ability to radiate a steady luster of spiritual light. The symbolic philosopher's stone is the instrument of divine change—the change that takes place in us when we are seized by divine love. We are responsible for mining our own philosopher's stone, which means we need to follow our longing to find our own spiritual roots, our true nature. We as alchemists are the most important secret ingredient in alchemy. It is up to us to cultivate the desire and ability to find and use our philosopher's stone—the invisible divine spark that brings about the desired transformation.

The philosopher's stone represents the touching of our consciousness by divine love from God and the angels. Interactions with angels create powerful changes in people's lives because the angels vibrate on such a high level that any contact with them raises our own vibration, changing our consciousness and repositioning us in the direction of the golden light of spiritual transformation.

An Angelic Reflection: **My consciousness has been blessed by the alchemical golden light of the philosopher's stone.**

WEALTH

An Angel Reminder: **Our greatest riches are the intangibles.**

A friend of ours was trained as a concert pianist. She was very talented and played with great feeling, and everyone loved to listen to her. But she couldn't afford the item of her dreams, a grand piano. One day she was at the home of a wealthy woman who was not a very good pianist but who had a beautiful, fifty-thousand-dollar Bechstein grand. When our friend sat down at the Bechstein she wanted to cry. Suddenly she was able to sound the way she'd always dreamed of sounding; the piano was as responsive as the most intuitive lover. Our friend was filled with anger, that this talentless woman owned the instrument she should have had. She wanted to shake her fist at God for allowing such crass injustice. But the owner of the piano was similarly envious. When our friend commented that she wished she could afford such a beautiful piano, the wealthy woman sadly replied, "Yes, I have the piano. But of the two of us you are the luckier one. Someday you may be able to buy a Bechstein. But I will never be able to buy your talent."

What does wealth mean to you? Do you see it in terms of money and possessions? Or do you value the intangibles that cannot be bought because no one can name their price? Make a list of your true riches—the talents and abilities, the love and friendship that no amount of money can buy. Realize how wealthy you really are.

An Angelic Reflection: **I am wealthy in the gifts of the spirit.**

GOOD REASONS
FOR MISSING LIFE

An Angel Reminder: "Faced with the choice between changing
one's mind and proving there is no need to do so,
almost everyone gets busy on the proof."
John Kenneth Galbraith

There are always reasons for not taking a risk, yet following those reasons sometimes leads to regret. If you're looking for reasons not to live fully, you probably will find them, because that is where you are training your attention. So we didn't take that risk to love or to get married or to have a child, and, wow, aren't we glad; think of all the reasons it would have been wrong. The fact is we will never know if it would have been wrong, and all our reasons may provide cold comfort in the end. Give life a chance, and it will surprise you in simple ways. That person you didn't go out with again because he or she didn't measure up in your critical mind could have been a great love in your life. Get rid of reason, and get into what is in front of you, leaving behind the need to prove it wouldn't have been good.

Where do we place our attention? Are we looking for reasons not to live fully, or are we letting the angels bring us into the exciting world of taking risks? There is no need to punish ourselves if the outcome wasn't perfect. Perfection exists only as a projection; good and bad are just games.

An Angelic Reflection: I will look beyond reasons and seek to live fully.

MEANS WELL

An Angel Reminder: Meaning is only half of doing.

You know how some people have the irritating habit of botching things up in their attempt to do good? We say of such people, "Oh, but they meant well." It's nice to mean well. But if the results of our efforts are the opposite of what we intended, we need to look closely at exactly what our intentions were. People who mean well may not really be aware of the needs of others. Instead they may be putting their own spin on a situation and then rushing in to fix things without checking to find out if this is what the person they're trying to help really wants. So Aunt Jessie sends you a horrible knitted sweater for Christmas because she meant well, or your mother nags and scolds you because down deep she's really concerned for your welfare. The angels appreciate good intentions, but they like it even better when we stop to tune in to the real needs of others. They think it would be great if Aunt Jessie sent you something you, not she, thought was beautiful. They think your mother might better exhibit her concern for your welfare by not projecting her own fears onto you but instead understanding and striving for honest communication. They gently remind us that meaning well may be just a little selfish and that it takes being truly willing to see things from the other person's perspective in order for real good to be accomplished.

How do you feel about people who mean well? Do you excuse their obtuse or misguided behavior because "their heart's in the right place"? That is certainly the polite thing to do. Or do you try, gently and lovingly, to make them aware of what you really need?

An Angelic Reflection: I try to approach another's situation from their perspective rather than my own.

REBEL

An Angel Reminder: "Orthodoxy is the death of intelligence."
Bertrand Russell

There is a part of you that is rebellious. You may have lost touch with that part of yourself, or you may be all too familiar with it. Being rebellious is a natural response when we feel too controlled and constrained. The word *rebel* comes to us from the Latin *rebellis,* an adjective formed from the prefix *re-,* "again," and *bellum,* "war." So a rebel is someone who after being defeated or beaten down reemerges and "wars" against the subjugators. Our spirit has a natural tendency to rebel. Spirit is our inner flame, the warming fire of our life force. People rebel in various ways, some by being aggressive and others by being passive-aggressive. We rebel instinctively through creative expression and humor. The human spirit fights against being broken and can barely tolerate taming. If we learn to tame and master our own spirit through spiritual study, then we will be able to save our spirit from being broken, for we will understand how important it is to honor ourselves, and our spirit, as a facet of *The* Great Spirit.

If you are feeling overwhelmed and hopeless, maybe it is time to rebel. Ask the angels to help you stay positive and life affirming. Think of an area in your life in which you feel defeated. Think of ways you can reemerge and stand up for your rights. If you use your imagination, you will be able to create a change within, bringing you a sense of having more power in life over these things. The angels will bring you humor to light the way.

An Angelic Reflection: **I am a rebel for the angels' cause of love.**

HOUR OF POWER

An Angel Reminder: **Know thyself; know thy cycles.**

Are there certain times in the day when you feel sharper and more alive, specific periods when you know you get more accomplished? Some people refer to themselves as morning people; others feel most productive in the afternoon or evening; and others are night owls, doing their best work in the wee hours. All of us have our hours of power—those times in the day when our mental and physical stamina are at their peak, when we operate at maximum efficiency and clarity. But we may not be aware of this, especially when work and family duties force us to keep running, even when our bodies want to retreat and recharge. When we need to be creative or we need extra energy to accomplish something, the angels suggest that we discover our hour of power and make it work for us. Or, we can dedicate a certain part of each day as our hour of power. We can begin by spending a few minutes in some psychic warm-up exercises like breathing, relaxing, and meditating, a few minutes energizing our bodies with some tai chi, yoga, or stretching routines, and a few minutes giving thanks for the power we are about to receive. The ensuing concentration that we will be able to devote to a project or activity will surprise us.

What is your hour of power? When in the day do you work most happily and productively? Is this convenient for you, or does it conflict with your daily schedule? For instance, do you have a day job, but your hour of power is midnight? If you can, try to make the most of your most productive time. If you would like to change your current hour of power to make it more amenable to your schedule, pick a time of day and make it your hour of power, doing things that will energize and center you so that you can live at your most creative.

An Angelic Reflection: **I use my energy wisely and efficiently.**

SEEDS INTO TREES

An Angel Reminder: "Every moment and every event of every man's life on earth plants something in his soul. For just as the wind carries thousands of winged seeds, so each moment brings with it germs of spiritual vitality that come to rest imperceptibly in the minds and wills of men. Most of these unnumbered seeds perish and are lost, because men are not prepared to receive them: for such seeds as these cannot spring up anywhere except in the good soil of freedom, spontaneity and love."

Thomas Merton

Think about the fact that every majestic tree on the earth came from a tiny seed. Is this not a miraculous event? Planting the seed of a tree is easy; it starts with finding soil that is ready to receive the seed. The soil is created from humus, which is formed by the decay of dead leaves and plants. Planting the seed of the tree of life in your waking consciousness is easy, too; the soil that nourishes our inner tree is created from our humility, which is formed from the decay of our dead outmoded patterns and attachments. If we approach life with humility, we head toward wisdom. Soon our tree starts to grow and send tender shoots up to reach the light, while the roots go venturing into the rich soil of the mysteries.

To fertilize our inner tree of life, we use growth enhancers that give our tree the best chance to thrive. The power of humor accelerates our growth and revitalizes our intelligence. Other growth stimulators have to do with contemplation, such as thinking through new avenues of reasoning, and communing with life. Most important, know that your tree is watched over by a guardian angel.

An Angelic Reflection: I will tend to my inner tree with positive qualities blessed by the angels.

LIVING IN THE CITY

An Angel Reminder: "We have met the enemy and he is us."

Pogo

There are many ways to navigate life in the city. One choice is paranoia. When we choose to be paranoid, life is a living hell, a place where every other person could be the one to strike you down. Another choice is to create a little utopia bubble, and close out the harsh realities of poverty and desperation that may reside little more than a mile away. We can live in a gated community, build a wall around our property, and leave the house with blinders on. The choice less taken is to stay awake and *to love.* To love the city you live in with all its ills and imperfections is a difficult choice.

Next time you go out into the city, pay attention. Get a true sense of the place. Ask the angels to let you see what is happening that you may otherwise miss. Accept the mixture of beauty, awe, and angst that it brings you.

An Angelic Reflection: I shall make where I live my home.

PSYCHIC HOT LINES

An Angel Reminder: **There are no luggage racks on a hearse.**

Psychic hot lines are a true phenomenon of our restless and insecure society. How eager some of us are to hand over our hard-earned money and our hard-won power to anyone who promises us that success, love, health, and wealth are all just around the corner! Yes, the psychic hot lines are quick to assure you that God is delivering everything you desire, priority overnight. But how many of those psychics would have the nerve to say, "I see many challenges for you that, if met in the right spirit, will bring you inner peace and joy. Maybe you won't have a lot of money, but your spiritual riches will be boundless." Whoops. We can just hear all the psychic phone lines going dead with predictions like that. But the angels remind us that when we leave for the next life, the only thing we'll be taking with us is our spiritual scorecard. And our eternal reward will depend not on how much money we made but how much we shared, not how self-important we were but how sincerely we loved.

What do you think of psychic hot lines? Have you ever called one? Have you ever been tempted to call one? If you think of the future in terms of the next life, what would you like to have predicted for you? What sort of things are you willing to do now in order to ensure that future?

An Angelic Reflection: **I know that when it comes to eternal life, the future is now.**

GRUDGES

An Angel Reminder: "I buried the hatchet,
but I never forgot where I buried it."
Old saying

Even the word *grudge* sounds cranky, something between a growl and a
drudge. A grudge is a sort of growl in the soul, and it is certainly
drudgery to hold on to one for very long. When we hold grudges, we hold
on to the past, which takes an extraordinary amount of energy away from
the present. Holding a grudge is also a way of keeping pain alive and well,
something that we don't ordinarily tend to do unless we're certified
masochists. When you have a headache, do you try to keep it going? Or do
you instead do the first thing you can to relieve the pain? Yet with grudges,
we almost worship the painful feelings they bring up because they seem to
justify our position. But the real truth is that it is the grudge, not its target, that is causing us pain now. We ourselves are giving misery a first-class
seat on the trip of life. And that's an awfully expensive way to go.

*Are you holding a grudge? If so, why and against whom? How do you feel when you
think about your grudge? Angry? Helpless? Righteous? Do you feel all the old feelings
associated with the person or incident rising up as if the entire affair is happening all over
again? What might happen if you let go of your grudge. Ask the angels if they hold
grudges, and listen for an answer.*

An Angelic Reflection: **I will put down the burden of a grudge so that I
can live in the present and not the past.**

THE BLAME GAME

An Angel Reminder: "Change comes not from trying to change, but from observing blame, who I am blaming, and who is blaming me."
Fritz Perls

Think about your life right now, right here: Who is to blame or praise for how things are? Think about the times in your life when someone blamed you for their unhappiness. There are times when people cause trouble for us or victimize us, and they are responsible for those actions. However, they are not responsible for our reactions and responses to the situation. Often in love relationships we blame our partners for our unhappiness, and this poisons the emotional waters of life. Whether you are the blamer or the blamed, each position holds a payoff. If you are the blamer, think of the self-righteous feeling you get with that power, and if you are the blamed, think about how you may feel like a innocent victim suffering a bad rap.

Study the issue of blame in your life. Who has that much power over you? Think about the things you want for yourself that you don't have, and ask yourself if someone is really standing in the way. Pay attention to when you manipulate with guilt and shame, and let it go. Ask the angels to allow you keen awareness of the blame game. If you can let go of the blame game, then you will participate more deeply in life.

An Angelic Reflection: **I have no one to blame.**

---　✦　---

FEBRUARY 13

NORMAL

An Angel Reminder: **It is normal to wonder what normal is.**

One of the strangest concepts humans have come up with is the idea of normal. Apparently some part of us is comforted by the thought that somewhere there is a distinct line separating normal beings from abnormal ones and that all we have to do to stay happy is to remain on the right side of the line. This would make life simple, all right. The only problem is, who decides what's normal? There was a time, not so long ago, when a healthy sex drive in a woman was considered abnormal. There was a time when the profession of acting, today revered, was looked down upon as an abnormal way to make a living. And a lot of guardians of normalcy would definitely not approve of people who talk to angels—although the angels consider it perfectly normal. The whole idea of normal is upsetting to the human soul; when we are forced into a mold, we will either suffocate or spill over. When it comes to normal, the angels allow for a wide range of definitions. Otherwise, what would become of creativity?

What do you consider normal or abnormal? Make a list. Who do you think is crazy? Are you ever tempted to do something bold or creative but worry about being labeled a kook? Do you know anyone who might be considered abnormal by boring, unimaginative people because they are so alive and interesting? The angels invite you to play around with your idea of normal and not to worry too much if you might sometimes be outside the range. It might be a good sign.

An Angelic Reflection: **If conforming to the norm inhibits my spirit, I prefer to be abnormal.**

VALENTINE

An Angel Reminder: Love is not blind.

The mad Roman emperor Claudius felt that married men made poor soldiers, because they didn't want to leave their families for battle. So he decided to abolish marriage. The bishop Valentine rebelled and invited young lovers to come to him in secret, where he would join them in holy matrimony. Claudius was impressed with Valentine's passionate conviction and tried to convert him to the Roman gods so he would not have to be executed. Valentine refused and was sent to prison where legend has it, he fell in love with his jailer's blind daughter. His love and faith miraculously restored her sight. After composing a farewell message "From Your Valentine," he was clubbed, stoned, and beheaded on February 24, 270. In the 400s the Catholic Church needed to usurp the popularity of a mid-February pagan rite of passage for adolescent boys, in which they would randomly pull the name of a teenage girl who would be their companion for a year for mutual entertainment and pleasure. So the mid-February festival was outlawed, and when a name was pulled from the box it was a name of a saint, St. Valentine.

The angels are happy about love and romance when it is honored as a sacred gift from God. Spend today honoring love and romance.

An Angelic Reflection: I will treat the powerful force of love with respect and devotion.

New Endings

An Angel Reminder: **Aren't all endings
really beginnings in disguise?**

We know a psychologist who works in the realm of myth and fairy tale. She and her client will explore a fairy tale and how it relates to the client's life. Then she will have the client write a new ending to the story—one the client would like to see. The ability to write a new ending—to create the future we dream of—is a powerful, self-liberating tool. How many times have we accepted the endings that have been handed down to us without asking why they are that way and without believing in our own immense power to change them to suit a broader vision? Isn't this power, after all, at the root of myth and folktales? The hero is faced with a danger, an unhappy ending, that he or she manages to reverse through seemingly miraculous means. In reality the hero has unleashed the power of his or her intuition and heeded the mysterious voices of wisdom that come to us when we learn to trust our inner knowledge. The angels remind us that endings can always be turned into beginnings and that we can always write new ones in the continuing story of our lives.

Are there any endings in your life that you would like to write? Any that you would like to rewrite? What or whom do they involve? Set aside some time to write those endings— to envision the future as you would like to see it and to change the past as well. Now envision the new life to which these endings can give birth.

An Angelic Reflection: **I know that endings and beginnings interweave in the endless circle of life.**

CAUGHT OR NOT CAUGHT

An Angel Reminder: "The measure of a man's real character is what he would do if he knew he never would be found out."

Thomas Babington Macaulay

Many people think of right and wrong in terms of getting caught or not caught. Instead of looking at the action or behavior that started the damage, we focus on the stupidity of getting caught. Here is a scenario: a man has been unfaithful to his wife and has even put an ad in the personal section for a sexual partner. He tells someone, and the gossip starts. Soon the wife finds out, but the husband gets mad at the person he told for passing on the information. Who is really wrong, and what was wrong in the first place? Are the gossipers who were passing along true information to blame? Is the man sorry for what he did, or is he sorry only for how stupid he was to tell someone? Perhaps we set ourselves up to get caught in order to stop certain behaviors that are not for our ultimate good and the good of all. We've all known someone who seems to advertise the trouble they are causing as a way of getting it stopped.

Next time you get in trouble for something, or you inadvertently become part of someone else's trouble, look for the "original sin" to find out what is really wrong. In the angels' view we are all one, connected in the web of life, so our actions ripple outward toward others. The angels want us to integrate our behavior and to base our ideas of right and wrong not on secrecy and betrayal, but on how our actions affect the whole.

An Angelic Reflection: I will focus my attention on the obvious signs and see beyond manipulations.

IN-TO-IT-NESS

An Angel Reminder: "Sell your cleverness and buy bewilderment, / Cleverness is mere opinion, bewilderment is intuition."

Rumi

Intuition is our passport into the realm of the unknown and mysterious. Because it is so mysterious and powerful, it is the new spiritual concept that people are trying to track down and use in their professional and personal lives. The trouble is that real intuition comes from being connected to the divine realm, so if we use it instead to manipulate a situation in our favor, we gain nothing but an illusion. Intuition is a feeling-based way to read the world around us, to tune into a new perception or insight for deeper understanding. Intuition is "in-to-it-ness," because you have to be in-to something on a deeper level to receive an intuitive hit. Sometimes intuition can be a very loud signal, with obvious messages, and other times it comes as a vague feeling that beckons us to look closer at something and use all of our senses for fuller understanding.

If you want to be intuitive, don't be afraid to not know, and let yourself venture into bewilderment. When you don't know, the angels do know, and they like to send you on a treasure hunt. To get their messages of where to go next, tune in and check in with your feelings. Stay in the feeling realm, and let the angels gently guide you. Intuition takes practice and the ability to not let your thinking mind fill in the blanks.

An Angelic Reflection: I am in-to my feelings and bewildered by the awesome knowing that arises from emptiness.

THE LAST WORD

An Angel Reminder: **The last word is often exactly that.**

You know how obnoxious people can be who just have to have the last word. They never seem to be listening to what you're saying; they're only interested in stating and defending their own position at all costs. Instead of promoting communication, they seem to be dedicated to promoting and maintaining conflict. Such people are so insecure that they equate losing an argument with losing their identity. They cannot separate themselves from their position, and in their skewed perspective, anyone who doesn't agree with that position is rejecting them. Unfortunately for them, the last word will often indeed be the last word, in terms of a relationship. People who have to have the last word will find others constantly leaving them, until there's nobody around to have a last word with. And as they are leaving this life, what do you think their real last word will be? The angels bet it will be, "Sorry."

How do you react to people who have to have the last word? Do you keep arguing with them, or do you walk away from them? Do you ever feel you have to have the last word? What does this concept really mean to you? Remember that the angels are always on hand to help us strive for true communication, based on acknowledging the opinions of others rather than having to be the one who is always right.

An Angelic Reflection: **I respect the opinions of others, even though I may not agree with them.**

THE GOD FACTOR

An Angel Reminder: "It is time to develop our
hearts not our intellects; it is time to experience life
and the true interchange of relationships."
Tony Gwilliam

What is the difference between intelligence and genius? It may be a matter of spirituality. Albert Einstein, whom we acknowledge as a genius, was quoted as saying that he wanted to know the thoughts of God. He also supposedly said that "imagination is more important that knowledge." Many studies have been done to find a particular factor that makes some people more creative and ingenious than others. Perhaps the biggest factor is the willingness of a person to listen to the thoughts of God, to tune into the angels, to allow themselves to vibrate at a higher spiritual frequency. This will have unique and varied results in each person, since we were born with unique gifts and talents. Sticking only to the facts will never promote genius. We discover the magnificently new by tuning into a higher source.

Genius takes a lot of courage. At times you may find yourself alone in your idea, without any support from others. Sometimes you may think that you are a bit crazy, when things happen that you cannot explain. Maybe our need to explain takes out the "God factor." The angels encourage us to seek out our own genius and let the God factor expand in our consciousness.

An Angelic Reflection: Each day I allow the God factor to expand my consciousness and bring me closer to the angels.

The Human Heart Has Its Own Timing

An Angel Reminder: "The heart has its reasons which reason knows nothing of."
Blaise Pascal

When it comes to the issue of time, people in modern society agree on very little, except for clock time. If the clock says three, we all agree that it's three. But we don't all agree on how long it takes to heal or how long it takes to fall in love or how long we are supposed to grieve. When it comes to how we have loved, our heart is not interested in clock time. The heart knows that once we have truly loved, that love stays, and when a loved one goes away by death or by choice, grief can visit whenever it likes, for grief is really a friend to the heart. Our heart is not going to play our game of time, but our saving grace is that if we let love grow, our heart grows, and there will be room to love some more, and then some, and then even more.

Many times we look back and think, "I wish I had loved more or spent more time loving." When you have a moment of regret, let it be. Then ask the angels to help you open your heart to love so that you will love differently in the future and there will be no regrets. Don't forget that at the end of your Earth time the angels will ask you, "How well did you love?"

An Angelic Reflection: **I shall use love as the eraser of regret.**

HAS IT HAPPENED YET?

An Angel Reminder: **Living in fear of the future robs us of the peace of the present.**

The human imagination is a pretty impressive asset. It has created great works of art, invented wonders, and opened windows onto dreams that have changed the world. Yet our imaginations can just as easily run away with us, setting a record for the hundred-yard mind dash by worrying about something in advance and creating a problem before one actually exists. Ninety percent of the things we worry about are simply fears that have not yet materialized and that may never materialize. When we are afraid, the angels caution us not to let our imaginations run away with us. Instead, they suggest that we stop and return to the moment, where the worst has not yet happened. Then we can calm down and see our fears more rationally, realizing that they may be nothing more than a projection of our own insecurities.

What are you afraid of? Have any of your fears materialized, or are they merely possibilities and not actualities? List some of the fears you have in terms of "purely imaginary," "possible," and "already realized." Which category wins out? Let the purely imaginary fears go. Figure out some actions you could take that could prevent the possible ones from materializing. As for the fears that have become reality, call upon the angels to help you meet the challenge and ride out the storm. The worst has happened; it's all up from here.

An Angelic Reflection: **I do not let fearful projections rule my life.**

ADJUSTING

An Angel Reminder: "If truth and love, mutual respect
and concern, affection and friendship have any value in life,
then the social, economic, political structures will have to be
changed and adjusted to these, not our inner life adjusted
to the outer structures."

Vimala Thakar

Certain human qualities are requirements for the soul and spirit, as important as vitamins for the body. Things like the exchange of loving affection, inner peace, reverence for the expression of life itself, deep friendships, and a spiritual foundation to build upon give us the values we need to be the best people we can be. We cannot ignore these important values because they are not supported or appreciated in the world. The angels know how difficult it is to maintain a spiritually integrated life, so they give us extra help when we hold the intention strong to keep the sacred qualities of human life from going extinct.

If we choose to accept the angels' mission—keeping love, laughter, happiness, and gratitude from going extinct—there will be days when it seems like mission impossible. At those times all we need to do is remember who is in charge of this mission. Then we will know that all things are possible with love, that love is God, and that the angels are an invisible army of love emissaries.

An Angelic Reflection: **Whenever I think my mission is impossible, the angels venture forward to lead the way.**

NOT ENOUGH

An Angel Reminder: **Enough *is* enough.**

Our consumer society tends to make us feel that we never have quite enough. If we have a house, we wish it were bigger. If we have one car, we want another. If we've got a 250 megahertz computer, we want a 500. If we're married, we wish our spouse were more this and less that. But the angels know that while there's nothing wrong with having goals and wanting to improve our lives, we will never be truly happy until we learn the art of not being attached. We can acquire more things and appreciate them, but we are at a disadvantage if we are not able to put our possessions in perspective and see them as merely temporary enjoyments and not absolute necessities. Similarly, if we are attached to wanting our friends and loved ones to be different instead of appreciating them for who they are, we will miss out on their unique contributions to our lives. The angels remind us that wanting to make our dreams come true is not a problem, as long as we realize that we already have enough, in terms of inner resources and divine assistance, to be happy on the deepest level.

Do you believe that you don't have enough of a certain commodity? Where do you feel you're lacking? In money? Friends? Health? Love? Try detaching from the idea of "not enough" and see yourself as already having enough of everything that you need. We predict that abundance will start appearing in your life.

An Angelic Reflection: **I have enough faith in divine assistance and in my own resources to know that my needs will always be met.**

THE ART OF COMMITMENT

An Angel Reminder: "Concerning all acts of initiative
(and creation) there is one elementary truth the ignorance of
which kills countless ideas and splendid plans: That the moment
one definitely commits oneself then Providence moves too."
Johann Wolfgang von Goethe

A true commitment is serious business. But to many people, commitment seems overwhelming. Goethe reminds us that when we consciously commit, Providence moves to help us. The trouble is that this help is usually in the form of a test, and who among us likes to be tested? A commitment will not be strong unless it has opposition to overcome; this is reality. The tests are difficult, and they come in many colors. Doubt is a dangerous test. It is natural to have a lot of self-doubt and questioning, because how do we know we are making the right decision? Sacrifice is another test we encounter. We often have to sacrifice fun opportunities in order to stay true to our commitment. This is no fun when we are bombarded with messages telling us we can have it all simply by sitting back and wanting it. We can't have it all if we have chosen certain commitments. But after you've passed the commitment tests, the joy and awe that you will be gifted with will be worth every sacrifice.

Don't let your commitments own you; you must greet them gently. When you are choosing a commitment, allow it to merge naturally into your calling, leaving dancing space for the angels. When you commit, you send out a message than you are truly ready to join and connect with something greater and are willing to be entrusted with what it will bring.

An Angelic Reflection: I am willing to commit, to meet the tests with courage and grace, and to respect my calling with the angels.

RIGHT EFFORT

An Angel Reminder: **Joy is in the process, not the goal.**

In Zen practice, there is the concept of right effort, or effort aimed in the right direction. In this instance, right direction means toward non-achievement, that is, away from accomplishing this or that goal through the practice. Achievement is regarded as an illusion born of pride, the child of ego, whereas the true Zen practitioner strives to free himself or herself from ego-based desires and to simply appreciate the process of the practice itself. This grounds the practitioner in the moment, which is the true birthplace of enlightenment. In our daily lives it's good to have goals. But it's even better to work toward them with right effort, appreciating the process rather than focusing all of our energy on the future. As we pay closer attention to how and why we are doing something, we become more proficient at it; we are clearer about our goals because we are clearer about who we are. So we don't have to put happiness on hold; satisfaction is in our practice, and we trust that it will lead us to where we are supposed to be going.

Do you have goals that you are trying to achieve? Is the trying sometimes frustrating to you? What if you were to stop trying and start living, in the process and the moment, trusting that the right effort will effortlessly take you to your destination?

An Angelic Reflection: **Delighting in the journey rather than rushing toward my destination, I discover that "when" is "now."**

COSTLY

An Angel Reminder: "It's only money."
Richard Margoles
(our accountant)

Have you ever thought about how much you cost to operate? You are probably quite expensive. Too often we are tempted to value ourselves by the money we earn or the investments we have accumulated. On paper we may look poor, rich, or somewhere in the middle. But there is no financial statement for our soul and spirit. If we assess our value by dollar bills, we will never have enough to match our worth. A teacher we know tells of a dream he had. In the dream he saw a huge ballroom filled floor to ceiling with dollar bills. At first he thought, "Great! This is how much money is coming to me." But the dream messenger told him something different: "If you had all this money, you still wouldn't approach your true worth." The angels want us to measure ourselves, not by our bank accounts, but by the depth and integrity of our souls.

What does the statement "It's only money" mean to you? Have you ever run out of money? It is a very scary moment when the bank account is on empty. Is there a financial issue in your life haunting you? The angels don't need money in their realm, but they can help us have a soulful perspective on the subject. Take a day and ask the angels to be your financial consultants. Imagine a running dialogue with the angels. Each time you spend money on yourself, have a discussion with the angels.

An Angelic Reflection: **My worth goes deeper than my bank account.**

GODSEND

An Angel Reminder: **Angels are sent from God.**

A godsend is a great blessing. We have many godsends when the angels are in our lives, because we appreciate all the things in our lives that represent love, and we recognize them as coming from God. A pet is often mentioned as a godsend. A close friend, a stranger bringing good news, a lover that heals our loneliness, an unexpected windfall—all are godsends, expressions of God's divine love for us. But some events we don't recognize as godsends. These may be times when we are resisting change and holding on to the past, and the godsend comes in the form of a break with the past, which at first causes us pain. But after the initial pain we see that God always sends us a new chance for love.

Think of the godsends in your life. Think of anyone you may be a godsend to. Ask the angels to send you on a mission to discover God in all the details of your life, and how precious each one is regardless of how painful its first visit was.

An Angelic Reflection: **God sends me all I need to heal.**

In One Ear and Out the Other

An Angel Reminder: "You look into his eyes
and you see the back of his head."
**Comedian Mark Russell,
on a well-known politician**

Some people are so clueless it makes us wonder what's filling up the space where their brains are supposed to be. You tell them something, and it goes in one ear and out the other, with no gray matter to block its path. The angels consider this a true tragedy, since God took great pains to fit us with brains. All of us go through times when we don't use our brains, when it seems as though all we can hear is the wind rushing between our ears. It's therefore a good idea to pay a visit to our brains every now and then, just to see if anyone's home. If we're not listening to others, not processing and making use of important information, it's a signal that we need to pay more attention to the supreme gift of intelligence. Combined with true sensitivity, it has the power to make us the higher beings the angels want us to be.

Has anyone ever told you something important that went in one ear and out the other? What were the consequences? Did you end up wishing you'd turned your brain on? What causes us to disregard good advice? Sometimes we're preoccupied with something else; sometimes we're simply self-absorbed or in denial. If the angels were to give you an important message, wouldn't it be awful if it went in one ear and out the other?

An Angelic Reflection: I listen, I reflect, I learn.

LEAP OF FAITH

An Angel Reminder: "In order to *become our visions,* we must go to the deepest core of who and what we are—observing everything with wonder. Then the leap of faith that brings emergence does not contain fear, but is based in personal trust and knowing."
Jamie Sams

When you ponder the word *leap,* all kinds of images may emerge. The idea of jumping over something or doing something impulsively may enter your mind. Life sometimes asks us to jump over the mundane and land in the infinite heavenly realm of faith. This means we must look past the mundane and see the true wonders of the world we live in. When we take a leap of faith, it doesn't mean we change localities, but it does mean we change realities. Once you take a leap of faith in your life, you can't go back. Even if you try to get back to where you once were, the leap of faith you took will change your consciousness forever, because you conquered a fear and put your trust in God.

Is it time for a leap of faith in your life? You don't have to wait for a leap year. A leap of faith is pretty much required in one way or another each day of our lives—especially now. Make an effort today to think about jumping over the mundane and living in the angels' world. We can't tell you how that will look, because each leap brings you into the realm of infinite possibilities.

An Angelic Reflection: I am ready to leap into the realm of faith and live in the angels' world.

DON'T JUST GO WITH THE FLOW

An Angel Reminder: *"Only dead fish go with the flow."*
Anonymous

We have all been told to just go with the flow. Be free, just let it happen. Well, that is great advice, but there are many times when our destiny demands that we cocreate the flow, step into the water, and not be swept away by the current. Sure, it would be nice just to put our little raft in the water and cruise down the river looking at the sights. The angels ask more from us than a simple sight-seeing cruise with the flow.

Fish don't go with the flow of the river; they dart around exploring the coves and sometimes even swim upstream. Learn to dance and sing with the flow. Explore the reaches of your river. Give to the flow, and the flow will give to you.

An Angelic Reflection: I will go with my own divine flow.

LEARNING THE HARD WAY

An Angel Reminder: **We all learn the hard way.**

Learning means gaining knowledge, comprehension, or mastery through experience or study. A lesson is something to be learned. When we learn our lessons the hard way, it means we had to go through the experience to gain the knowledge, even though we were warned that the experience would be a tough one. True mastery usually comes through experience; we need to learn firsthand what the lesson is about. Experiencing something means we are present physically, mentally, and spiritually. Sometimes we experience something several times before we feel we have learned a lesson, and then in the back of our minds and hearts we know there is a possibility that we may just go back and do it again.

The angels want us to know that awareness is change and all experiences are unique. If we understand that, then we won't need to analyze and group all of our behavior into one lesson plan. The angels give us courage, enabling us to see beyond difficulties and simply learn from experience.

An Angelic Reflection: **I will not be hardened by life's lessons.**

WATCHERS

An Angel Reminder: **You are being watched.**

One of the most ancient words for an angel is the Aramaic word *ir*, which translates as "watcher." Lately in movies we have seen angels depicted as watching humans from the tops of buildings and in libraries (angels like books and knowledge). When they notice a human in trouble, they respond accordingly. The angels read the special intentions of our heart. If we are closed down, refusing to leave a negative way of being, the angels watch but are unable to respond. On the other hand, if we are honest and real and open to change, they respond by bringing us light and love for the situation at hand.

If you are being watched by angels right now, what would they see? How would they respond to your feelings? What would they notice in your actions? If you are living an authentic life, the angels will be well entertained.

An Angelic Reflection: **I will open my heart so the angels can see—and help—the real me.**

VULNERABLE

An Angel Reminder: The truly strong summon
the courage to face and honor their feelings.

A man we know used to be heavily armored and not in touch with his feelings, until increasing unhappiness and loneliness led him into therapy. As he began peeling off his protective emotional layers and discovering his feelings, he was frightened. But he pushed on, and gradually a new person began to emerge—one who was far more open and compassionate, who could state his needs and communicate better with others, who was no longer afraid to feel. The good side of this newfound vulnerability was that his friendships and other relationships deepened and he felt more profoundly alive than he ever had before. The "bad" side was that once he took off his armor he seemed unable to maintain the facade necessary in the corporate world to get promotions and advances. He was a bit worried about this change, but he knew in his heart that it was for the best. The angels love this man for his courage to become vulnerable, and they assure him that his openness and self-honesty will lead him to the work he is meant to be doing.

Fear of being vulnerable stems from childhood, when we learn at an early age to adopt personas that will protect us and get us love and approval. So, we often unconsciously don masks that disguise the real us, forgetting to take them off as we grow older. Remember that you don't have to wear a mask for the angels. They appreciate the real you, and besides, they can see right through it.

An Angelic Reflection: I am not afraid to know myself and to share that knowledge with others.

HELP

An Angel Reminder: Heaven help us!

Remember when you were young and your parents told you not to yell for help unless you really needed it? Remember the story about the boy who cried wolf? When do we really need help, and how do we get it? Have you ever thought about what help is? Some of the synonyms for help are *assistance, aid, guidance, backing, advice, comfort, befriend, uphold,* and *support.* These are all things the angels do for us, and they are also things that we need from our friends and family in order for life to be connected and rich.

Next time you need help with something, take a look at how you go about getting it. Do you come right out and ask for it? Do you first ask the angels, and then let yourself be guided to the best solution? Do you ever "cry wolf"? Remember, being a human doesn't come with a user's manual; we need help being the best human possible.

An Angelic Reflection: I could use some help.

A House Is Not a Home

An Angel Reminder: **"There's no place like home."**
The Wizard of Oz

How do we know when we are at home? Is it simply a matter of showing up at our address? Our feeling of home is what matters. Some of us feel at home just being on the planet; wherever we go, there we are. Some of us don't feel at home anywhere; we are restless and unsettled no matter what. The angels teach us that our real home is in our heart. Our heart is where we generate love and stay connected to heaven. The more we love, the more at home we will feel, no matter where we are physically.

Think about where you live for a moment. Does it feel like home? Think about the feeling in your heart. Are you content where you are? How could the angels help you feel more at home here on Earth? Ask them to help you find a home base from which to spread your love.

An Angelic Reflection: **Wherever I go, I am down home.**

SEVEN DEADLY SINS

An Angel Reminder: **Pride and self-absorption mark the path away from inner happiness.**

Pope Gregory the Great gave us a list of seven sins that have become famous as the seven deadly sins, and they are reexamined each time someone reads Dante's *Purgatorio*. The seven sins are pride, envy, anger, sadness (which later became sloth—spiritual sloth, or apathy), avarice/greed, gluttony, and lust. They were considered "wicked human passions," and they were represented originally as a progression of greater self-fixation, with pride as the worst offense. It is interesting to note that Lucifer fell from heaven because of his pride. Human life is a balancing act, and these sins represent a serious imbalance. We are here to work on getting past our self-fixations and the kind of pride that interferes with our relationship with God and the angels.

Think about the seven deadly sins; examine why and how each one can be deadly to either the person owning the sin or to a person accidentally associated with the sin. Have any of these sins messed up your life lately? Do you know anyone who has actually died as a result of one of the seven deadly sins?

An Angelic Reflection: **The angels make me feel proud without pride.**

JUST BREATHE

An Angel Reminder: **Calm is just a breath away.**

Sometimes we are moving too fast to think before we speak. At times like these, we need an internal editor, a voice inside reminding us to take care with our words, to consider their effects on others before they're out of our mouths. We can develop more care with our speech by taking a moment to center ourselves, making sure that head and heart are connected. One of the best ways to do this is to say to ourselves, "just breathe." Each time you say it you can simply take a breath. It can be a gentle breath; you don't have to hyperventilate for it to be beneficial. A good "just breathe moment" can center you so that you can speak simultaneously from your heart, mind, soul, and spirit.

Pay attention to your editing skills. The angels are very good editorial assistants, and if you ask them to help you they will. Practice breathing with the angels. You can imagine each conscious breath you take as a peace bath for all the cells in your body.

An Angelic Reflection: **When in doubt, I shall breathe a deep breath of wisdom.**

YOUR GARDEN

An Angel Reminder: **A garden is meant to be left behind.**

One of our friends loves to garden. At one point, when she was renting a house, she transformed the backyard into a fragrant wonderland of fresh herbs, beautiful flowers, and luscious vegetables. When it was time for her to leave the house, her neighbor exclaimed, "But how can you leave your beautiful garden?" Our friend replied, "I'm not leaving it. My garden is inside of me; wherever I go I recreate it. In the process I am also creating something for others to enjoy when I move on."

Do you have a garden inside of you? What kinds of seeds are planted there? What kind of fruits do you harvest? What are the gifts you carry within you that you can always use to transform and uplift your environment and nourish and nurture others? These are the things that will be remembered about you when you pass on.

An Angelic Reflection: **I scatter seeds of kindness, compassion, humor, and tolerance wherever I go, and I leave their fruits for others to enjoy.**

CIRCUMSTANTIAL EVIDENCE

An Angel Reminder: "Growth is the only evidence of life."
Thomas Cole

Think about who you are for a moment. Consider the evidence of your life, the facts or signs that lead others to draw conclusions about you. Often in our society we look for evidence of wealth, health, beauty, job level, or education. Is this the evidence that defines you? If we look only on the outside, we may find this kind of evidence and form our opinions about someone based on it. But in the court of the angels, this outward evidence is considered circumstantial; it has no direct bearing on the facts of the case. In a legal dispute, circumstantial evidence is the kind that is gotten from inference, not from direct experience. Our life is not a legal dispute, but it can feel that way when we are burdened by debts, divorce, past mistakes, current failures, or other painful circumstances. The good news is that heaven is not a court of law. The angels know you by your character, not by the outward circumstances of your life. If there is evidence that you are a kind and caring person who puts love first on their list, then there is no dispute.

What circumstantial evidence are you carrying that is weighing you down? Perhaps you are giving more weight to the outward circumstances than the angels do. Today, try to notice each time you are kind to someone; be aware of each of the good wishes you send to friends and acquaintances—and that includes you! Each time you are patient with yourself or someone else, you are showing love, the true evidence of your heart.

An Angelic Reflection: **I am not on trial; I am on an angelic assignment for love.**

COMPROMISE

***An Angel Reminder:* It is true wisdom to know
when to compromise and when to stand firm.**

Compromising is an important skill. We can't have everything we want, so we often have to adjust our expectations and remain flexible. In negotiations, compromise is essential in order to assure that all parties have their needs met. Daily life is a series of compromises. You want to go to the movies, but you have to work; you want a new car, but your kid needs braces; you want that piece of pie, but you also want to lose ten pounds. The ability to compromise helps us not to become too attached to our desires and to explore alternative avenues toward gratification. But when we compromise our nonnegotiables, like our values or our health and happiness, it's time to put the brakes on. There are times when compromise is not appropriate, and the angels want us to have the courage to stand up for the things that are dearest to us, that define who we are as spiritual and moral beings.

Where are you compromising in your life? Are these compromises reasonable and healthy? Or do you feel "compromised"—forced to take a position or an action that goes against your grain or your deepest wishes? Take a look at the role compromising plays in your life. If you tend to be unwilling to compromise in areas where it would be appropriate, you might want to explore why you feel the need to always get what you want and have the last word.

***An Angelic Reflection:* I compromise in the interest of peace, not tyranny.**

TRUE GRIT

An Angel Reminder: "In the real (as opposed to the ideal) world, a tender heart needs to be balanced by a tough mind; good feelings, by a willingness to struggle."

Sam Keen

Grit is an interesting word. It means gravel or sand as well as courage, pluck, fortitude, and heroism. If you say someone has true grit, you are noticing their indomitable spirit. Have you been taught to fight a good fight, have courage, and forge ahead when you feel overpowered or defeated? What about when the going gets tough, are you tough enough to get going? We can all have indomitable spirits. If you find yourself faced with the gritty truth of life, stop running to all the usual places to hide. Live with the grit, and you will end up with a pearl.

A pearl starts when a little piece of shell or sand gets inside an oyster and annoys the smooth lustrous lining of the shell. Pretty soon the cells of the lining start to layer themselves over the piece of grit, resulting a beautiful iridescent pearl. If you were to cut a pearl in half you would see layers, and then the original grit. Let the angels help you know that real courage is a beautiful pearl formed by the gritty encounters we have had along the way that strengthen our resolve.

An Angelic Reflection: My courage is formed by the true grit of life.

THE BEST MEDICINE

An Angel Reminder: "Among those whom I like or admire,
I can find no common denominator; among those I love,
I can: all of them make me laugh."

W. H. Auden

Laughing is one of the most intimate things we can share with someone. It is intimate because it is a moment of letting go and just being who you are. When two people can have a good laugh together, it means that they are sharing humorous insights and perceptions—something we can't do with just anybody. Therefore laughter is a good indication of compatibility in friendship and love. Another truth about laughter is that it cannot be forced or faked very well; when we laugh at something, it is a spontaneous and real response. Laughter doesn't need to be left behind when we are sad. We do not have to commit to one emotion at a time; we are multidimensional, and laughing and crying are good partners.

Take a moment and think about the people you love. How often do you laugh together? The angels love to hear our laughter, and they will encourage bouts of hilarity whenever they can. If you haven't laughed for a while, it is due time. Go rent a movie you know you can laugh at. Call up a friend and reminisce about something funny you did together, and laugh again. Go on a laughing quest with the angels, and make sure to laugh at least once a day.

An Angelic Reflection: **Laughter is my angelic medicine.**

PRAYING FOR OUR ENEMIES

An Angel Reminder: **Having compassion for the oppressor as well as the oppressed is known in Buddhism as the Unusual Attitude.**

His Holiness the Fourteenth Dalai Lama has told of the terrible stories his people have shared with him about their suffering at the hands of the Chinese invaders of Tibet. Often, he said, he has cried with them as they recount their horrific experiences of torture, rape, murder, and other atrocities. Yet he continues to pray for his country's oppressors. When asked why, he replied emphatically, "Oh, because they are the ones who are most in need of prayer! We must pray for them unceasingly, for their souls are in the gravest danger of all." To most of us, this logic sounds insane. Why would we care about the souls of murderers, torturers, people who have destroyed our lives? In his book *Path to Bliss,* the Dalai Lama explains, "For a Buddha, all sentient beings are equally dear. Also, when you examine deeply, you will find that it is in fact the delusions within the enemies and not the enemies themselves that actually cause harm. Therefore there is no justification at all for you to hold grudges against those who cause harm, and neglect the welfare of such beings." The angels would add that in praying for our enemies we are, in a strange way, praying for ourselves, for our own enlightenment through total compassion.

Is there anyone who has hurt you and for whom you bear great hatred? Would you ever consider praying for them? If not, why don't you give it a try? It can't hurt, and the angels predict that the more willing you are to care about the soul of someone who has wronged you, the more deeply you will experience the healing power of love and the ennobling power of compassion.

An Angelic Reflection: **I know that all human beings are ultimately one soul under God.**

WILLING TO CHANGE

An Angel Reminder: "When you are walking the tightrope
of change it is important to not look down or back."
Ken Kalb

We have to remember when using affirmations prayers that our affirmations need to reflect a spiritual change *we* are willing to make within. Too
often in our chants and affirmations we demand that external events
change in our favor. God has in mind a much more interesting idea for us,
and it comes to us through trust and faith and the willingness to change.

*To receive blessings from God, one must know how to greet and recognize them. The angels
work with God to bring you the highest gift, and it often comes at the last minute, when
you are ready to give up and look back. Next time you pray, examine your focus and ask
God to give you the elements necessary for you to change and receive your blessings.*

An Angelic Reflection: I will walk the tightrope of change with the angels
ready to catch me if I fall.

A WEALTHY SOCIETY

***An Angel Reminder:* To have a rich culture we
must cultivate prosperity close to home.**

Do we really live in a wealthy society, as we're so often told? A truly
wealthy culture places education, learning, creativity, and teachers above
Wall Street. Children are listened to and mentored. Individuals are
accepted as such, and individual cases are just that. In a rich society no
one needs to be out on the street for lack of job skills, and there are long
enough grace periods after losing a job to get back in the swing of things.
Drug abuse is not made a criminal offense but is seen as a need for real
help. There is no racism, classism, hatred, or ageism in a truly wealthy
culture. Compassion and mercy are the law of the land, and spiritual
practices are encouraged and honored. People are not judged or given
power based on their financial status. Jobs are kept close to home, and
buying locally and supporting independent businesses are the rule.

*When was the last time you heard a politician really touch on these ideas? Mostly you hear
about fear-related issues that they promise to take care of, like making sure the death
penalty stands and that any criminal who might get near you is put away for life. If we
lived in a wealthy, richly resourced culture, a lot of the criminal problems would take care
of themselves. Take a look at your community, and find out where the real wealth is and
the spiritual poverty. How can you help expand the wealth?*

***An Angelic Reflection:* I will learn how to give to my community in small
but important ways.**

ENABLERS

An Angel Reminder: **The angels ennoble us.**

To enable means to provide the means for and make it possible for something to happen. It also means to empower or sanction. *Enabler* has become a standard word in the language of the recovery field. An enabler is someone who helps us do something that may not be so good for us. By labeling someone an enabler, we are bringing in the right to blame. But let's look a little more closely at this idea of enabling. Don't we always have free will? And doesn't the enabler also have a choice in the matter? Furthermore, how do we know that enabling is always wrong? In other words, if someone has a drinking problem and they choose to drink at home where they are enabled to do so, isn't this better than drinking out in public where they may injure someone? In the realm of sickness and disease, we have to be careful with strict renditions of right and wrong. Perhaps the angels have a bigger plan. Perhaps the challenge for both the enabler and the enabled is to exercise their free will in the wisest possible way. Then we can become ennobled instead of enabled.

Before we jump into the label game, let's study the big picture. The angels know that each situation is unique, and they are waiting to enable us with courage and love. Love enables us to be our best, while blame throws us overboard. Think of a situation that you are tempted to view in black-and-white terms. How might the angels see the bigger picture? How might they assist you in leaving blame and labels behind?

An Angelic Reflection: **I will allow the angels to ennoble me with help, clarity, and guidance.**

PAINKILLERS

An Angel Reminder: **In killing the pain,
we are sometimes killing the messenger.**

The fact that we can cut down on or be spared physical pain by the simple act of taking a pill is undeniably a great boon to humanity. But as we well know, emotional pain is not so easy to eradicate. So we often resort to a variety of methods to escape unhappiness. We may use food, drugs, or alcohol as emotional painkillers. We may use relationships to escape from pain. We may go on shopping sprees, trying to fill a psychic or spiritual void with material acquisitions. We may submerge ourselves in work or busyness, to the point where we don't have time to even think about our problems, let alone solve them. Yet it is a curious irony of life that when we don't make time for our pain, our pain will make time for us. Then we must look pain in the eye and ask why it has come into our lives and what it has to teach us. And we must also ask ourselves how much of our pain is due to circumstances or to our attitude toward the circumstances and our way of looking at life.

When you are in emotional pain, how do you deal with it? Do you try to kill it, avoid it, escape it? Do you ever "sit with" your pain? If there is a painful situation in your life right now, what role is it playing in your growth? How much of it is unavoidable? How much pain could you kill by simply changing your attitude and expectations?

An Angelic Reflection: **I am not afraid to listen to my pain.**

"I" LEVEL

An Angel Reminder: "If we were to give up the 'self project' so dear to many therapies and theories of psychology, education, and spirituality, we might see angels once again; for the blazing light of self-interest blanks out the glow of angels. . . . Whether we're concerned about our own 'self' or the 'self' of others, that attention blocks our appreciation of the angel who stands at the doorway of the truly deep and intimate."

Thomas Moore

So much of our time is spent at "I" level, instead of "Us" level. "Us" level is the whole picture: you, me, God, the angels, the Earth, the heavens, the animals, and the mystery. Thomas Moore suggests that we give up our self project so that we might see the angels once again. This is good advice for all areas in our lives, because when we are operating in the "all about me" terrain, everything we do is compromised. Our relationships cannot go deeper because we only ask, "What is comfortable for me, what can I handle?" We forget to ask, "What is the dynamic of this relationship really asking for?" The angels operate in our lives when we give them room to do so by holding the expansive attitude of recognizing *Us*.

Take an honest look at your current relationship with the big picture. Are you mostly interested in your self project, or are you truly interested in what the world needs now: love?

An Angelic Reflection: I will contemplate *Us*.

Heavy Loads

An Angel Reminder: **It all comes out in the wash.**

Sometimes we are forced to carry heavy loads. We may have to care for sick children, parents, spouses. We ourselves may be faced with a serious illness. We might be up against a financial crisis that has taxed us to the limits of our resources. Perhaps we're trying to raise a family as a single parent; perhaps we are dealing with a devastating death. Whatever the burden, when we find ourselves breaking under its weight, it's time to stop and hand it over to the angelic laundry service, which has washers big enough for any size load. The biblical saying "My yoke is heavy but my burden is light" refers to the truth that no matter what befalls us, we are always in partnership with divine forces, which are there to add the extra detergent—in the form of newfound courage and strength—we need to do our loads and carry on.

Are you carrying a heavy load right now? Is it one that you cannot avoid? Or is it one that you don't need to shoulder but have chosen to do so? Ask yourself why your load is so heavy and if there is anything you could do to lighten it. Imagine sending this load to the Angel Laundry and having it come back fresh, clean, neatly folded, and all ready to put away.

An Angelic Reflection: **No matter how heavy my load, the angels are there to lighten it.**

SYNCHRONICITY

An Angel Reminder: **The mystery is the message.**

One byproduct of being spiritually awake is that we tend to encounter meaningful coincidences or synchronistic events. These events seem to hold a magical meaning, going beyond mere chance. You've probably had the experience of thinking about someone you haven't seen for a long time and receiving a phone call from them an hour later, "just by chance." Or, you may have needed a certain amount of money and received the exact amount unexpectedly, in the form of a refund check or some other totally unplanned windfall. These synchronicities, as Jung called them, are a form of proof that our lives are guided by forces that are not always "sensible," that is, of the senses or explainable. Knowing that the mystery is the message and that something else is always going on under the guise of everyday life is an exciting antidote to the relentlessly predictable march of time.

What synchronistic events in your life can you recall? Did you appreciate them as synchronicities, or did you pass them off as coincidence? How does it make you feel to believe in the possibility of spiritual intervention in your life and the idea that your own thoughts and needs are a powerful transmitting device that can draw unexpected responses from the cosmos?

An Angelic Reflection: **I know that unseen forces are always there to answer my requests and reward me with the unexpected.**

Do unto Others

An Angel Reminder: **"On earth as it is in heaven."**
from the Lord's Prayer

Much too often in our quest for personal power, we let our ego guide the way and we don't stop to look at how the outcomes we desire will affect others as well as ourselves. We need to bring in the Golden Rule if we are to expect help from the angels. When you are looking to create a positive change, look at the whole picture. Put yourself in the place of anyone else involved, and ask yourself, "If I were that person, would I want this outcome?" Sincerely look at the effect your actions could have on the world around you. Does your quest involve competition, taking advantage of others, or a hidden agenda?

What if heaven treated us based on how we treat others? How do you treat people, the Earth, and animals each day? Think beyond your good intentions, and examine what you are really doing to help heaven. Have you followed the Golden Rule in all that you do— do unto others as you would have them do unto you? Ask the angels for guidance, and the Golden Rule will bring gold to your consciousness.

An Angelic Reflection: **With the angels in my life, I notice how my actions affect others.**

BLAST FROM THE PAST

An Angel Reminder: Our demons give us
endless opportunities to conquer them.

Have you ever had the experience of thinking you'd finally overcome a difficulty that was impeding your progress, only to have it craftily resurface again and again, in different guises? For instance, just when you thought you'd given up relationships that weren't good for you, another wrong person enters your life to tempt you. Or, every time you've made the vow to finally quit your boring job and do what you've dreamed of doing, your boss offers you a raise you can't refuse. It seems like one of fate's cruel jokes that our past mistakes should keep coming back to entice us to make them again. But instead of a joke, could this instead be God's way of keeping us on our spiritual toes, by periodically reminding us of the traps that it's all too easy for us to fall into? If we've really changed our ways at the deepest level, such little tests won't bother us. Instead, they'll just make us even stronger in our commitment to change. But if down deep we're still susceptible to the lure of the problems we were sure we'd conquered, those problems will keep on coming back to us until we have truly moved beyond them.

What sort of past troublemakers keep coming back to you in different forms? People you thought you'd left behind? Desires you thought you'd overcome? Have you been able to discern a reason for this pattern? Are there any things that used to tempt you but that don't anymore? Remember that the angels are here to help you grow, in insight and wisdom. When unwelcome visitors from the past come knocking, look at them as mere remnants of a bygone era, and send them back to where they came from.

An Angelic Reflection: I am not tempted to resume unhealthy patterns in my life.

THE LEAST FAMILIAR

An Angel Reminder: "Individuation is a natural process. It is what makes a tree turn into a tree; if it is interfered with then it becomes sick and cannot function as a tree; individuation does not shut one out from the world, but gathers the world to oneself."

C. G. Jung

It is very important to meet the lesser-known aspects of ourselves. In our quest to understand ourselves, we often focus too much on what is seen, known, and comfortable. We overdevelop what is obvious and easy for us to grasp, and we overlook what is mysterious to us and may feel alien to our elemental makeup—what Jung called the inferior function. Whatever feels the least familiar to us may be a way to great creative fire, the gateway to inspiration for our lives. What heals us may entail going back to what made us ill. Our weakness can become our biggest strength, for a brittle bone when broken heals to be stronger than the rest.

When the angels come into our life, we begin to explore the least familiar parts of us. We may find out that we are destined to do something we have resisted in little ways our whole life. There are wellsprings within us remaining to be tapped. We can discover that the parts of ourselves that we don't know yet, and may be a little afraid of, are where the magic is.

An Angelic Reflection: I am not afraid to discover new areas in my psyche.

WORDS VERSUS FEELINGS

An Angel Reminder: "Anxiety is the word. The feeling is you."
J. Krishnamurti

The great Indian philosopher Krishnamurti often makes the distinction between words and feelings. For instance, when we are anxious, he says, we are really reacting to the word *anxiety.* In an attempt to define our feeling, we confuse it with a word, which in and of itself has no power save the feeling we attach to it. So, if we do not saddle our feelings with definitions—if we merely observe the feeling itself without words or judgment—a mysterious thing happens. Instead of identifying with the feeling as a positive or negative experience, we become an observer, of both the feeling and ourselves. We detach from bad or good, painful or not painful. In the process we are able to rise above the emotions that keep us in pain or cloud our awareness of what is real—our infinite consciousness—and what is merely passing sensation.

Can you think of any times in your life when you were overwhelmed by a feeling? Are there feelings that you are having right now that instantly engender reactive emotions? If so, try this trick: Think about the event or person that seems to be causing this feeling in you. Then let go of all definitions of the feeling. Don't see it as anger, sadness, excitement, bliss, whatever. Simply feel the feeling as a physical sensation. Step back from it and observe it; watch how you react to it and what it is doing to you. The angels predict that soon you will feel a sense of calmness and detachment that will surprise you.

An Angelic Reflection: I am not my feelings.

AGITATORS

An Angel Reminder: **Be different; stir up
the positive wherever you go.**

Some people are basically agitators, and others are peacemakers. Agitators
are those who disturb and cause anxiety to others. Sometimes it is difficult to recognize an agitator because she or he is disguised as an interesting or highly conscious person, apparently interested in the peace of all.
Sometimes agitators may not even know that they have an agitating effect
on others; they may know only that they like the feeling of stirring things
up and that drama is somehow created around them. Agitators can drain
us if we let them. It is our responsibility to recognize the feeling we get
around others, then choose how to respond. Keep in mind that we cannot
control the behavior of those around us, but we can choose our response.

*To know if someone is causing agitation in your life, think about how you feel after a
simple discussion with that person. How does she or he leave you feeling? Think about how
you leave others feeling—in peace or vaguely upset?*

An Angelic Reflection: **I will be aware of my presence and absence and the
feelings I leave behind.**

GOD'S WRITING

An Angel Reminder: "I am a little pencil in the hand of a writing God who is sending a love letter to the world."

Mother Teresa

Mother Teresa was a true love letter to our world. Each human life can be a love letter from God. Our lives can be a statement of love when we are helping the angels here on Earth. The world can seem very dark and cold at times, but it also is very warm and beautiful. When so much of the writing on the wall is bleak, we may have to look intently to find God's writing. Seek and you will find that love is ever-present when our hearts are full. Joy, smiles, laughter, hugging, and all exchanges of real kindness are verbs in God's love letter.

Are you part of God's love letter? You can be if you want to. Start each day with a moment to center yourself in the hand of a writing God. Ask the angels to help you leave proof of God's love wherever you go.

An Angelic Reflection: **God's love is a verb in my life.**

KEEPING OUR FRIENDS

An Angel Reminder: "A friend is someone with whom
I may be sincere. Before him I may think aloud."
Ralph Waldo Emerson

What is the secret of friendship? The angels say, two things: acceptance
and trust. This may not seem too difficult. But how many of us trust our
friends at the most profound level, which is to have complete faith in
their essential meaning in our lives? The hallmark of friendship is loyalty—being there for your friend through the years, through thick and
thin. Loyalty is an outgrowth of acceptance and trust. Those who tend
to keep their friends throughout their lives have learned to value them as
unique individuals who make a vital contribution to their happiness and
growth. When we make our friends feel prized above the most precious
jewel, seeing the jewel within them—their soul—and allowing it to
sparkle, we will have their undying devotion.

*Do you have long-standing friendships? What do you think has made these friendships
endure? What qualities do you appreciate in your friends? What do you give to them? If
you want to be a better friend, imagine the angels as your friends and try to emulate the
virtues of friendship that they embody.*

An Angelic Reflection: **I value, respect, and honor my friends.**

SOBRIETY

An Angel Reminder: **Sober doesn't have to mean boring.**

Serenity is not a state of robotic homeostasis; it is a state of natural and honest tranquillity that comes from staying awake. Staying awake doesn't mean not resting, but it does mean not being asleep. When we wake up in our consciousness to certain truths we didn't want to acknowledge, it is difficult to go back to sleep. After we wake up and suffer the shock that life isn't going away just because we can't handle it, we get sober so that we can approach life honestly and clearly. This is when the angels are most active in our consciousness. Sobriety becomes of the utmost importance if we have abused a chemical substance in our quest to sleepwalk through life. The journey toward staying awake becomes a hero's journey. The path toward being awake lies in front of us at all times, and when we take one step forward on this path our guardian angel calls in all the help we need to keep going until we wake up one day with serenity in our heart.

Getting sober does not have to be so dark and foreboding with the angels in our life. No matter where you are or what you are doing, sobriety and serenity are available. Twelve-step programs are in a town near you, as a gift from the angels. Sometimes we get a sobering wake-up call when something dear to us is lost or threatened. If we heed the wake-up call, our gift will be the natural high of God's peace in our soul, which equals serenity.

An Angelic Reflection: **I will sober up to the beauty in life.**

ACTION

An Angel Reminder: **A man is the origin of his actions.**
Aristotle

Action is movement. It is the exertion of energy or influence. As humans we are in action a lot of the time. We take action, or we go in and out of action. If we are the origin of our actions as Aristotle said, then who are you? What have your actions in the past hour said about you? How about in the past year? How about your actions toward certain people? What is it that your actions are trying to get across? Once we take action in response to something, we can't undo the action. We can know many things, but we will never really know the effect of and extent of all our actions.

Think about your actions today. Think about the actions of the angels. Is it always possible to think before we act? Do you recognize all your actions, or do you sometimes look back and ask, "Did I do that?" Ask the angels for help in acting consciously, with courage and compassion.

An Angelic Reflection: **With the angels in my life, I can be a true action hero.**

PILING UP THE PLATES

An Angel Reminder: **If you want to balance a pile of plates on your nose, join the circus.**

Sometimes our lives get crazy not only because we've just piled too much on our plates, we've also piled up too many plates. The myriad of duties and obligations we've taken on gets to be overwhelming, and we feel like those Chinese acrobats who balance a tower of spinning plates on their noses while riding a bicycle and juggling ten balls. What we have to remember, though, is that the acrobat trains for years to achieve the awesome precision that allows him or her to achieve seemingly impossible feats of balance. By contrast, when we are trying to balance too many plates and juggle too many balls, everything is sure to come tumbling down on us unless we possess that unshakable sense of inner balance that somehow keeps everything in a state of harmonious intersection. As the Earth's center of gravity assures that the planets will never spin off course and the many worlds in the cosmos won't collide, so we must turn to our center of gravity in order to keep the disparate elements in our lives from crashing into one another and exploding. When we center ourselves we begin to see the folly of having too many things to do, too many plates to balance, and we instinctively begin to find ways of unpiling those plates without breaking them. Thus are we restored to balance and sanity.

How many plates do you have spinning in the air? Can you balance all of them without losing your own balance? Or do you have too much going on at once? When you're trying to do too many things and juggle too many balls, life does indeed become a circus. What are some ways you could streamline your life and restore balance to it?

An Angelic Reflection: **I do not let my obligations and activities go spinning out of control.**

APRIL FOOL'S DAY

An Angel Reminder: "God looks after fools,
drunkards, and the United States."
Anonymous

In the early sixteenth century, France observed New Year's Day on March 25, the advent of spring. Following would be a weeklong celebration ending with parties and dinners on April I. With the reformation of the Gregorian calendar, King Charles proclaimed that New Year's Day be moved back to January I. Many people resisted the change and continued to party on April I. The rest mocked the resisters by sending foolish gifts and invitations to phony parties. Years later, when most of the country had adjusted to the change, whimsical April fooling remained, and the tradition reached England two hundred years later and then finally America. It is easy to be mocked and considered a fool when we refuse to change and go with the new. However, sometimes the old traditions have a lot more meaning.

Pay attention today to the essence of fooling around, the mocking, the so-called practical joking, and the whole idea of tricking someone and then saying "April Fool's." How does it all feel? How would the angels view an April Fool's joke? Always be careful when you judge someone else a fool; it can turn around on you pretty quickly.

An Angelic Reflection: I'm no fool.

TRAGIC OPTIMISM

An Angel Reminder: "He who has a 'why' to live
can bear with almost any 'how.'"

Nietzsche

In 1946, Holocaust survivor Viktor Frankl published a small book entitled *Man's Search for Meaning.* Through the years the book has become a huge best-seller and a guidepost for those trying to make sense of out life's often inexplicably cruel curve balls. Frankl, a medical doctor and psychotherapist who survived Auschwitz and other concentration camps, used his terrible experiences to create a new form of psychoanalysis, which he called "logotherapy," designed to help people focus not on the past but on the present and future, not on their neuroses but on the meaning that life holds for them. Frankl called this attitude toward life "tragic optimism"—optimism in the face of tragedy. Such optimism allows us to remain hopeful in the face of seemingly unendurable suffering because we know that we can still make a difference, that we can still, in Frankl's words, "turn suffering into a human achievement and accomplishment."

If you have suffered loss or some other form of tragedy, how did you respond to it? If you accepted it as a test, how did you score? Are there any events in your life that seemed like tragedies at the time but that, in retrospect, turned out to have their own meaning and purpose? What good things emerged to fill the space that loss left open?

An Angelic Reflection: I know that suffering is meant not to be explained but to be transformed into meaning.

REBIRTH

An Angel Reminder: **Our true self never dies;
instead, it is always being reborn.**

We tend to look at rebirth as a singular phenomenon of epic proportions. The ceremony of baptism, for instance, is a solemn ritual that signifies the rebirth of the soul into newly cleansed life. Or, we may believe in rebirth after death, in the form of reincarnation or new life in new worlds. But the angels want us to realize that rebirth is a continuing gift of life. We are always being reborn on some level, even if we're not aware of it. Our cells are continually regenerating. We are always receiving new insights and experiences that can lead to life-altering awarenesses. This is good to remember when we feel like we're in a rut or that we're too old to change our ways. We can always give new birth to our creative selves; our spirit is always there, to lead the way to new life.

Think of some of the ways that you have been reborn in your life. Were there special events or people who changed your life? Did the birth of a child give you new life? Did a new career or a creative project revitalize you? Is it time for you to be born again on some level? If so, think about how this might happen, and bring in an angel midwife to facilitate the process.

An Angelic Reflection: **My life is always in the process of re-creation.**

RESURRECTION

An Angel Reminder: "The resurrection is nothing if not a conquest of time and place . . . where grief comes to an end, where life, new but mysterious, is resurrected against all odds and all pessimism and all cynicism and all sadness."
Matthew Fox, *The Coming of the Cosmic Christ*

Resurrection means "to rise again." We usually use the word to refer to something that has been given up for dead and suddenly gets a burst of new life. There may be times when something from our past needs to be resurrected, when a relationship, a need, or an issue rises from the grave seeking either rejuvenation or closure. Or, we may believe, after the loss of a love or something else dear to us, that our ability to experience love, hope, and happiness is dead forever, only to discover that these emotions, which constitute the life force, can always be resurrected. The angels remind us that resurrection is a call to address the idea of death in our lives and to acknowledge those things we have left behind that were perhaps not ready to die and those aspects of our being that cannot and will not die. Just as Christ was resurrected, so the good and godly part of us is always ready to rise again and give us new life.

Is there anything from your past that has been recently resurrected or that you have been thinking about resurrecting? If so, what do you think are the reasons for this? Is there anything within you that needs to be resurrected, like faith, hope, passion, or courage? How does resurrection spell new life in your life?

An Angelic Reflection: Every day my soul rises anew.

THE RIGHT TO GRIEVE

An Angel Reminder: **Grieving is our right and our salvation.**

However valid the truth that tragedy is opportunity disguised as loss, it does not ease the pain of that loss. Before we can accept the hidden blessings that loss may bring, we must first go through the process of grief, allowing ourselves to feel and deal with our pain. This is both practical and healthy. Since grief is the new companion that will be with us for a while, it is to our advantage to get to know it. By surrendering to our grief and allowing it to take us by the hand as a friend and teacher, we are letting it work strange magic on us in deep, unknowable ways. The healing process following loss is not quick and easy; a Band-Aid and a kiss won't take care of this deep psychic wound. We have to let ourselves trust the long and arduous process of shock, denial, numbness, despair, and finally acceptance that is common to all survivors of loss. But the angels assure us that as painful and even hopeless as things may seem, healing is taking place, quietly under the surface, and that one day we will discover, as if by a miracle, that we are ready to laugh again, love again, live again.

If you are grieving the loss of someone or something, do you allow yourself to feel the grief, or do you try to avoid or suppress it? There are many confusing and distressing emotions that make up grief, like anger, depression, lethargy, loneliness, and despair. The angels say, don't be afraid of these feelings. When you are angry, let yourself rage. When you are depressed, let yourself cry. When you are lethargic, let yourself sleep and recharge. When you are lonely, let yourself feel the emptiness down to the last drop. When you are despairing, let yourself despair. Then let yourself turn to the angels for comfort, hope, and new direction.

An Angelic Reflection: **I know that in honoring the grieving process, I am honoring the thing I have lost and the heart within me that needs to heal.**

GOING ON

An Angel Reminder: "I'm trying real hard not to indulge in self-pity. . . . Why, I have had so many blessings in my life!"
Sarah Delaney, *On My Own at 107*

The Delaney sisters, Bessie and Sarah, were a truly remarkable pair. They were born into an African American family in Boston in the 1880s, and they put career above everything, never marrying and instead living together for over one hundred years, until Bessie's death at 104 forced her 107-year-old older sister to confront life alone for the first time. Sarah could have easily given up the ghost and joined her lifelong companion. But as she reflected to Bessie's spirit, "I guess I could have died very easily. I suppose I could have just given up, succumbed. But I fought it. I'm not sure why. Much as I want to join you in Glory, I knew it wasn't my time yet." The angels want us to know that it is all right to grieve, even to want to die, when death parts us from our beloved—but it's a true act of courage to live productively instead and let God take care of our final travel plans.

Have there been times in your life when you didn't feel like going on? What kept you going? Was it a person? A goal? Was it that you were too chicken to take your own life or, in the words of "Ol' Man River," tired of living but scared of dying? If you are currently bowed down with sorrow, remember Sarah Delaney's words, "Being alone is a challenge. It's a difficult road to travel, but not impassable."

An Angelic Reflection: I know that life, however painful, still belongs to God and not to me.

THE GIVING TREE

An Angel Reminder: "Praise and blame, gain and loss,
pleasure and sorrow come and go like the wind. To be happy,
rest like a great tree in the midst of them all."

Jack Kornfield

Trees have been symbolic and sacred to humans from as long as we have been here on Earth. A tree's branches reach up to heaven, and its roots venture deep into the sacred ground. Think about a tree in a storm. It can withstand great assaults from nature, but it continues to stand strong, continuing to give to us. Sometimes our position in life is that of a strong giving tree. Other times the wind picks up and hurls the usual insults of life on us, and we feel unappreciated, which diminishes our ability to give. After the wind and rain, though, the sun will warm our branches and we will again be able to provide shade for those who need it.

If you are interested in angels, you are very sensitive and are happiest when you are able to give love. What if you are asked to keep giving until finally there is practically nothing left of you? For a special treat, read The Giving Tree, *by Shel Silverstein.*

An Angelic Reflection: **I will give and be given great love.**

SPIRITUAL LITTERING

An Angel Reminder: **The reward for spiritual smugness
is not paradise but a bad case of tunnel vision.**

Spiritual litterers are people who think they and they alone have all the
answers to everyone's spiritual questions. They are the ones who scatter
their tracts in the streets trying to foist their solutions on others. Since
humans tend to try to avoid discomfort, many like the idea of a solution
to their problems. The only trouble is, this reliance upon solutions or
fixes too often leads to becoming addicted to one set of beliefs and
dependent on what we perceive is the answer to our difficulties. Shooting
up on dogma makes us unable to accept the validity of others' beliefs or
growth processes. At the same time, it may blind us to our own need for
self-exploration. The angels don't like spiritual littering because it invariably involves pitting one belief system against another so that somebody
has to come out a loser. They prefer that we respect spiritual choice as
the domain of providence and that we simply behave according to the
highest good, allowing God to manage the conversion department.

*When someone else has to lose so that we can win in the spiritual arena, how do you think
God is reacting? You better believe he or she is reaching for the spiritual Alka-Seltzer!
What function does your present spiritual belief system play in your life? Do you think
you have the one true way to God, or do you allow for alternative routes? How do you
feel when somebody tries to convert you to their spiritual belief system?*

An Angelic Reflection: **I know that all spiritual roads ultimately lead to God.**

COURT OF FOOLS

An Angel Reminder: **There is such a thing as a spiritual buffoon.**

Some people believe that giving themselves over to a spiritual teacher or religion grants them automatic admission to heaven. These people are often very conscious about going to regular services and following every ritual; some even live in religious communities. Then they go out and act in all sorts of unspiritual ways, lying, cheating, putting one another down, being thoughtless, and generally behaving like typical humans. The problem is, they honestly believe that because they are followers of a spiritual discipline, they are naturally leading a spiritual life. The Bible has a name for such people: hypocrites. We have another name for them: spiritual buffoons. Instead of being models of right conduct, they are living jokes, unintentional self-parodies. We don't know if the angels are laughing at these jokes or just are smiling with infinite patience. We do know though, that it's God's honest truth that people who think they are saints would try the patience of a saint. The angels remind us that the last thing God wants is to preside over a court of fools.

Do you know any spiritual buffoons? How do you feel when they preach to you? Do you lead a life of congruence in terms of your spiritual philosophy and the way you practice it? What are some of the hardest things, to you, about living a truly spiritual life? If you sometimes have difficulty being completely true to your spiritual principles, remember that cultivating the spirit of humility is your most powerful tool in achieving proper perspective.

An Angelic Reflection: **I try to practice what I preach, or better yet, to practice without preaching.**

TRUE LOVE

An Angel Reminder: **"We love the things we love for what they are."**
Robert Frost, "Hyla Brook"

Robert Frost's poem "Hyla Brook" is about a brook that is old and dried up. Yet those who grew up by the brook remember it in its prime—fertile, vibrant, water rushing and singing—and still view it as a grand old brook, despite the fact that it is no longer functioning. Isn't this the true way of the heart? We do not desert those we love when they become old or ill or fall on hard times. Instead we continue to find them beautiful, to love their souls and the inner light that drew us to them in the first place.

Who is beautiful to you? Why? Can you think of people in your life who have loved you simply for who you are, in any and all situations? If so, thank them now. Feel their love coursing through you and warming your heart. Feel yourself generating this beautiful unconditional love toward anyone with whom you come in contact today.

An Angelic Reflection: **I am able to love myself and others not for what they do but for who they are.**

CALLED

An Angel Reminder: **When God comes calling we'd better be in.**

Those who decide to enter the religious life usually say that they were "called" to the vocation. It is fortunate that they took the call and that God wasn't forced to put it on their voice mail or, worse, be subjected to call waiting. We don't have to be a religious to be called to our life's purpose; each and every one of us has a calling. What that calling is, however, may take much time and discernment to figure out. Sure, some people have always known they wanted to be a doctor or a teacher or a musician ever since they were little. But a lot of us are still struggling to discover what we are meant to be doing with our lives. The angels ask us to listen more carefully for the call that will lead us to our fulfillment. God is always trying to reach us; if she hasn't it's most likely because she wasn't able to get through. When we take time to ask for direction, the call will come in. It may not be completely clear at first; there may be static as we try to tune in to the higher vibrations of the celestial phone lines. But eventually we'll get our instructions clear. Then it's our choice whether or not to hang up or trust the call and make a commitment to a new life.

What do you think is your calling? If you're still waiting for the call, the angels suggest that you take some time to think about directions in which you seem to be pulled. Do you have an urge to do something but are afraid you can't make a living at it? Are you afraid to commit your life to anything at all? Our callings don't always take us along a comfortable path; those who live lives of service, for instance, must often make great personal sacrifices. Are you willing to make sacrifices for the sake of your contribution to the world and your soul's satisfaction?

An Angelic Reflection: **I keep my spiritual phone lines open.**

DAYDREAMER

An Angel Reminder: "Laziness goes with mental brilliance.
Long hours of waste that accompany intellectual
activity, inertia, and dullness, are necessary."
James Hillman

We have a name for those who sit and do nothing; we call them day-dreamers. The position of daydreamer is not an honored one in our society. However, it ought to be. Daydreamers dream possibilities. The angels remind us that we are all connected, we each have a special role to play, and for some of us that role is daydreaming. Just because a daydreamer doesn't seem to be providing society with hard copy or three-dimensional money-making items does not mean the dreaming is not important. Many people think daydreamers are lazy. Some people seem to think that laziness is a serious crime; our society has developed all kinds of synonyms for the word *lazy*, and they're all very insulting. The angels are pleased when we allow a bout of laziness, for then they can finally drop by and talk to us. And when they do, they will probably tell us that if we are in the right light, laziness, dullness, and daydreaming are like compost for a good crop of creativity.

Have you ever been accused, or accused yourself, of wasting time? What about those days that pass and you don't get a lot of work done? Are those wasted days? How can we waste time? Next time you feel like doing nothing but daydreaming, contemplating, staring out the window, invite the angels and really get lazy.

An Angelic Reflection: I will help dream the day with the angels, for deep within me I know that this is all a dream of choice.

APRIL 13

MISTAKES

An Angel Reminder: **"May you always make mistakes—just not the same ones."**
A wise spiritual teacher

Mistakes can't be avoided. They are part of the grand scheme of things. When we make mistakes we can almost imagine the angels rubbing their hands with glee at the opportunity we've created for ourselves. Now is our chance to really learn and grow, to discover more about who we are and why we act the way we do. The only problem is when we persist in making the same mistakes over and over. This is a little grating to the angels, like forcing them to listen to a record that's stuck in a groove. Our mistakes can be our salvation or our undoing. The angels encourage us both to admit our mistakes and to examine them honestly. Then, instead of getting ourselves into the same old fixes, we can get ourselves into nice new ones!

Have you made any mistakes lately? Were they helpful in any way? Did they clarify important issues or even take you in an unexpected and better direction? Or do you tend to repeat your mistakes? Try looking more closely at your beliefs and choices and noticing which ones tend to get you stuck in less-than-optimal situations and which are noble risks that propel you to a new level of understanding.

An Angelic Reflection: **I am not afraid to make and learn from mistakes.**

YOUR OWN WORST ENEMY

An Angel Reminder: **If I am not for myself, who will be for me?**

What does it mean when we say someone is their own worst enemy? The word *enemy* comes from the Old French *enemi,* meaning "not a friend." So, when someone is their own worst enemy, the bottom line is that they are not being a friend to themselves. You probably know people who seem to create all their own problems without being the least bit aware that the cause of their misery lies not in the stars, dear Brutus, but in themselves. The sad thing is that this misery is self-perpetuating; they are their own worst enemy precisely because they refuse to acknowledge their responsibility in creating their life and their power to recreate it. So the problems continue and the victim mentality is reinforced. The angels want many things for us, but above all they want for us to be our own best friend, not our own worst enemy. When we are working against ourselves, it becomes that much more difficult for the angels to work with and for us.

Are there ways in which you may be your own worst enemy? Some of the ways we act as enemies and not friends to ourselves include self-deprecation, feeling worthless, self-absorption, insensitivity to others, spreading negativity instead of hope, and addictive behaviors. You may be able to think of others that apply to you or to someone you know. How can you become a better friend to yourself—supportive, ever encouraging, unconditionally loving?

An Angelic Reflection: **In loving myself I find it easier to love others and to draw love to me.**

TERRIBLE THINGS

An Angel Reminder: "I have been through some terrible things in my life, some of which actually happened."
Mark Twain

The legacy of Mark Twain is abundant with insights into the irony and humor of the human journey. What terrible things have you been through lately? Were you actually there during the upheaval, or did you experience it vicariously—in your imagination or on your TV? Most of what happens "to us" is experienced in our mind. The rest of us—our soul, spirit, heart—may be on to other things while our mind is dragging us through one frightening scenario after another.

If you want to go through some terrible things, it is not hard to do, for awful things are only a thought away. If you don't want to go through terrible things, it is not hard to do, for it is only a thought that will change your perspective. The angels are alerted when a truly terrible thing is at hand, and they will be right beside you—heart, soul, spirit, mind, and body.

An Angelic Reflection: **I've been through some wonderful things in my life.**

DO YOU REALLY WANT PEACE?

An Angel Reminder: **Peace can be achieved
only if it is truly desired.**

It's a curious thing, how peace treaties always seem to be stymied or violated. Just when it looks like the Protestants and the Catholics or the Arabs and the Israelis or the Serbs and the Muslims are getting close to negotiating a peace, a bomb goes off in a British embassy or a Jerusalem marketplace or a Bosnian street. We may think that any sane person, given the choice between peace and war, would automatically choose the former. But when it comes to our egos too many of us are insane, opting to live in hatred rather than forgiveness, intolerance rather than tolerance. And this is not just the terrorist minority. How many times in our own lives have we preferred to stay angry because we simply liked the feeling and didn't want to give it up? The angels plead with us to rise above anger and hatred, to transcend the overpowering impulse to be right no matter what the cost.

Begin to see your emotions as energy fields, radiating out into the atmosphere. What colors do they have? Anger is often seen in hues of red or black, while peace is associated with the colors of white and blue. When you are faced with a conflict, concentrate on sending out healing, calming blue-white light, which acts as a cooling breeze on the red heat of anger. See what effect it has on the situation.

An Angelic Reflection: **I willingly offer up my ego on the altar of peace.**

Doing Our Part

An Angel Reminder: **The school janitor is just as important as the President as far as God is concerned.**

There are moments we might feel that our lives are insignificant—that if we disappeared tomorrow the world wouldn't be any the poorer for it. These are the times when angel courage comes in the form of the knowledge that as long as we are on the Earth, each and every one of us has a unique part to play in its progress. The entire planet might not depend on us for its survival; as Eliza Doolittle contemptuously sang to the arrogant Henry Higgins in *My Fair Lady,* "The sun will come up without you . . . the tides will roll in without you. . . ." But on the level of infinite mystery, we are a vital ingredient in the grand scheme. We don't have to be doing great things to make our contribution. It's in our daily interactions and choices that we have the most impact. Even the seemingly low-level job is high level if it is performed in the spirit of higher consciousness. At the final judgment, if there is such a thing, it's the people who gave of themselves with compassion, sensitivity, and a smile whose contribution will be considered the greatest, no matter how much money they made or how much power they wielded.

Think about the effect that you have on everybody around you, every day. If you look back on your life, there's a good chance you can recall many instances in which your influence was felt. Today, become conscious of how you interact with people and the actions that you take, however small, that have an effect upon your environment.

An Angelic Reflection: **I appreciate the gift of life and the chance to make a difference.**

WHAT'S REAL?

An Angel Reminder: **It ain't necessarily so.**

We all think we know what's real. That table over there is real. The sun up above is real. This life is real. But talk to a Buddhist and you get a very different version of reality, one in which our earthly existence, with all its supposedly tangible accoutrements, is merely an illusion, and the things that are not necessarily visible to the naked eye are the true reality. The point is that reality is as flexible as a Peking acrobat, able to be turned and twisted into all variety of probability-defying positions. "Real" can be a clever trap. When we get locked in to one version of reality, we severely limit our capacity for vision, change, and compassion. It may be real, for instance, that you and your partner are not getting along. But is the reality of the situation that "this relationship can't be saved"? Or is the reality, "This relationship is making me so uncomfortable that I'm forced to grow and change"? The angels are around to remind us that reality is a perceptual choice. We can always change our reality, and in so doing we open up whole new vistas of hope. It may feel safer to set clearly defined boundaries around reality, because then we believe we have control over our lives. But it's when we have the courage to admit that nothing is really as it seems that we become far more creative in shaping our destiny.

Do you tend to view reality as being carved in concrete? Take a moment to assess your view of what's real. What happens when you think about the possibility that what seems real may not be? How much do you have invested in your notions of what's real?

An Angelic Reflection: **I am constantly open to new and more interesting versions of reality.**

PEOPLE ACTUALLY CHANGE

An Angel Reminder: **Do people change,
or do our impressions of them change?**

Have you ever met someone and formed a firm impression of them, then met them a year later and found that they are nothing like the role you cast them in? If you meet someone when they are thick in a depression, you may not realize it and think they are that way all the time. Think about what happens if you meet someone after they have had a few alcoholic drinks, and then the next time you see them they are sober and they seem so different. We can't help forming a first impression, but we can help getting attached to it. It is not easy to let people change in our minds. It isn't a character flaw to change with time; it is a character flaw not to allow it.

Next time you meet someone new, try to look deeper into who they are, even if you are with them for a short while and it is supposed to be only business. We don't like others' impressions of us to be stuck in the past, so we have to practice the Golden Rule and not stick others in the cement of past perceptions. The angels give us the courage to let our minds change in an instant.

An Angelic Reflection: **I will change my mind.**

OBSERVER

An Angel Reminder: "It is all movies—a movie within a movie."
Paramahansa Yogananda, *The Divine Romance*

Sometimes the angels think that when a human being is born, there should be a sign posted on the Earth's doorway that reads "Warning! You are now entering the sea of life. Swim at your own risk!" Total immersion in the raging waters of daily life can lead to drowning if we're not careful. That's why it's a good idea to step back every once in a while and trade the role of participant for that of observer. Paramahansa Yogananda said that once, when he was taken to see a movie, he suddenly became a complete observer of all of life. "The theater, every motion, the people sitting around me—I could see them all as pictures on the vast screen of cosmic consciousness." It is when we detach ourselves from material reality that we are able to connect fully with our divine consciousness. Paradoxically, at the same time we are better able to understand fully what's going on around us. You'd be surprised at how refreshing and eye-opening it is just to watch humanity in operation—yourself included—without preconceptions or judgments, as though you're at a movie. It's quite a show, isn't it? And once it's over, you step out of the dark and into the light.

Try a little experiment. Just stop what you're doing and look at your life as if it's a movie. See yourself as a character on-screen. What are you engaged in and why? What other characters are around you? What does your room look like? What would the camera pan in on as being important indicators of who you are? Do this for a few moments, or even longer if you feel so inclined. Later you might want to jot down some of your observations.

An Angelic Reflection: **I sometimes sit back and enjoy the show of my life.**

WEEPING

An Angel Reminder: "A time to weep, and a time to laugh."
Ecclesiastes 3:4

To weep means to shed tears as an expression of emotion; it also means to ooze or exude moisture. Emotions are watery, and feelings are deep like a well. If we are feeling emotional and weepy, no amount of logic will help us change the situation. Sometimes we just have to give in to the weeping and let the tears ooze out of us when they begin to well up. It can be scary when we are weepy. We think we may never get past it. But if we feel weepy it is for good reason, regardless of what our intellect may tell us or what someone may project onto us. If you stop water when it needs to flow, it builds up and the dam will break, so let your watery emotions weep. When you weep, remember the angels are there watching you. They count each tear that falls from your beautiful eyes.

Sometimes a good weep may turn into a wail. Let it go. Allow yourself privacy to weep and wail and cry out to God. We weep because nothing lasts forever, and weeping too will not last forever. Let the angels shine their light through your tears and make a rainbow. A rainbow is a sign of hope and a sign of the sacred covenant between God and us.

An Angelic Reflection: I will let my tears fall freely from the depth of my feelings.

DOWN TO EARTH

An Angel Reminder: **When we are really down to earth we are close to heaven.**

We and the Earth are one. We are made of the same substance as the Earth; we get our food, our oxygen, our minerals from the Earth. So it is important to maintain our connection to and respect for the Earth, our source of life. The angels want us to become aware of our particular role in the ecosystem, for every living thing contributes in its own way to the maintenance of creation. How we treat our environment is ultimately a mirror of how we treat others and ourselves. We are communal, not autonomous, beings; life is a continually interactive system of cause and effect. Many of us have lost contact with the Earth, our natural environment, and as a result we are not grounded. Appreciating the Earth helps us to become centered and focused in our work and purpose. Letting our bare feet connect with the grass, feeling the soil between our fingers as we plant a garden, harvesting the fruits, vegetables, and herbs that we grow ourselves, walking down the majestic tree-lined halls of the forests—all of these actions bring us closer to the Earth and, simultaneously, to the angels and God.

Do you appreciate the Earth? Or have you become disconnected from your true source? Are there difficulties in your life that might be resolved if your feet were planted more firmly on the ground? Think of what "down to earth" means to you. Putting down roots? Being more practical? Doing reality checks? Try connecting to the actual Earth more, and note how this helps you to be more grounded in the rest of your life.

An Angelic Reflection: **I take advantage of the strength and solidity of the Earth, and I know that its tremendous energy is part of me.**

Put Them in Their Place

An Angel Reminder: "Great spirits have always found violent opposition from mediocre minds."
Albert Einstein

Bright shiny things cause trouble. Bright shiny people get in trouble. Bright children intimidate dull adults. When someone seems excessively lucky, on a certain level we think it unfair. Low-level luck can stay invisible, but grand luck is obvious. Being invisible is safe, being visible is dangerous. We can "know too much for our own good," and when we do, count on the fact that we will be put in our place sooner or later. But where is our real place? When we shine, do others get envious? Do the angels want us to dull our radiance? We can never be free from the mediocrities, but we don't have stop shining when the angels are in our consciousness.

The cauldron of jealousy, envy, and entitlement gets stirred up when good fortune befalls someone. The angels want us to be careful with what we say and do in the realm of great blessings. It never does us any good to brag about our good fortune. Staying humble when we are blessed will help protect us from the envy of others as well as allow us to develop gratitude for our blessings.

An Angelic Reflection: **I have a place with the angels.**

HOPELESS PEOPLE

An Angel Reminder: **Hope implies trust,
in the essential rightness of the universe.**

Hopeless people are the angels' greatest challenge, for the most important ingredient in angel courage is hope. We can't have courage—we can't have anything, really—if we don't have hope. Hope goes hand in hand with joy, dreams, goals—all the things that propel us forward, make life worthwhile, and give us the strength to get through the bleaker times. If you've ever wondered why your body and psyche feel worse when you're around a hopeless person, the answer is simple. It's because they're trying to rob you of the essential fuel that keeps your inner fire burning brightly. Hopeless people are like smog: they spoil natural beauty, obscure the horizon, and choke us with the insidious fumes of perpetual despair. They are so depressing that even the angels need a double shot of courage to remain in their energy field. Of course there are times in everyone's life when things look hopeless, when hope seems more like a luxury than a birthright. But most of us find ways to pick ourselves up and sift through the rubble of our dashed hopes for some treasures to remind us that hope is never lost, only buried.

Do you know any hopeless people? How do you feel being around them? Do you some-times feel hopeless yourself? What are some of the things that give you hope? The angels prescribe the following antidote to hopelessness: (1) See the humor in things; (2) be encouraging, not discouraging; (3) believe in the virtue of happiness; (4) have faith in the unknown; (5) believe in miracles, not statistics; (6) allow yourself and others to express themselves without fear of criticism or ridicule; (7) be loving and generous, and watch love and generosity fill your life in return.

An Angelic Reflection: **I make it my business to generate hope.**

CRUTCH

An Angel Reminder: "You break your leg,
you need a crutch for a while."

Jai

Needing a crutch is obvious when you have broken your leg, but when your heart, spirit, or soul is broken, then it gets a little confusing. A crutch is something we depend on for support for however long it is needed. After the past twenty years of pop psychology and the "one minute get back out there and conquer the world" solutions we have been fed, it is difficult to realize that there are times we have to be dependent on others or on a crutch. We think it is a sign of weakness if we allow someone to care for us after we have been hurt or knocked off the merry-go-round of life. Why is weakness a bad sign? Why is weakness something we immediately set out to fix? Why is it wrong to let someone take care of our soul and heart for a while? Love is what heals; we will let go of our crutch when it's time.

If you need a crutch, let yourself use it. If you are lucky enough to have a human angel to look after you, let that person love you. Love needs to be given and shown. Ask the angels to help you with your inner work so you can be conscious of your crutch—using it and not abusing it. The fact is we are all fragile and easily broken, so let's not force a healing. With the angels around, everything will be taken to higher ground. Don't worry about dependence or independence; just be honest with how you feel and the angels will help you with what you truly need to heal.

An Angelic Reflection: I will rest on the angels' invisible crutch of love.

HEAD VERSUS HEART

An Angel Reminder: "If you prefer book learning, go ahead. But you will wither away and neither love nor kindness will emanate from you. You will be nothing but a cold, dried-up intellectual who discusses, criticizes and dissects everything but who is incapable of escaping from his own inner disorder."
Omram Mikhael Aivanhov

We know a philosophy professor, a highly learned man, who has taught and lectured on Buddhism for nearly fifty years and prides himself on knowing all there is to know about his subject. But this professor is also one of the worst academic snobs you will ever meet. He is condescending and critical and also given to holding grudges against anyone who offends him, intellectually or otherwise. What do you suppose a real Buddhist would say about this professor, who has undoubtedly never seen himself in the countless Zen stories that poke fun at head-versus-heart knowledge? The angels remind us that spiritual knowledge is lived, not intellectualized. In their eyes an uneducated person is closer to enlightenment than an educated fool, for it is our intellectual pretensions, more than any other vice, that put up the biggest block on the road to God.

Do you know any educated fools—people who prefer "rationality" to feeling, intellectualizing to empathizing, or who wear their intellect like a medal, showing it off as though it entitles them to special privileges? Education is a wonderful thing when it is combined with compassion, humility, and empathy. Then we have a real opportunity to uplift both the minds and spirits of others, which is what real teaching is all about.

An Angelic Reflection: I think with my heart as well as my head.

PRODIGAL

An Angel Reminder: "And the son said to him, 'Father, I have sinned against heaven and in your sight; I am no longer worthy to be called your son.' But the father said to his slaves...'let us eat and be merry; for this son of mine was dead, and has come to life again; he was lost and has been found.' And they began to be merry."

Luke 15:21–24

Sometimes it is difficult to choose to take gallant risks in life when you feel that you might do something wrong and be punished for it. Yet, who would do the punishing in that case, and who judges us wrong? Why was the prodigal son honored when he came back from his reckless journey? He chose to find out about life, to live it and experience it—to learn his own lessons. The results of our actions, whether prodigal or profitable, teach us the value of life and point us to our own values. The angels will always welcome us back from any reckless journey just as the father of the prodigal son did. They want us to be alive and awake, and a good sign of this is when we question authority.

Next time you find yourself listening to an authority figure, ask yourself if you feel right about what this person is saying. Have you wanted to do anything reckless lately and felt held back by convention? Look at the reasons.

An Angelic Reflection: With the angels in my life, I am more interested in those who think differently.

THE BOGEYMAN

**An Angel Reminder: Fear is often nothing
more than misdirected potential.**

Sometimes fear is necessary for survival. If we had absolutely no fear of anything, we would not know the difference between safe and dangerous. We would do foolhardy things, like running into the street in front of a car or going right up to a hungry lion. But fear, while necessary in times of physical peril, is nothing more than a bogeyman when it comes to our emotional and spiritual lives. So often what we're afraid of hasn't yet happened and is thus a projection of our overactive imaginations. The angels urge us to examine our fears and decide which ones are in our best interest and which ones are merely bogeymen, waiting to be exposed by our courage to face them and laugh them in the face.

Remember the old childhood game The Bogeyman? A bunch of kids get together as twilight is descending, and one of them is picked as The Bogeyman, who goes and hides while everyone else closes their eyes and chants, "Twilight, twilight, the Bogeyman won't come out tonight." And of course, at the climactic moment, the Bogeyman does jump out from his or her hiding place and runs after the screaming, fleeing children. But what happened when the Bogeyman got you? Nothing! The next time you have a fear that's become a Bogeyman, try playing this game. Pretend the Bogeyman has gotten you, and then see yourself as still standing, still breathing, still alive, still perfectly all right. Then realize that your fear is only fear and you have the power to create your own reality.

An Angelic Reflection: My fears can never catch me if I face them and do not run from them.

PROCRASTINATION

An Angel Reminder: **Never put off till tomorrow
what you can do the day after tomorrow.**
Mark Twain

Have you ever thought about why we procrastinate? The word *procrastination* means "for tomorrow," and the verb means "to put forward to tomorrow." What are the things that we most often put off until tomorrow? Paying bills, doing taxes, cleaning up, making phone calls are some of the things most of us put off. We may tell ourselves that we like to work under pressure, and so putting these things off gives us such a sense of emergency when we finally get to them that we are propelled into action. The trouble is, these objects of procrastination are tormenting us and causing anxiety all along, and the truth is that our bodies don't really like working under pressure.

Think of things in your life that you have been putting off, and then ask yourself why. Is it because these things just are not fun and meaningful? Putting something off doesn't mean we have an innate flaw. The stuff we put off is put off for a reason. If we choose to face that reason and not give ourselves a dose of guilt, then we can see into other areas of our life that may be feeding the procrastination spiral.

An Angelic Reflection: **My life is on time.**

KNOWING THAT
YOU DON'T KNOW

An Angel Reminder: **Not knowing anything is ignorance;
knowing that you don't know anything is wisdom.**

There's a classic moment in the 1951 movie *A Christmas Carol* when
Scrooge, played by the great Alastair Sim, realizes that he's still alive after
his spooky visits with the ghosts of Christmas past, present, and future
and that he still has time to turn his mean-spirited life around. In this
moment he sheds his nasty, old self and begins prancing wildly about the
room, singing, "I don't know anything, I never did know anything, but
now I know that I don't know!" His terrified housekeeper shrieks, "Mr.
Scrooge, have you lost your senses?" To which Scrooge replies, "No, dear
lady, I haven't lost my senses. I have come to them." What an exquisite
moment of enlightenment Dickens created: the moment at which we
shed our false selves, our egos, and step into the light of pure awareness
of our nonknowing! We are like a child once more, full of awe, wonder,
and curiosity, open to all new experiences, willing to learn. This is the
point at which we are most receptive to the angels, who no longer have to
beat at the closed door that was once our mind but can now walk freely
through an open one.

*How do you feel about not knowing something? Okay? Inferior? Are you able to admit
when you don't know something, or, better yet, can you welcome the possibility? Are there
any know-it-alls in your life? What do you think of them? Wouldn't you rather be a wise
know-nothing than a smug know-it-all?*

An Angelic Reflection: **I allow myself the freedom not to know so that I
may be truly open to learning.**

CANDLEPOWER

An Angel Reminder: "You are the light of the world."
Matthew 5:14

Candle power, technically, is the intensity of a light source expressed in candelas. But candle power is also a term we use when someone seems to shine very brightly in all that they do. Candle light is wonderful. When someone shines with candle power they allow those around them to glow also. Candle power gives beauty to the spirit and a gentle warmth to the soul.

The angels see all of us as having candle power, and they like to help us increase the candelas. True candle power is a divine gift, so be careful when and where you choose to shine. If there are some around who can't stand the light, they may try to blow out your flame. Ask the angels to shine with you. This way if you are attacked, your attackers will get a blast of love light.

An Angelic Reflection: **They can't hold a candle to me.**

HISTORY

An Angel Reminder: **History is always in the making.**

We know the old phrase "history repeats itself." We also know that we can learn from history. If we are indeed learning from history, though, it shouldn't have to repeat itself. We should have learned our lessons and ceased to duplicate past errors. Unfortunately, or fortunately—for who knows what is fortune?—human beings will always be human beings, acting according to innate mechanisms that remain the same through the centuries. So there's a good chance that here and there we will probably repeat the past, taking two steps forward and one step backward on our journey toward enlightenment. The angels suggest that history isn't only something in the library. We all have our own history, and it can be very helpful to study it once in a while. As we look over our own lives, key events that have shaped us and patterns that we have tended to repeat jump out from the pages of our past, bringing awareness. In the process, we may be able to see the present more clearly and to create the future with foresight instead of hindsight in the making.

If your life were in a history book, what would the entry say? What are some of the pivotal events in your personal history? What are the things you'd like to have recorded for posterity? The things you'd rather weren't remembered? How would you like to "make history"? Have some fun, and write your own entry in "The History of the World." You may be surprised at what you learn.

An Angelic Reflection: **I study the past, live in the present, and learn for the future.**

IDOL WORSHIP

An Angel Reminder: **Ye shall have no other gods before me.**

In the best sense of the term, *worship* should mean to look up to or aspire to, with regard to other people, and to revere and praise, with regard to God. Unfortunately, we sometimes mistake other humans for God. This leads to trouble, for we then give our power over to them. This is the way Hitlers are created; it is also the way false gurus and other charlatans are able to hoodwink the multitudes. The angels remind us that only God is worthy of worship. Humans may be worthy of admiration; there is no harm in wanting to emulate someone who is a model of conduct. But we have to remember that an idol is really an ideal to which we aspire, not a god to whom we bow. When we worship a fellow human, projection is almost always at work. We are investing them with godlike qualities and looking to them for salvation instead of cultivating the godlike qualities within us that make idols unnecessary.

Do you have any idols? Do you merely admire them, or do you worship them? When you worship something, does it tend to have power over you? Ideally, the act of worship should both humble us and remind us that we have a divine partner to whom we can always turn. When worship strips us of our sense of self and turns us into a blind follower, we must question its validity.

An Angelic Reflection: **I cultivate inner strength instead of giving my power to others.**

HATE

An Angel Reminder: "There are six things which the Lord hates, yes, seven which are an abomination to Him: haughty eyes, a lying tongue, and hands that shed innocent blood, a heart that devises wicked plans, feet than run rapidly to evil, a false witness who utters lies, and one who spreads strife among brothers."

Proverbs 6:16–19 NASV

Hatred is not a pleasant feeling. It is a state of extreme detesting and loathing and at its worst results in violent hostility. Although none of us wants to feel hatred for another, there are times when it creeps into our consciousness. Usually when we feel hate it means that someone has attacked us or our loved ones. The Proverbs quote above lists seven things that God hates. If we think about it, these are the things that lead to hate in our own lives. If someone has done these things to us, it may cause us to hate them; if we do these things to others, we will end up hating ourselves.

Evil begets evil, hatred begets hatred. It is up to us, with the help of the angels, to change the direction of evil energy. Don't let hatred stay very long in your consciousness. If it is there acknowledge it. Be honest with yourself, and examine all of the evidence. Then resolve to step onto higher ground. As soon as you do, the angels will come in and help you leave hatred behind.

An Angelic Reflection: I will release my angry feelings and clear the air with the angels.

ECONOMY

An Angel Reminder: **Don't let your assets make an ass out of you.**

To manage an economy means to manage resources carefully, to reduce expenses, and to set up a system for the production of goods and services. Think for a moment about your own economy, that is, the system by which you manage your resources. Is it a healthy economy? Is it something you feel comfortable about? How do you manage your emotional economy? Do you receive as much nurturing as you give to others? How about your physical economy: Are you taking care of your body so that you don't waste your resources? Is your spiritual economy healthy, so that you are producing the goods and services that are yours to give the world? Would you be happier if your system for management in your life were a little stronger or a little simpler?

We can best be open to the angels when we have a sense of sacred management in our lives. Now is a good time to manage our resources and economize where necessary. Ask the angels for insight on better ways to manage your personal economy. Are there places where you might be able to save your resources? Do you need more balance between the goods and services you receive and those you send into the world? With a balanced personal economy, you are better equipped to remain open to what the angels have to offer.

An Angelic Reflection: **I am ready to manage my own economy.**

LOANS

An Angel Reminder: Before God we are all in debt.

Have you ever loaned someone something that they didn't return? Money is a good example. Many of us have loaned a friend or relative money, only to be frustrated and resentful when they neglected to pay it back. What is the best way to respond in this situation? If we demand repayment, we may risk putting the other person in an embarrassing or defensive position. If we say nothing, we risk destroying the relationship by poisoning it with suppressed and misdirected anger. In such awkward instances the angels advise us to release our attachment to the money, trusting that as long as we continue to love our debtor, the loan will be repaid. Many people have found that if they sent blessings to someone in their debt, the money was repaid soon afterward without their ever having to ask for it. The angels remind us that everything in life is on loan to us anyway; to believe that we really possess anything is an illusion. If we are sorely in need of the money that is overdue, we need only to ask God to intervene and surround the issue in light, not anger and fear. The angels promise us that with this attitude we will never fail to attract all that we need.

Does anyone owe you money? How has this affected your relationship with this person? If you are angry that the person hasn't repaid you, send out loving energy right now to him or her. See your anger transforming into a ball of light that surrounds your debtor like a warm embrace. Communicate psychically to this person that you need the money and that you know they want to repay you. Then hand the matter over to the Angel Collection Agency.

An Angelic Reflection: When it comes to loans, I subscribe to the philosophy of the dollar: In God We Trust.

SAME OLD SAME OLD

An Angel Reminder: **When you reach a plateau in life, don't get too comfortable; look for a mountain to climb or a valley to explore.**

Some people have a very limited repertoire, and once it has run through they have nothing new to offer. This is often the case when people stop growing or experiencing life in an honest and real way. Maybe they develop an addiction, or maybe they shut off when hurt by a loss. Whatever the reason for the shutdown, what results is a repetition of old stories and insights that eventually end up boring others. When we live as real as we can in each moment, we accumulate new insights and stories to share, and our repertoire expands.

With the angels in our lives we don't need a repertoire. All we need is a reserve of love. Love is never boring. To approach life with love and courage means to remain open to each moment, ready for our old insights to be challenged by new truths. Who needs old stories when we can tap into our angel consciousness and love in the here and now?

An Angelic Reflection: **My repertoire is as vast as the wings of angels.**

POWER

An Angel Reminder: "Nearly all men can stand adversity,
but if you want to test a man's character, give him power."
Abraham Lincoln

Think for a moment about somebody who you think has power. Do they
have power in your mind because of how much money they have, the job
or position they hold, or the way they handle their life? Think about
someone you know who abuses the power they have. Perhaps they are
mean-spirited or forget about the less fortunate as soon as they gain a little
influence. Or perhaps they try to control others, using their power to
mold others into their likeness instead of using it to love others into their
highest good. The angels remind us that power is temporary. We never
really possess it, because life can turn on a dime and present us with a situation that no amount of money, fame, or position in life can resolve.
When these situations arise we are humbled and reminded that there is
one true Higher Power.

*Think about a time you felt powerful in a situation. How did you use your power? The
angels remind us that the Higher Power is available and works toward the highest good of
all. Ask the angels for help in remaining open to the source of true power—love.*

An Angelic Reflection: I know where the Highest Power is when I need it.

MOTHER'S DAY

An Angel Reminder: **"Angels—we call them mothers down here."**
Title of an old Eddie Cantor song

The old song above was typical of the sentimental mother reverence that prevailed in the early part of the twentieth century, when Mother's Day came into existence. Corny cards and hearts and flowers became the standard method of honoring mothers—to the consternation of Anna M. Jarvis, the founder of Mother's Day. She griped that her original intent—to remind us of the importance of our mothers and to challenge us to treat them with love and respect every day of the year—had been commercialized and trivialized beyond recognition, to the point where sending a card had become a substitute for meaningful relationship. The angels are the ideal mothers, unconditionally loving and nurturing. Our mothers are not angels, and we should not expect them to be. We should love and appreciate them for who they are. If we haven't had adequate mothering in our lives, we can always turn to the angels for the comfort and support that our own mothers may have been incapable of giving to us.

Today, think about the qualities associated with the ideal mother. Then, if your mother is still alive, try mothering her on her day. Instead of brushing her off with a card or a bouquet, give her the wonderful gift of unconditional love and understanding. If your mother is no longer alive, you can still send these gifts to her and she will feel them in spirit and be grateful.

An Angelic Reflection: **I adopt the best qualities of motherhood in my own life, and I extend them to others.**

ZIGAZUNDT

An Angel Reminder: You shall live and be well!

Zigazundt is a Yiddish word meaning, roughly, "live and be well." It is a blessing one wishes others in parting. We can look at this word as having a magical capacity to release someone into God's hands. This way we can let go of any worries or negativity that might be left behind, and both parties receive a healing. Others often disappoint us, and we may keep the connection alive with bad feelings. When we part with someone, we need to make it clean and healthy. A blessing is the perfect way to clean things up.

Use the magic of Zigazundt to release painful connections with someone that may reside in your mind. If you want a blessing for yourself, then bless those who curse you. Say "Zigazundt" each time a negative thought enters your mind about someone with whom you're angry, and imagine the angels expanding the blessings. Keep it up, and you shall live and be well!

An Angelic Reflection: I know that God holds us in health and love.

REMORSE

An Angel Reminder:

**"When such as I cast out remorse
So great a sweetness flows into the breast
We must laugh and we must sing,
We are blest by everything,
Everything we look upon is blest."
William Butler Yeats**

Having remorse means that we have done something that we regret. Our regretful action may have brought us shame and guilt—two feelings that can eat away at us. The word *remorse* means, literally, the "biting" of conscience; it comes from the Latin *remordere*, "to bite again." So whenever we feel remorse it means we were bitten once and if we can't let go of what we did and move forward, it will continue to bite us and torment our conscience. The angels want us to know the good news about remorse: it means we care about how our actions affect others and the world.

If you are feeling the bite of remorse, let it go. Don't carry around shame. Ask the angels to give you the positive version of remorse, which is the courage to ask forgiveness for wrongs we have committed and to seek to make things right. If there is action you can do to help change the chemistry of the situation, think it through and then do it. The bottom line is that we need to drop the heavy burdens of remorse. This way we are free to create a better situation in the future.

An Angelic Reflection: **I shall not be bitten again; I am on my way to the future.**

INVOLVED

An Angel Reminder: "Any man's death diminishes me, because I am involved in mankind; and therefore never send to know for whom the bell tolls; it tolls for thee."

John Donne

To involve means "to draw in, embroil, include, entangle." It comes from a Latin word meaning "enwrap." To get involved is to get mixed up in. It can also mean to get more complicated and complex. When we are involved we have mixed our minds, hearts, spirits, and souls into the complex. We need to be careful about what we get involved in, for what we give heart and soul to tends to hold us in its grasp, making it difficult to get out of, if necessary. When the involvement is good for us, then the various parts of us will flow together in harmony. But if the involvement is harmful to us, then our heart, mind, and soul will not be aligned, and the various parts of us may look for their own escape routes.

Have you gotten involved in something that was so entangled it felt like it was choking you? If so, it is time to get mixed up in positive things that come from the angels. Get involved with art classes, prayer, sacred dance, singing, happy people, and anything else that involves spiritual inspiration.

An Angelic Reflection: I will get involved in conscious connection with the angels.

THE OTHER PERSON'S SHOES

An Angel Reminder: **If the shoe fits, wear it.
If it doesn't, take it off.**

You know the old expression "putting yourself in the other person's shoes." This is another way of saying, try to understand what someone else is feeling; try seeing things from the other person's perspective. But we've always found this expression curious, because nine times out of ten when we step into someone else's shoes they don't fit. It would be like putting on someone else's glasses; we can't see a thing. The fact is, we can't walk in someone else's shoes without getting a bad case of bunions. Everyone's experience of life is unique, molded to their soul's specifications. The angels would rather we seek to understand the viewpoint of others by allowing them their journey and giving them both support and space. Then we can wear our own shoes as we walk alongside them.

Have you ever tried to walk in someone else's shoes? Did they fit, or were they too tight or too big? Are there times you can think of when you just couldn't put yourself in someone else's place—when their actions were understandable only to their own souls? At times like this, we must allow others to walk their own walk while we continue to love and support them even without understanding where they're going.

An Angelic Reflection: **I accept the mystery of the individual soul journey.**

GRACE PERIOD

An Angel Reminder: The most important
grace period we have is right now.

Grace is a gift bestowed upon the soul from God. It is a divine impulse, a
prayer, an abiding glow within, the presence of the Holy Spirit. The
word *grace* is from the Latin *gratia*, meaning favor or thanks, and it's related
to the Sanskrit *grnati*, meaning "he praises." A grace period is thus a time
for showing gratitude and praise. Who needs a grace period? We all do!
Our planet appears to be in trouble, human beings are destroying one
another and the rest of creation, and so many of our human institutions
are corrupt. We need a grace period, a last chance to pay our dues and
start to reverse some of the corruption. The meaning of the word *grace*
suggests that the way to reverse our course is to start by offering thanks.
When we give thanks for the way the Earth nourishes us, when we offer
praises for the differences between our races and peoples, we will have
entered a grace period. For things to change we need to honor love, commit to love, and love will bring us grace.

*To encourage grace, and to help the angels, we need to practice daily gratitude, praise God,
pray, and always choose love.*

An Angelic Reflection: I am always living in a grace period.

DIFFICULT TASKS

An Angel Reminder: "The difficult we do immediately.
The impossible takes a little longer."
U.S. Armed Forces motto

Difficult things are things that are hard for us to do. They may be things we have psychological blocks about doing, like paying bills on time or returning phone calls—things we put off because they are necessary but no fun. Other difficult, hard things are the challenges we face that we think we will never be able to overcome. There is always something in our life that we can label difficult. The angels remind us that when we don't do the difficult, we actually become hard—stubborn and rigid. They want us to know that when we do the difficult, the impossible turns into glorious possibilities.

If you were to take one hour each day to do the difficult, at the end of the month you would have spent thirty hours taking care of the things that have been causing stress and worry. Choose one thing today that you have been putting off because it's too hard, and spend a few minutes tackling it. Then notice how your courage rises to meet the next challenge.

An Angelic Reflection: **Bring on the difficult; I am getting ready for the impossible.**

PROVIDENCE OR PROPHECY

An Angel Reminder: "Heaven and earth will pass
away, but my words shall not pass away. But of that day
and hour no one knows, not even the angels of heaven,
nor the Son, but the Father alone."
Matthew 24:35, 36

We are told in the Bible not to foretell the end times but to take care of the present with reverence. Often these days you can hear people say it is the end of the world and that there is no hope for our survival on this planet. People are often quoting the latest prophecy or the newest date for the end of life as we know it. But keep in mind that prophecy is big business, too, with people stockpiling supplies and weapons out of fear for the future. The angels really wonder what we are preparing for, when we stockpile supplies because we fear dying at the end of the world. The fact is, we can die at any moment, and our only saving grace is to live in love at each moment.

Each of us chooses which reality we are going to live in. If we choose prophecy, then we are living in fear of demise. If we choose providence, then we will live by the truth that all things are possible with God and that God is love.

An Angelic Reflection: I shall help cocreate God's mysterious plan with the angels.

MADE THAT WAY

An Angel Reminder: **Know thyself.**

It is good to know ourselves as well as possible. When we are aware of our own patterns, behavior, personality, likes, and dislikes, then we will understand the deeper sense of the way we are made. Often we spend a lot of effort trying to live up to a new image, yet the change just doesn't happen. Maybe we read a book that says we should be out conquering the business world, and we get inspired by this philosophy but we can't seem to find it in us to actually implement this new idea. The reason is that some of us just aren't made that way. We might better spend our energy learning to know what it is we truly need and want. When we know and accept ourselves at a deep level, we will choose goals that match up with our own purpose, and the angels will open doors we never even imagined.

Look around at the people you know, and ask yourself if they seem made for what they are doing. Then ask the angels to help you understand the way you were made, the talents you were born with, and your natural inclinations. Do you accept yourself as you are? Do you believe your gifts matter in the world? They matter to the angels, who are waiting to help you use them for the benefit of all.

An Angelic Reflection: **I am happy to be made this way.**

INSINCERITY

An Angel Reminder: "The most exhausting
thing in life is being insincere."
Anne Morrow Lindbergh

Have you ever encountered someone who just couldn't tell the truth?
Some people find it hard to be honest with themselves and with others.
Even when circumstances allow an honest and true response, an insincere
person will choose to abuse it and lie. Some people turn into pathological
liars, and their lies start to corrupt those around them. Most pathological
liars move around a lot—from town to town, or relationship to relationship—because once they are found out their game ends. It is difficult
to be compassionate to a pathological liar. They are so disingenuous you
can't find the true person inside. The angels suggest that someone devoted
to living a lie probably experienced something terrible in the past, and
they are trying to get away from anything real within themselves in order
to be protected from the original horrible memory. Insincere people need
the angels' love.

*The angels want us to find compassion for all of God's creatures, including the insincere. If
you come across someone who won't be sincere, remember the first thing to do is to say a
prayer for that person. Then honor the truth by refusing to get caught in the web of dishonesty.*

An Angelic Reflection: **I am sincerely God's.**

ENCHANTMENT

An Angel Reminder: Some enchanted evening
you may find enchantment.

The word *enchantment* has interesting roots. It originally meant "to surround with song," which is where the word *chant* comes from. The act of chanting can take us to another dimension, an altered state of consciousness, which could explain why the term *to enchant* eventually came to mean "to cast a spell over." Enchantment is a magical, mystical state in which joy and wonder prevail. The angels are certainly agents of enchantment and are happy to reconnect us to the delightful feelings of magic and mystery that take life out of the mundane and into the exhilarating. Many of us have not experienced enchantment since the days of childhood, when fairy tales and hope were our food and drink. The angels remind us that enchantment is not just the province of childhood; it is a vital ingredient in human happiness.

Are you in need of some enchantment in your life? Have things grown stale, boring, habitual? Do you feel starved for the touch of the extraordinary? If so, the angels invite you to let go of your dependence upon the "real," rational, tangible, and predictable and let yourself believe a little more in the unseen world of mystery, which beckons to us everywhere we look. Surround yourself with enchanting people and enchanting activities, and see what happens.

An Angelic Reflection: I find ways to keep my life fresh and surprising.

EN-LIGHTENING UP

An Angel Reminder: Humor is the supreme balancing mechanism.

Enlightenment has been described as coming out of the darkness of illusion into the clear light of true consciousness. *To enlighten* also means "to lighten up." How do the two connect? We believe that when we cultivate lightness of heart, we move more quickly toward the light. At the same time, we bring light to others. When we are en-lightened, we not only see clearly; we are lighter in spirit. You might say the three essential aspects of enlightenment are clarity, humor, and lightness of being. Of the three, humor does the most to promote the other two. In a tense situation humor lightens the atmosphere, helping people to get a broader, less self-centered perspective. Humor liberates us from the prison of tunnel vision; laughter is a proven health benefit that can cure illness and heal the psyche. God and the angels love laughter and humor. They know that the truly en-lightened person is not harsh or critical but full of the joy, having discovered his or her eternal self.

If you'd like to practice en-lightening up, here are some ideas. (1) When you're having an attack of seriousness, counteract it immediately with an absurdity attack, in which you let yourself see the absurdity of the entire human condition. (2) Do something fun for someone else. (3) Make a pact with yourself to have a good laugh at least once a day, and make a conscious effort to find the humor around you. (4) Send light to the trouble spots in your life. See the difficulty surrounded in angelic light. We guarantee that in a very short time you will see the light and feel lighter and freer.

An Angelic Reflection: I dwell in the light and I am light of heart.

SALAD DAYS

An Angel Reminder: "My salad days,
when I was green in judgment."
Shakespeare

The color green in nature means something is new or unripe. In the game of life we are all green, and our salad days never really end. Just when we think that we have gained a bit of ground and can sit back and sagely eat the main course, some little glitch shows up and we are eating salad again. It is good to stay green and not pretend to know everything. Green will keep us young. Our judgment ripens when we develop a strong spiritual foundation and consider how our actions affect others. If we follow the Golden Rule it will never matter how green or new to life we are.

Green is the color of healing, of the heart chakra; it is the proof of life in nature. Green is both warm (yellow) and cool (blue). Think about being green. Start to allow yourself to recognize the different hues of green in your approach to life and wisdom.

An Angelic Reflection: **The angels give me the wisdom to know when I don't know.**

WARNING SIGNS

An Angel Reminder: **Stop. Look. Listen.**

Many of us have found ourselves in relationships that started off like a dream but somewhere along the way turned into a nightmare. We start to ask, "Who is this person? When did they suddenly change? What happened to those days of bliss?" The truth of the matter is that the other person didn't become someone else overnight. The warning signs were always there; we just failed to heed them. You're familiar, of course, with the expression "Love is blind." Well, sometimes it's a good thing to be blind—to see only with the heart and soul. Then again, when we are blind to things not because we don't see them but because we don't want to, an unpleasant surprise inevitably lurks up ahead. The angels ask us to summon the courage to be aware early on of danger signals in our relationships—disturbing behaviors in the other person that set off a warning bell inside of us—and to pay attention to our intuition. We may want to confront the person and talk about our feelings. But if their behaviors are too much a part of their overall makeup, we should realize that what we're seeing is going to be what we're getting and adjust our expectations accordingly.

Are you involved in any problematic relationships? What were some of the warning signs that might have clued you in to the possibility that there could be trouble up ahead? With the benefit of hindsight, can you see how you might have avoided the current situation by reading the warning signs correctly? How can you deal more honestly with the situation now?

An Angelic Reflection: **I view my relationships through the lens of intuition, not projection.**

LIFE BEFORE DEATH

An Angel Reminder: Are you alive or just going through the motions?

Many people are very concerned with the question of whether or not there is life after death. But the angels would like us to be more concerned with whether or not we are having a full experience of life *before* death. We're not talking here about simply breathing in and out, but about taking part in the wonderful mystery of human existence and exploring the full range of exhilarating possibilities that it offers. From early childhood, many of us have been conditioned to suppress the curiosity, wonder, and joy that are natural components of our being. We do things that are socially acceptable without stopping to ask ourselves whether they are in alignment with the deeper needs of our soul. The angels offer us the courage to explore who we really are, what we really need. When we are living in a way that makes our heart sing, we know we are truly alive.

Are you an active or passive participant in life? Do you pursue activities that give you joy and bring meaning to your life? Or does life seem to be passing you by? Think about the things that make you feel madly, truly, deeply alive. How can you incorporate more of them into your life? What is keeping you from doing them?

An Angelic Reflection: I am open to the deep beauty of life, and I accept my right to happiness.

DEATH TOLL

An Angel Reminder: "The purpose of human life is to serve
and to show compassion and the will to help others."
Albert Schweitzer

When monumental disasters strike, the media always keep us informed of
the latest death toll. There is another toll we never hear about on the
news, and it is the toll of all the people who have died of broken hearts,
spirits, souls, and psyches. Many die because they never learned how to
get it right after a childhood of abuse. Think about the souls who did
what they were supposed to do, worked hard for a company for many
years, then just when everything is going great—the college fund is set
up, one of the parents can stay home with the kids, and so forth—their
job is sold down the river and they can't find another. Some die from
causes that others attribute to a lingering illness. The angels are aware of
all these broken hearts. They know the death toll, and they will do anything they can to stop it, but they need our help. We help ourselves by
not letting our broken heart kill us—by asking for help when we need it
and being open to change. We help others by praying for those who are
broken down and asking the angels to help them.

*Strength comes through being flexible in body, mind, and spirit. Those who die of a broken
heart are not being punished; they were not weak; they did their best. If you find yourself
dying from the blows of life, open your heart and let the angels in. Give yourself one last
chance to see things differently, and pray for the strength and courage to change.*

An Angelic Reflection: No matter how terrible the change, the angels are
with me.

SPELLS

An Angel Reminder: **Too often our life resembles
a long stretch of driving under the influence.**

A spell is an incantation or formula, or a bewitched state, or a compelling
state of attraction. It is a powerful message that has somehow taken up
residence in our psyche, dictating our behavior on an unconscious level.
To some extent all of us are under spells—beliefs that have been
ingrained in us and that we cling to for reasons we've never stopped to
question. Some common spells include projections from others, psychic
predictions, or labels from childhood that we've somehow never shaken.
When we are under a spell our vision is limited, and we may indeed
become victims of self-fulfilling prophecies rather than agents of change
and renewal. In fairy tales and myths, spells typically paralyze their victims or put them into a deep, years-long sleep. The angels remind us that
we don't need a mythic hero or fairy tale prince to rescue us from spells.
We are our own heroes, on our own journey; we have the power to change
our beliefs and awaken from the deep sleep of unconscious behavior.

*Are you under any spells? Think about beliefs that might be immobilizing you and pre-
venting you from moving ahead. Who cast this spell upon you? When you're ready to
break the spell, ask the angels to help you expand your belief system and shift your life
from past to present tense.*

An Angelic Reflection: **I am open to the new self that is always emerging
within me.**

TIPPING

An Angel Reminder: "Generous people are rarely mentally ill people."
Dr. Karl Menninger

A tip is a small amount of money given as an acknowledgment of services rendered. It is also a helpful hint or inside information. The angels want to give us some inside information on tipping. Don't pass up the chance to give a tip, and don't decide whether or not the person you are tipping deserves it or not. See your action as being a part of the economy, of giving someone buying power and helping him or her make a living. Many people working for tips are in school working toward a future job they will love; many others are supporting a family. When we stiff someone who works for tips, we are stiffing ourselves—because we are all connected. Give freely when the opportunity presents itself, and you will be richly rewarded in generous mental health and peace.

Next time you find yourself driving around the block because you don't want to tip the valet, ask yourself what you are really avoiding. Next time you are out to dinner and the waiter is having a difficult time, don't repay with stinginess. Ask the angels to bless the person as you leave a good tip. Tipping is a chance for us, not to sit back in judgment, but to help our fellow travelers on the journey of life. After all, you may be working for tips someday.

An Angelic Reflection: I know in the sight of the angels that a gratuity is a gift to all.

WANNABE MARTYRS

An Angel Reminder: "**All have not the gift of martyrdom.**"
John Dryden

Probably all of us know a wannabe martyr—someone who takes on the burdens of the world and makes sure to let everyone know how heavy the load is. The definition of *martyr* is "a person who chooses to suffer or die rather than give up faith or principles." True martyrs transcend themselves for a greater cause; their heroism is characterized by humility, and it is indeed a gift given to few. Wannabe martyrs, on the other hand, are their own cause, and their false humility is as transparent as a glass pane on the soul. True martyrs do not go in search of suffering; wannabe martyrs glorify suffering and believe that God has chosen them to receive a bigger cross than everyone else. The angels caution us not to allow wannabe martyrs to rain on our parade, making us feel guilty or insignificant if we choose to look for joy rather than join the procession toward a self-inflicted Calvary.

Do you know any wannabe martyrs? How do they make you feel? How do you handle them? The next time you come in contact with a wannabe martyr, try this prescription from your angel doctor: one dose each of love, patience, and detachment, to be taken as often as needed.

An Angelic Reflection: **I choose not to suffer but to learn from suffering.**

COMPARED TO WHAT?

An Angel Reminder: **Authentic life has no comparison.**

When things happen that upset our balance, someone well meaning will say, "Well, at least such and such didn't happen; you should be grateful." We search for comparisons to make us feel better, but comparisons often don't. We spend a great deal of time comparing products—wines, food, restaurants—as well as comparing people. When something calamitous happens we can get out a chart and check out our trouble on a list of stressors to see how upset we should be. If we're getting a divorce, we think we shouldn't feel as bad as someone losing a spouse through death. The problem is that there are no comparisons. Our paths are unique, and what stresses one person may shatter another. The angels invite us to honor our own experience and refrain from comparing it to that of others.

Think of all the work that goes into comparing, and ask yourself if you are caught up in the comparison game. When you are in pain, honor it and cease the comparison. Your experience will always be unique to you, and even now the angels are bringing something new and incomparable into your life.

An Angelic Reflection: **The angels teach me that comparisons are a trick of the intellect and my heart can not compare the love that comes from the Great Creator.**

THE OTHER SIDE OF THE FENCE

An Angel Reminder: **If the grass looks greener on the
other side of the fence, it's time to water yours.**

Sometimes it's hard not to believe that the grass isn't greener on the other
side of the fence, that other people don't have it better than we do. The
problem is that envy puts the responsibility for our happiness "out there"
instead of inside. We are constantly looking wistfully over the fence
instead of living on our side in the here and now. How often have we
been impressed by the seemingly wonderful marriage of this person or
the prestigious job of that one, only to see the marriage crumble in
divorce or the big CEO indicted for embezzlement? How many times have
we tried to cure our problems with a move, thinking that once we were on
the other side of the fence things would be better, only to discover that
our problems have a mysterious way of following us wherever we go, and
that grass, wherever it is, will wither and die if we don't give it proper
attention and nurturing? The angels remind us that we can never trust
appearances; we can only trust God to lead us to that place of inner satisfaction based on spiritual, not material, reality.

*Have you been looking over anybody's fence lately? Do others seem to have it better than
you? In what way? What do you have that they don't? (There's always something!) If
there's anyone whom you particularly envy, send that person a blessing and a big congratu-
lations. Then realize that they have nothing to do with your own happiness or unhappiness.*

An Angelic Reflection: **I take care of my own lawn.**

KILL IT

An Angel Reminder: **Are we all natural born killers?**

There is a tendency in our society to try to destroy anything that gets in our way. We kill pain, kill enemies, kill thoughts, kill insects, and kill cancer cells. We declare war on poverty, war on drugs, and war on disease germs. But setting out to kill things, such as when we imagine cancer cells being destroyed by our "natural killer" cells, may not be the best way to promote healing. People studying the effects of thought and prayer on cells have found that loving energy sends a message to cells to return to balance, whereas the energy of killing and destruction may simply upset the balance further. Balance and wholeness are the true keys to healing.

Think about how different it feels to solve a problem through love rather than destruction. Being constructive is important in all our affirmations, healings, and intention work with the angels. Using the energy of killing to right a wrong or achieve balance may not be the way to attract angels. The angels want us to love something into balance. Next time you set out to kill something, whether it's the mice in your attic or the virus in your body, take a moment and realize what you are doing. Is there another option that is more constructive?

An Angelic Reflection: **I shall not kill.**

MEMORIAL DAY

An Angel Reminder: "The life of a soul on earth lasts beyond his departure. You will always feel that life touching yours . . .
Angelo Patri

Memorial Day has become little more than one more excuse to party. We are far more concerned with the big barbecue than we are about the original meaning of the event, which was to commemorate those who died in the armed services. The spirits of the dead probably have nothing against having a good time, but they'd undoubtedly appreciate it if we remembered to include them in the day that was meant for them. Today we can take some time to remember all those who have passed on who were special to us. We might want to have our own little ceremony, lighting a candle, looking at photos, talking to our loved ones in spirit and sharing with them whatever comes to mind. As we connect to our deeper feelings of appreciation and loss and keep our connection to our loved one strong. Above all, the angels want us to remember that those who have left the Earth have merely gone before us. They are not dead; they have only shed their physical bodies and moved to the country of the spirit.

Is there anyone in particular who has passed on whom you would like to remember today? What memories do you cherish most about this person? How would you like to honor him or her? You could have a ceremony, or you could do something this person would have loved, or you might help a cause your loved one held dear. Think of your own memorial you could create to this person.

An Angelic Reflection: I remember those who have gone before me with love, and I honor them in my own way.

NECESSARY ESCAPES

**An Angel Reminder: If our wheels are going to spin,
they might as well be taking us somewhere.**

Do you ever feel like you "just have to get away"? When things seem to
be closing in on us, when we feel like all we're doing is spinning our
wheels, it may be time for a necessary escape. Necessary escapes are different from just escapes, period. When we make a necessary escape we are
not running away from a problem. Rather, we are running to sanity and
perhaps, in the process, a solution to our problem. A necessary escape
can take any form, from actually going to your favorite getaway place and
checking into a hotel for a night or two, to just putting all the have-to's
on hold and indulging in the luxury of doing absolutely nothing. The
angels say, when it's time for a necessary escape, do whatever you feel like
doing but *don't feel guilty*. Realize instead that in giving yourself breathing
space and thinking time you are probably doing the most productive
thing possible to help you meet and conquer your difficulties.

*Do you ever feel like getting away from it all? Do you feel guilty about taking time off or
"wasting" time? Necessary escapes are safety valves to be turned on when you're in danger
of short-circuiting. Make a list of ways or places that can give you some R & R & R—
rest, relaxation, and refocusing. Put it on your fridge with a note that says, "For use in
the interest of self-preservation. Angels' orders."*

An Angelic Reflection: I appreciate the healing value of getting away.

No Itinerary

An Angel Reminder: "A good traveler has no
fixed plans and is not intent on arriving."
Lao Tzu

Why would a good traveler not have fixed plans and not be intent on
arriving? With too much focus on plans and arriving, we miss the lessons
along the way. When we make an itinerary, the travel agency of the angels
runs into problems, because God's travel plans might take us someplace
completely new. And we need not be eager to arrive, for in life there is no
arrival; life is constantly moving. The adventure lies in traveling with the
angels—no itinerary.

*Think about how we usually make plans. We set a time and a place, we ask others to go
along with our plans, and we hold preconceived notions of how the plan will go. All of this
is one step removed from true experience on the journey of life. Ask the angels to be your
travel guides. All they ask is that you slow down and pay attention, and forget arriving.*

An Angelic Reflection: I am a cosmic traveler; I will leave my itinerary to
the angels of God.

BEGINNER'S LUCK

An Angel Reminder: "Every search begins with beginner's luck. And every search ends with the victor's being severely tested."
Paulo Coelho

At the beginning of a new phase in our spiritual journey, it seems as if we are charmed and blessed in ways we never knew possible. People come into our lives to help just at the right time, and we find ourselves drawn to things that open our minds to God's imagination. The beginning stage of anything is known as a honeymoon period. Our relationship with the angels is this way also. At first they bring truckloads of magic into our consciousness, and then after the honeymoon it seems like the magic stops coming. We may forget that the magic came with a bargain—that you will be tested further down the road. Every test you encounter will require you to use your inner gifts, which include the magic you received at the beginning of your journey. When tests come, draw for courage on your memories of the time when life was so sweet.

You are not being tested because life is cruel and unusual; you are being tested because in order to help God you need to have strength, courage, and wisdom. We don't receive these qualities for free; we earn them. When the tests get the most difficult, it means we are on the horizon of realizing a dream, and another honeymoon period is just around the corner.

An Angelic Reflection: When testing comes, I draw for courage on the gifts I received at the beginning of this journey.

EVOLUTION

An Angel Reminder: We evolve spiritually
by choosing the larger good.

Humans are designed to evolve; it is programmed into our cells. *To evolve* means "to develop or work out," and it comes from the Latin word *evolvere,* which means "to unroll." We were rolled up in the womb, and our life is a process of revealing and unveiling what we were protecting in the womb—our spirit. The notion of evolution also includes the idea of getting better and improving through trial and error. The angels protect us during our long unrolling process, as we move toward a larger mind and spirit.

We each follow a process of personal evolution, and we are all part of the larger evolution of humanity. The evolution of each is equally important, and each one supports the others. Spiritual evolution requires that we make personal choices leading to the betterment of the whole. Evolution that leads to the divine light is a noble choice and demands that we trust that things are getting better and will continue to expand in love.

An Angelic Reflection: I am evolving with the angels.

THE MAN BEHIND THE CURTAIN

An Angel Reminder: **"Pay no attention to the man behind the curtain."**
The Wizard of Oz

In the late eighteen hundreds the phenomenon of snake oil came into being, heralded by the flashy medicine show and its amazing cast of salespeople. *Snake oil* has become a term we use for anything promoted and peddled as a cure-all that is basically worthless. One can imagine it sold well, since charismatic showpeople were convincing people that this oil, collected from the snake sharing the stage with them, could cure any ill. What really happens when we encounter charisma—a divine gift—is that it sparks our life force; it hits a hope button within us, and the healing energy starts flowing. It has been said that God works in mysterious ways, and even off-the-wall characters, like charismatic showpeople, can be God's instruments of change.

Snake oil can heal. Its secret formula lies not in the oil but in the ritual between two people and the excitement generated when we are sold something that gives us hope. Humans are easy to trick, and we all secretly want a cure-all or a quick fix. The angels are always on hand to help us heal, which really means to restore balance. If we fell for a trick of healing, it may mean we needed it; we needed the excitement and prompting of our life force. If you have been tricked, don't blame the man behind the curtain. Look at what you really needed, and then have a good laugh, because in the trick something has been healed.

An Angelic Reflection: **I know that the man behind the curtain has as much healing magic as I do with the angels in my consciousness.**

CHEAP

An Angel Reminder: "He's so cheap he made his daughter get
married in the backyard so the chickens could eat the rice."
Old joke

Who hasn't had the dubious pleasure of coming across cheap people?
These unfortunate souls live in a constant state of deprivation created by
a poverty mentality. They won't spend a penny on themselves or others,
and they are hoarders of the first degree. Many times the cheapest people
have tons of money, because they are such experts at accumulating without giving. But sadly, their money is of no real use to them because they
are incapable of enjoying it. We know rich people who wear the same old
clothes until they fall apart, use the same piece of packing tape twice, and
spend their lives searching for the best deal. One man we knew was a mil-
lionaire, yet he would drive all over town looking for gas that was a penny
or two cheaper. Cheap people essentially do not value life, and consequently others do not value them. They are the opposite of the angels,
who spread generosity and abundance wherever they go.

*Do you know any cheapskates? Is it easy or worthwhile to remain friends with them when
you always seem to be on the giving end? Do you have a fear of spending money? There is
a difference between frugal and cheap. If it's hard for you to use money for your own or
others' enjoyment, think about what good your "pile" will be to you when you are gone.
Then, like you, it will be nothing more than dead weight.*

An Angelic Reflection: In sharing my riches, I make the world a richer place.

MISTAKEN IDENTITY

An Angel Reminder: **We are always more than
what we appear to be, even to ourselves.**

Mistaken identity has always been a popular theme in literature and movies. The hero is mistaken for someone else, and all sorts of adventures and fantastic plot maneuvers ensue. In the process, lives are invariably changed as someone falls in love with someone who isn't what they seem, or the hero is able to accomplish deeds he wouldn't have been able to achieve as his real self. Many of us live in a perpetual state of mistaken identity, keeping our "real" self or selves under lock and key. In an effort to maintain an image we think is desirable, we don't allow others to see us as we truly are. The problem is that it takes an awful lot of effort to live a dual life. Look at all the time and energy Superman could have saved for other more useful pursuits if he hadn't had to run around pretending to be Clark Kent! The angels know and love as we are, with all our amazing personas and possibilities. They ask us to do the same and not to be afraid to reveal who we really are, to others as well as to ourselves.

Take a moment to reflect upon all the different personalities that make up the total you. Are there some that you are shy about revealing? Some that you're ashamed of? Some that you have difficulty even acknowledging? If so, try allowing these personalities to exist without judging them. Don't try to hide them or make them go away; just observe their behavior, and see if they have anything to tell you.

An Angelic Reflection: **I appreciate the complexity and mystery of my human nature.**

SELF-ESTEEM OR SELF-AGGRANDIZEMENT

An Angel Reminder: "Too much praise can do damage just like too much criticism."

Philip Toshio Sudo

We have a great need to "feel good" about ourselves and the way others treat us. That seems harmless enough, but it skews the picture when it becomes our main focus. Parents are afraid of hurting their children's feelings if they correct them after the children have done something wrong, yet receiving this kind of correction is the very way we learn how to treat others with respect. If we experience pain and then can appreciate that others feel it, too, we learn the Golden Rule: "Treat others as you would have them treat you." Not, "Others better treat me right or I will punish them (or sue them)." Self-esteem is a good quality, yet we need to understand that life is not just about our feeling good or attaining pleasure. Let's exalt what is truly noble.

Self-esteem is something that is earned, not handed to us in the latest toy. Ask the angels to help you develop true self-esteem: the strength of knowing yourself and operating from a higher reference point.

An Angelic Reflection: I feel good about life and myself when I operate from my highest reference point.

FOUNDATION

An Angel Reminder: "I'll huff and I'll puff
and I'll blow your house down."
The Wolf to the Three Little Pigs

A foundation is a base that upholds and sustains a structure. Homes and buildings built on shaky foundations tend to collapse. Correspondingly, lives built on shaky foundations are in danger of coming apart at the first threat of danger. This may seem like stating the obvious, but it's amazing how few of us take the time to examine our own foundations—the spiritual and psychological support systems that give us the tools to maneuver positively and productively in an often adverse universe. What is our life really based on? What are our values, our beliefs? What holds us up when the wolf is at our door? What do we fall back on when things get tough? We all encounter situations that demand fortitude, clarity, and a strong sense of commitment and purpose. But if our foundation is insecure, we either will avoid dealing with these situations or will crack under the strain of emotional challenge. The angels ask us to inspect our foundations and to reinforce them with extra faith and courage. Then we can be sure we'll remain standing, no matter how strong the winds are.

How strong is your personal foundation? Have your values and beliefs sustained you in times of crisis and guided you through your daily life? Does your foundation have any cracks? Where? What sort of attitudes and actions could you take that would strengthen your foundation?

An Angelic Reflection: **I build the dwelling place for my soul on the solid ground of faith and commitment to a higher power, higher consciousness, and higher purpose.**

JUNE 10

UNIMAGINABLE CIRCUMSTANCES

An Angel Reminder: "Sometimes at that moment a wave of light breaks into our darkness, and it is as though a voice were saying: 'You are accepted.' *You are accepted,* accepted by that which is greater than you, and the name of which you do not know."
Paul Tillich

Some of the trials humans face seem so unimaginable that they render everything else on the scale of horrors meaningless. It is easy to say that God only gives us trials we can handle, but what are we handling? No one needs to remind us how fragile life is, how in one moment everything in one's life can change by way of tragedy. When tragedy strikes, we may fall completely apart at the seams, but those seams exist so that we *can* fall apart. The pieces will come back together in time, and our seams will be stronger. When you are faced with unimaginable circumstances, let yourself fall apart smack into the fire of God. Just when you see you are about to hit the ground, trust and know that you will be guided by your angels into the loving hands of God.

It's good that many tragedies are unimaginable to most of us; otherwise our focus would be only fear. When you come across a thought that brings fear, remember it is only a thought. When you come across a situation that is horrendous, ask yourself if you are in it or if it belongs to someone else. If you are in it, the angels are there with you, so consciously ask them for help.

An Angelic Reflection: I know that adversity comes with many angels.

SPIRITUAL MOMENTS

An Angel Reminder: **Spiritual moments are like babies;
there's one born every second.**

When we are in tune with the angels, we are living not just in the moment but in the spiritual moment. Spiritual moments can occur when we least expect them. They may be as huge as an epiphany, an instantaneous, life-altering enlightenment such as the one Saul experienced on the way to Damascus. Or they may be as simple as feeling a burst of wonder and reverence upon noticing the divine artistry in a flower's petals. The point is, we don't have to make a big deal out of praying or meditating in order to find ourselves in the middle of one. When we allow ourselves to have spiritual moments, we unite our spirits with the moment and free ourselves from the imprisonment of time. Instead of waiting for time to pass and the future that may or may not come, we exult in the pure awareness of the present instant, where time ceases to exist and life is truly eternal.

Are you in the habit of having spiritual moments? Can you recall some key spiritual moments in your life? Try having a spiritual moment right now. Put down this book, breathe deeply a few times, and look around you. Let yourself experience the moment. Where are you? What's around you? Where are you headed? Where were you a moment ago? What thoughts are passing through your mind? Feel yourself becoming part of the moment—the timeless moment.

An Angelic Reflection: **I pay attention to the now and the wonders that are occurring in every moment.**

CRUISING

An Angel Reminder: "We must be willing to get rid of the life we've planned, so as to have the life that is waiting for us."

Joseph Campbell

To cruise means to sail about for pleasure, to patrol, or to drive around at moderate speed checking things out. When we cruise, we are in a special mood where we are not concerned about time. Cruising around is fun because we take time to watch life happening all around us. Cruising means we can be observers without seeming intrusive. To cruise well, you must be in a state of mind to just roll with it, take a break, and kick back.

Sometimes in life it is appropriate and good for us to go on cruise control with the angels. Take some time to just go cruising, and let the angels show you pieces of life happening around you that you would otherwise miss. Take a notebook on your cruise, and write down everything that you notice or encounter.

An Angelic Reflection: I am on cruise control with the angels.

FORTUNE COOKIES

An Angel Reminder: "The joyfulness
of a man prolongeth his days."
The Peking Noodle Company

You'd expect to find the above maxim in the Bible, wouldn't you? It's probably there, but Mary Beth received it in, of all places, a fortune cookie. This led us to ruminate upon what, exactly, fortune is. While fortune cookies generally make predictions like "Success is just around the corner" or, in a particular favorite we once got, "You will attend a party where strange customs prevail," whoever wrote this fortune had an evolved consciousness. He or she knew that fortune is largely up to us and our attitude. If we believe in fortunes. we become pawns in the capricious hands of fate instead of intelligent beings with the creative power to shape our destinies. It is true that we don't always have control over events. But the angels remind us that our ability to remain optimistic and positive gives us the power to transcend any writing on the wall or on a piece of paper in a cookie. In fact, when we have a joyful outlook, good fortune is already ours.

Do you believe in the power of someone or something else to predict your future? If so, why? The angels invite you to cultivate the kind of uplifting behavior that will always draw good fortune to you, no matter what your circumstances.

An Angelic Reflection: I am fortunate to be able to create my own good fortune.

THE CHALLENGE OF BEING

An Angel Reminder: "I am; therefore, I continue."
Theodore Roethke

"Just being" is a challenge, because when we try to live in our own true being, many forces tend to oppose us. At times we are working against the force of the personal history we have created, and possibly the most difficult force is when others are challenged by our being and want us to be different. Our own inner force toward freedom gets stronger when we feel forced to be something other than we are. Getting free of the driving forces against being is a lifelong quest. Angels are required.

Are you allowed to just be? Do you feel in sync with destiny and circumstances? How well are you doing in your quest for the freedom to be? Freedom brings us the possibility of choosing how to be and how to live, and the angels bring us the courage. The angels are happy to let us be.

An Angelic Reflection: **I am free, courageous, and in sync with my destiny.**

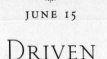

DRIVEN

An Angel Reminder: **If you are driven, who is doing the driving?**

We probably all have come across driven people. These individuals are sometimes labeled workaholics, compulsives, or fanatics because they are consumed by their careers or missions. Being driven is a scary scenario because those who are driven are obviously not in the driver's seat of their lives. Something else is in control, taking them to their destination at breakneck speed. But what is this destination, and why is it so important to race there without even one pit stop? Driven people think they know where they are going and why, but the angels know that they're really like wanderers in the desert, dying of thirst, hoodwinked by a mirage. They are searching for satisfaction, but it is of an outward rather than an inward nature and so will always elude them. The angels ask, what is the benefit of not being in control of your own life? What is the point of being driven nowhere?

Do you know any driven people? Are they fun and uplifting to be around? Or do they drive you nuts? Are you driven in any way? If so, does your lifestyle make you happy? Drivenness and stress always go hand in hand. Do you really want to live a high-pressure existence? Or would you rather be less driven and more at peace with who and where you are?

An Angelic Reflection: **I prefer to walk to where I'm going rather than being driven there.**

IMPOSED CONFORMITY

An Angel Reminder: "But now and then, somehow, through a grace beyond comprehension, we break out of this self-perpetuating cycle, touch another dimension of understanding, and become filled with a new realization."

Dorothy Maclean

Picture a pod of dolphins swimming happily and contentedly in the vast ocean. Along comes a famous dolphin trainer and says, "I know what is best for these dolphins. We must take them to the animal park and teach them to perform." Now the dolphins live in a small tank, which for a human would be like living in a house of mirrors. They are given silly names and are taught to do stupid pet tricks for food. The once free and happy dolphins are now mechanical performers, sick, tired, and afraid. Now think about a group of children playing free in a meadow. Pretty soon teachers and parents start to impose the regimens on these children, and their free spontaneous ways become replaced with the stress of trying to please others with a performance they never wanted to be a part of. They become afraid of life, and find themselves sick and tired. The angels value uniqueness more than conformity to a boring group standard. They are standing by to free us from the dullness of conformity.

Humans have a knack for bringing conformity into their spiritual practices, too. The spirit wants to move us, and the angels want to free us. If you feel like a tired-out performer, barely able to get the energy up for one more show, then you need to stop the show with a new response to life. Ask the angels to help you find the response that is uniquely yours.

An Angelic Reflection: I will raise the vibration of my spirit far above the sickness of imposed conformity.

SACRED SPACE

An Angel Reminder: "Fundamentally there is just open space. . . .
Our most fundamental state of mind before the creation of ego,
is such that there is basic openness, basic freedom, a spacious
quality; and we have now and have always had this openness."
Chögyam Trungpa

Space is, by its very nature, sacred. The Buddhists talk of the enlightened
state as one of infinite space. The space we allow ourselves and others to
have gives us the freedom to explore who we really are. The wide open
spaces—the meadows, beaches, mountains, deserts—are sacred in their
natural beauty and their unobstructed connection to their Creator. Outer
space—the infinite universe—is a profound miracle, the testament to an
existence beyond time. The angels revere space, and they make sure that
there is enough of it between them and us to allow us to make our own
discoveries and grow at our own pace. They want us to rethink our concept of space, not as a mere room to fill or a gap to close but as a sacred
opportunity to get closer to our own spirits.

*How do you see space? Do you respect your own space? Do you give others theirs? What
are some ways you can make your own personal space more sacred? You might want to
create a sanctifying ceremony in your home that will make you more conscious of the
meaning and privilege of space.*

An Angelic Reflection: I welcome and honor the sacredness of space in my
life.

No Sweat

An Angel Reminder: "It's all small stuff."
Richard Carlson

Have you tried to get something accomplished lately that involved others' participation and been met with total frustration? Have you noticed that simple things seem difficult to complete? Do you often feel like you are on the *Twilight Zone*'s merry-go-round when you try to make a simple phone call? Some days things that we used to take for granted refuse to go smoothly. All of this adds to the daily stress of life, and the source of this problem stems from the stressors of life. So how can we stop the downward spiral? Is our only choice to settle for less than we have been used to expecting? Another solution, which is a bit more difficult, is to find some humor in these ridiculous situations. If we practice diligently, the angels will join us.

Compromising can lead to frustration, hurt, and resentment. These three feelings lead to anger if we don't acknowledge them and change the chemistry. The angels don't want the daily frustrations of life to make you sick. They are working overtime to help, so help them by "not sweating the small stuff."

An Angelic Reflection: **When everyday stresses threaten to get me down, I relax into a good laugh with the angels.**

DOUBTS

An Angel Reminder: **The line between doubt and fear is a fine one.**

Doubt isn't all bad; sometimes it's a necessary cautionary tool. If we doubt the accuracy or validity of a statement or promise, we will not be prone to gullibility and can make choices based on reality rather than false hope. But too much doubt inhibits the imagination and the possibilities for new experience. The angels caution us not to let doubt rule our lives, to the point where it justifies inaction or, in its more extreme mode, becomes outright suspicion of everything and everyone. They ask us to be as objective as we can when we have doubts and to nip in the bud those that are not healthy before they blossom into fear.

Are you the kind of doubter who, like Thomas, just needed a little proof in order to believe? Or are you the kind of doubter who's always setting up roadblocks in the path of possibility and spoiling someone else's imagination party? Take some time to explore your doubts and figure out where they come from. Ask the angels to help you balance the virtues of doubt and trust in your life.

An Angelic Reflection: **I exercise good judgment in making the choice to either doubt or trust.**

HOLDING PREFERENCES LIGHTLY

An Angel Reminder: **In the long run our preferences may prove to be the opposite of what we want.**

We have many preferences each day, and when we don't get what we prefer we are disappointed. Often our preferences clash with the reality of the way things are, and we feel hurt by this. If we started out the day with no shoulds, no preferences, no preconceived ideas of what must happen, then we would greet each happening in our day with the knowledge that we can take care of it. We invite the angels into our daily lives when we hold our preferences lightly. That way they have more room to bring us the things that are truly good for us, not just the things we prefer.

When we consciously try to hold our preferences lightly, the angels rejoice because they know we will be happier and freer. Letting go of preferences is not easy, because we are trained to bring our preconceptions to the world and to try to make things happen to match them. We always want others to be safe and controlled around us. Yet this is out of our control. Ask the angels to help you stop clashing with reality and start merging with the magic of the mystery.

An Angelic Reflection: **The only preference I have is to accept the way things are.**

RITUALS

An Angel Reminder: "Ritual, when it's
heartfelt, is like a time capsule."
Pema Chodron

Spiritual ritual has largely gone by the wayside in Western society. We consider ourselves above the kinds of "superstitious" and "naïve" behaviors of "primitive" and past cultures, which might have revered rocks or danced for rain. But ancient practices of ritual and prayer can still serve us well by reminding us that every breath we take, every action we make, is a gift from a higher power. Grace at meals, for instance, is probably the most common of these time-honored rituals persisting into the present day. Many religions have different prayers for different times of day, reminding us of the natural cycle of birth, childhood, maturity, old age, and death of which we are an inexorable part. Through praying and incorporating the sacred into our everyday affairs, we learn to move with and respect the rhythms of the universe. This connects us to the past as well as the future, so that our rituals become, as the Tibetan teacher Pema Chodron observes, a time capsule linking us both to our ancestors and to generations to come.

Do you practice any spiritual rituals, such as saying grace or daily prayer and meditation? You might want to experiment with creating your own rituals that would bring you in closer contact with the sacred and deepen your reverence for life. This could be anything from walking in the woods to simply giving thanks upon awakening each morning. Begin to take note of how reverence changes your focus and attitude toward your life.

An Angelic Reflection: I revere and give thanks for the sacredness of life.

MISUNDERSTOOD

An Angel Reminder: "One should expect to be misunderstood and surprised if you're not. You have to work at communication."
Ed Wortz

Feeling as if we have been really heard and acknowledged is like a magical healing balm. It doesn't matter if the person listening agrees with us; we feel validated when we sense that someone really heard what we said. It isn't easy to get to this place of validation in friendships and relationships, because if we have something to say that might be uncomfortable for the other person to hear, then their self-defense mechanisms come zooming in. Have you ever told someone something that they did to upset you, and immediately they start to chant "that isn't true"? Have you ever jumped in and used that chant? Whether or not the thing actually happened, the fact is that the problem is true for the person bringing it up. When we can just listen to someone's truth, acknowledge it, apologize, or indicate that we have heard them without dismissing or patronizing them, then we are on our way to true communication—one of the rarest things on Earth.

Remember that the angels hear you and validate your existence. If you feel misunderstood, ask your guardian angel for help. You may want to imagine your guardian trying to reach the other party for you or giving you a new approach in communicating. To be heard is to be validated.

An Angelic Reflection: **I shall be heard.**

DOORS

An Angel Reminder: **God can open doors,
but we still have to walk through them.**

Sometimes opportunities that we weren't expecting present themselves to us. This is called good luck. But then we have to take advantage of these opportunities. This is called good judgment. Doors are always opening in our lives, but unless we walk through them we can never discover what's on the other side. It's not always obvious when something is a good opportunity; we may not always be sure whether or not we should take the plunge and just go for it. This is a good time for us to trust our intuition and also to make an inventory of the pros and cons of the situation. If we have fears that are keeping us from making the most of opportunity, we can explore them. If we want to trust in divine guidance and protection but have trouble believing in it, we can discuss the matter with the angels and see what answers we get. If we just aren't ready yet to walk through the door, we can look at that, too. The bottom line is, life happens to us—but we make things happen.

What doors of opportunity have swung open for you, in the past or lately? Did you walk through them? If not, why not? Do you wish you had? Was it a case of seeing the opportunity but being afraid to take advantage of it, or not seeing it at all? You might want to examine the reasons you don't walk through the doors that God opens, asking the angels to give you the courage to trust in providence and take more risks. Then, be on the lookout for any open doors.

An Angelic Reflection: **When it comes to opportunity, I support the Open Door Policy.**

PROTECTION

An Angel Reminder: **"If our methods of protection have not love, others need protection from us."**
Larry Dossey

Do you feel protected? If so why? What is protecting you? Are you protected by another person, by your bank account, your job, your parents? We spend a lot of time protecting ourselves and our stuff from the world. Often the need for protection is real. We may have made an enemy, and that enemy is out to get even. Joseph Campbell reminds us: "Jesus said, 'Love your enemies.' He didn't say, 'Don't have any.'" If we turn to an enemy with fear, suspicion, and hatred, the enemy has already won. If we can turn in love, faith, and compassion, we win.

Do you have any enemies? You may not know it if you do. If we can respond with love, even during the greatest threat, we will have much more in the end, even if death is the outcome. The angels watch out for us when we respond with love. Are you aware of your guardian angel, who works overtime protecting you in a multitude of ways?

An Angelic Reflection: **I will reward my guardian angels for their generous overtime by expressing my gratitude often.**

INSOMNIA

An Angel Reminder: **When we cannot sleep,
we may need to be awake.**

Many people are plagued by insomnia. No matter how hard they try, they can't sleep. So, they often resort to drugs or alcohol to "knock them out." But then they find they have a new problem, as they have become dependent on substances that are undermining their body's natural resources. Sleep is the body's natural way of recharging, and when we are deprived of it we cannot function well. The inability to sleep is a sign that we are seriously out of balance. Drugs are not the solution, but an honest examination of our life is. We may be insomniacs because we have worries that keep us awake. We may be tormented by guilt. Or, we may be lying awake with all sorts of ideas, frustrated and longing to flex our creative muscles. The angels suggest that if we're unable to sleep, it may be a message from our unconscious telling us to wake up to what's really going on inside of us. If insomnia is a symptom of imbalance, the way to cure it is by balancing ourselves—giving equal time to our physical, emotional, and spiritual needs.

Do you ever suffer from insomnia? If so, what do you generally do about it? If insomnia is a problem in your life, take a look at where you really need to be awake. Do you take good care of your body, giving it enough healthy food and exercise? Do you take good care of your spirit, giving it exciting and meaningful work to do? Do you take good care of your soul, giving it time and space in the form of prayer or meditation? If you begin to do all these things, chances are that your insomnia may go away all by itself.

An Angelic Reflection: **I keep my physical, mental, and spiritual selves in harmony so that I can sleep when I need to sleep and wake when I need to wake.**

JUNE 26

SCHEMES

An Angel Reminder: "We are all born brave, trusting,
and greedy, and most of us remain greedy."
Mignon McLaughlin

Many of us are tempted to fall for get-rich-quick-schemes and to follow
the ten easy steps to enlightenment. But who is really at fault if these fail
and we lose money and enlightenment? Is it the people offering the lies, or
is it us, led by our greed and shortcut mentality? It is easy to be duped at
times, and it is nothing to be ashamed of if we learn our lesson quickly.
In a world of lies and illusions, the truth is always there burning a hole
with its light. It takes courage to go beyond denial and naïveté, and that is
why we have angels, to help us turn the lights on and look at the truth.

*If you want to work and play with the angels, be willing to seek the truth and then not
hide when you find it. Life may not be easy and fair all the time. Ask the angels for
courage to resist being greedy—for either money or enlightenment—and to see past illusions to the truth.*

An Angelic Reflection: **Whenever I think life is unfair, I will remember
that life is only interested in balance.**

CONTRADICTIONS

An Angel Reminder: **The truth can often be contradictory.**

Life, as they say, is full of contradictions. What does this mean? A contradiction is a statement that is the opposite of another statement. Theoretically two statements can't be valid if they are opposing each other. But life is rarely so pat. Opposing truths are a fundamental part of the human experience. The very coexistence of the forces of both good and evil, for instance, is the biggest contradiction by which we are forced to live. And how often have we contradicted ourselves, saying one thing and then another? When we're caught in a contradiction, we may feel extremely foolish. But isn't it possible that we could feel two ways about something? Purists would argue, no, because all that means is that you're confused. The angels would counter, not necessarily. Our experience of reality is always open to change; as we grow, we often find ourselves contradicting former perceptions and beliefs. Life is open to many possible interpretations, which is why you may even occasionally find contradictions in this book. If you do, the angels welcome you to choose the position that rings most true to you. And then not to be too concerned if the opposite one appeals to you tomorrow. It's all part of being human.

What is your opinion of contradictions? Do you allow them to exist? Or do you expect everything to be black or white, right or wrong? Contradictions are interesting phenomena because they force us to think and expand our minds. Can you think of any contradictions that you find illuminating? What are some contradictions in your own life? How might they make you a more complex and interesting person?

An Angelic Reflection: **I know that fluctuating feelings and opinions are part of life, and I allow myself to express different views at different times.**

CENSORSHIP

An Angel Reminder: "The books that the world calls immoral are the books that show the world its own shame."

Oscar Wilde

Censorship has been a problem ever since the first thought-provoking book was written. Oscar Wilde points out that shame may be the culprit, since we don't want to look at the dishonor in ourselves. A censor is an officious meddler, one who seeks to ban, stifle, and suppress information that may be offensive to some. Sometimes we have an officious meddler living in our own psyche, waiting to stop us from bursting forth with something controversial. The angels teach us that it is difficult to be ruined by a "bad" book or movie; if we are spiritually grounded, it takes a lot more than that. We need to learn how to exercise discretion in the art we view instead of trying to ban or censor it. Censorship defeats its own purpose in the end, since without education or choice we don't learn how to think independently. The best way to live is with our own sense of discernment of what is good for us, then good for the whole.

What points of view are you tempted to censor? Which voices in yourself or others do you want to stifle? Is shame the driving force behind this need to suppress something? The angels know that what is controversial today may be commonplace tomorrow. Ask them for the courage to love all the parts of yourself and to be patient with the parts of others you may find controversial.

An Angelic Reflection: I exercise discretion in what I view, and I welcome many points of view.

AWAKENING TO YOUR MYSTIC SELF

An Angel Reminder: "For now is the hour when we are in danger of forgetting for what purpose we are on earth."
Herbert Weiner, *9 ½ Mystics: The Kabbala Today*

What does being awake really mean? The origin of the word *awake* is the old English *wacan,* which referred to a watch or vigil. In Buddhism, being awake means being free of *samsara,* life's illusions that parade as reality. When we are asleep, we believe that material reality is the only reality; when we are awake, we understand that our true self, our "nature mind," is immortal and eternal, that we are part of everything and that everything is part of us. Mystics of every religion speak of the profound bliss that comes with truly awakening to our larger nature, our infinite self, the oneness of everything. No longer are we imprisoned in a finite identity. No longer are we alone, separate from others. We are all, and we are endless. What a magical, liberating realization!

Would you like to become acquainted with your mystic self? If so, begin cultivating the ten characteristics of the mystic within you: (1) Feel at one with the universal life force; (2) know that you are timeless; (3) rejoice in the beauty of the universe, even in the midst of suffering; (4) expand with life instead of contracting with fear; (5) remain physically based and metaphysically directed; (6) enjoy a good mystery; (7) always be in love; (8) want what you have, not what you don't have; (9) see God as your playmate; (10) trust that you will always be given what you need, in ways you cannot imagine.

An Angelic Reflection: **I am not afraid to take the magical mystery tour.**

GERM WARFARE

An Angel Reminder: **Love is the best antiseptic.**

Germs are things we don't see, but we have all heard of them and felt their wrath. Seeing every germ could drive us crazy, and we do get crazy when we imagine them everywhere. Health and welfare exist in a delicate balance. Studies have shown that children who grow up in houses where one could eat off the floor because it is so clean get sick more often than children growing up in houses that are not cleaned regularly. The reason is that exposure to germs as a part of normal living helps to build immunity. Living a sterile life isn't the answer to a germ problem, because then we compromise both our immunity and the balance of nature.

When we are overprotected from life, we don't learn how to ride the storms. Life is not meant to be sterilized. It is meant to unfold and be messy—grow, ooze, die, be born, decay, repair. Life is a balance dance. Next time you get the urge to sterilize something, think about what you are doing. The angels don't like to see everything neutered, clean, orderly, and linear; they like life to look like life.

An Angelic Reflection: **I need more protection from negative thoughts than I do from the thousands of germs living around me.**

OUT OF TIME

An Angel Reminder: **If time can be lost, it can also be found.**

Often we get caught in the trap of thinking that we don't have enough time for something. Well, not having time means we're out of time, which we can't be unless we're dead. "Out of time" is an interesting concept in this context; when we're no longer part of the physical world we are indeed out of the restrictive boundaries of temporal time and living in eternal timelessness. The angels remind us that we are never really out of time while we're here on Earth and that when something is really important to us we seem to be able to find or make the time for it.

Do you ever fall into the trap of thinking that you don't have enough time? How are you using your time now? Have you structured your life so that you are "too busy to think"? Are you the slave of a never-ending schedule of events? Do you waste time? You and you alone have decided what kind of life you're currently experiencing, so it's up to you to make more time if you don't have it. Think of some ways right now that you could restructure your life so that you could have the time you need and use the time you have more meaningfully.

An Angelic Reflection: **I am not a slave to time.**

GROWING UP

An Angel Reminder: "Everyone wants to be
somebody; nobody wants to grow."
Johann Wolfgang von Goethe

A lot of people advance in years but forget to grow up spiritually and mentally. A grown-up is an adult, someone who is mature. With maturity comes wisdom. Growing up is a process of knowing yourself and going upward. Intelligence and wisdom come with learning how to think, and this takes effort and a brain that has been allowed to develop. When we grow up we stop being wimps and stop waiting for others to make things happen for us; we take the initiative and make our own life happen with the angels as copilots.

When you take an active part in shaping your life, with the help of the angels, you take another step toward growing up. You are less likely to fill a void in your life with unhealthy relationships or habits. By doing things you love and keeping your priorities and values in order, you earn a good feeling about yourself that you cannot not get in any other way.

An Angelic Reflection: **With the angels, I grow upward and expand in love.**

WEIGHT

An Angel Reminder: **The soul is weightless.**

Weight is a big issue in our society. Being thin is definitely seen as a virtue, while being overweight has been called the only visible vice. It's true that lots of extra poundage isn't terribly healthy. But the issue isn't the pounds so much as what they represent. Some heavy people like to "throw their weight around." For others, extra weight means a "wait," in terms of putting dreams on hold. And "holding weight" is one way in which we convince others of the validity of our positions. The angels don't judge us according to how thin or how fat we are. They don't judge us, period. If we have a weight problem, they merely ask us to look deeper into the issues surrounding our associations with weight, whether or not we're overweight. We may be at a perfect weight but remain convinced we're fat. If we're obsessed with not gaining an ounce, the angels ask us why we need to starve ourselves and what virtues we equate with excessive thinness. Then they remind us that our souls have no weight in the physical dimension, but they certainly carry a lot of weight where God is concerned.

What role does weight play in your life? Do you think you're too fat? Too thin? Do you equate being overweight with weakness of character and thinness with moral strength? Are you always trying to look a certain way in order to have the approval of others? You might want to examine the different meanings the word weight *has in your life.*

An Angelic Reflection: **I am worth my weight in gold.**

INDEPENDENCE DAY

An Angel Reminder: **Today, let us declare our independence from oppressive beliefs.**

On this day that we traditionally celebrate our country's independence, the angels ask us to take a closer look at the word *independence*. What does it mean, to be independent? Not oppressed? Not dependent on anyone or anything? Totally, completely free? Independence is a relative term; we may feel like independent beings when in truth there is always something or someone we're dependent upon. Our country may be independent from British rule, but it is certainly dependent on the rest of the world for many other things. As citizens, we may not be oppressed in the political sense, but we may indeed suffer under the tyranny of oppression in all sorts of different ways, whether it's a bad employer or a bad marriage, financial difficulties or ill health. In other words, independence is a fluid concept that changes constantly depending on our circumstances. The angels suggest (a) that we will always be moving between independence and dependence in our lives and (b) that true independence involves freeing ourselves from oppressive beliefs that inhibit our spiritual freedom. We are our own worst tyrants; when we allow our spirits and souls the freedom of imagination, when we unbind ourselves from the chains of negative and restrictive thinking, then we have a crack at knowing real independence.

Where do you think you're independent in your life? In what areas are you dependent? Is it a healthy balance? Do you have beliefs that are holding you down or back? Are there any people in your life who tyrannize you? Examine the idea of independence as it relates to your own life. Are you less or more independent than you thought? What or who would you like to declare yourself independent from?

An Angelic Reflection: **I live in the free country of independent thought.**

FISHHOOK

An Angel Reminder: "Bait the hook well: this fish will bite."
William Shakespeare

One of our most odious inventions has to be the fishhook. It is a metal hook with a barbed end to make sure that once it has hooked the fish it won't come back out on its own. So when you have caught a fish, you can work out the hook only by ripping the poor fish's mouth apart. Sometimes we find ourselves attached to a barbed hook, and it is no easy task to get free. It is usually in the form of a hurtful relationship, where we feel as if the other person has a hook in us. When it is of the barbed kind, we can pull on it and try to rip it out, but all that does is cause much damage and pain. We feel helpless, as if the hook has a line attached that the other person tugs on to cause us pain. Sometimes we supply our own hook; this happens when we will do anything to stay connected to somebody, even if it means staying hooked to a painful situation. When we feel unexplainably hooked to a hurtful situation, the angels guide us to be very conscious of the attachment and to take our time getting over it. In time the hook will start to dissolve and leave, but we have to do our part in not pulling it back in.

If you find you are hooked, breathe deeply, quiet yourself, and do your best not to over-react. Ask the angels to help you live with the attachment until it changes and you can go in peace.

An Angelic Reflection: **A hook is only temporary; I will soon be free.**

SOUL RETRIEVAL

An Angel Reminder: **Our souls are the angels' message center.**

In ancient times, healers considered depression and psychosis to be so unusual that the only conclusion they could come to was that the afflicted person's soul had been lost or stolen. In the shamanistic practice of soul retrieval, the shaman goes into an ecstatic trance and moves between the two worlds of life and death, finally bringing the lost soul back to the person who has been disconnected from it. Often we use the term *lost soul* to refer to someone who seems without direction or is at a loss as to how to cope with life. In reality such a person has lost connection with his or her soul, which functions as our center of spiritual gravity. At certain points in life we may need to do a little soul retrieving. If we are in unfulfilling relationships, experiencing ill health or depression, if we feel blocked in any way, it is usually a sign that we need to bring ourselves back into alignment with our souls, which often call to us through discomfort. When we choose to listen, we may at first have to make some uncomfortable alterations in the way we have been living. But we can rest assured that such changes ultimately lead to a newfound sense of freedom and purpose.

Are there places in your life where your soul seems to be lost? If so, practice retrieving it by sitting with it awhile and asking it what it is trying to tell you. Is it perhaps calling you to give up something that is no longer furthering your growth in order to receive something that is? Begin cultivating a relationship with your guardian angel, who is the official protector of your soul. Don't be afraid to go to him or her for guidance and reconnection to your soul.

An Angelic Reflection: **I am always within earshot of the call of my soul.**

FORCED INTIMACY

An Angel Reminder: **Forced intimacy leaves us feeling used.**

There is nothing more frustrating than the feeling that we need to change and that it has to happen now. Forcing growth and change is futile. But sometimes, if we feel a deficiency of love, we may feel forced to be intimate in situations where it may not be right or real. It is not necessary to force yourself to be intimate in any situation, whether with another person or a group of people or with the Divine. Take your time to plant the seeds you choose. Make sure you have cultivated the soil, and know what seed you are planting and what to look for as it grows. Don't feel bad if it takes years until you feel a shift. This is natural, and time is not relevant here. Anyone who claims to have a special line on divine teachings is out of line, because true spiritual teaching leads to "don't know mind," one of the highest states of being.

The angels suggest that anytime you feel forced or frustrated in your spiritual growth, stop a moment and look at it. Sometimes the energy of frustration is useful, because it signals the storing up of creative energy, and it often leads you to a breakthrough of some kind— that is, if you use the energy instead of sinking back into depression or resignation. But, even if you do that, it will be okay. We learn and grow from life, in whatever configuration it is taking. Remember that the angels know you and your pace; they do not want you to suffer or to force yourself to step into something that doesn't fit.

An Angelic Reflection: **I am growing at my own pace.**

LUXURY

An Angel Reminder: "Spirituality without discipline
is nothing but a hobby. So we should find a way
to ritualize our connection to the spirit world."
Geoffrey Menin

Having the time to think about spirituality and happiness and to ponder
philosophical questions is often seen as a luxury. Some, however, have the
time because they are in prison. Others have the time because they can
afford it; they have hired others to take care of the little things that might
distract them. Technology and affluence have freed many of us from
physical labor—not many of us are up at five o'clock feeding chickens
and plowing fields and communing with the rhythms of nature—but we
often use this time in self-indulgent ways. Do those in a war zone or a
ghetto have the luxury of contemplating happiness? Certainly they want
happiness at least as badly as those lounging around their houses in safe
neighborhoods do. We cannot say people living in horrendous conditions
are not contemplating happiness; Anne Frank is one who did. We always
have the luxury of contemplating the spiritual if we are brave enough to
make the choice.

*We have the luxury of thinking about what we want to, unless we are in a dangerous
emergency. Give yourself a chance to luxuriate in the lap of angel consciousness. While you
contemplate, the angels will remind you that happiness is all about sharing love with others.*

An Angelic Reflection: With discipline and ritual I will luxuriate in spiritual happiness.

THE COMPLEXITY OF GOD

An Angel Reminder: "To 'God's world' belonged everything superhuman—dazzling light, the darkness of the abyss, the cold impassivity of infinite space and time, and the uncanny grotesqueness of the irrational world of chance. 'God,' for me, was everything—and anything but 'edifying.'"
Carl Jung, *Memories, Dreams, and Reflections*

When he was a teenager, Carl Jung was already wrestling with the most weighty philosophical question of all: Who or what is God? Jung could not help but see God as the embodiment of opposing forces both wonderful and terrible, and if humans were made in the divine image, those opposing forces, for good and evil, must exist in us as a strange sort of divine perfection. It is tempting to want to reduce God to a comforting definition or description, but God is full of all the contradictions that inhabit the world He/She created, and those contradictions can never be understood, only appreciated. With this attitude we cannot label even evil as unworthy of existing, for God allows it. So we open ourselves to the beautiful and terrible forces within us, and we allow them to guide us to a deeper place of self-realization.

Do you appreciate the many different and sometimes seemingly contradictory aspects of God, as benevolent and harsh, ruler of both darkness and light, suffering and joy? Do you appreciate the complexity of your own nature, with its numerous personalities and dualities? When you have some time, you might want to write about how you see God and how you see yourself as made in the image of God.

An Angelic Reflection: I embrace the different aspects of my nature, and I explore the different energies they hold.

INVISIBLE HELPERS

An Angel Reminder: "As you work with courage and patience in your particular corner, so will you be rewarded by an ever-increasing consciousness of the companionship, and the very real help in your material lives, given to you by your invisible brethren."

White Eagle

Many people believe that human beings have spirit guides, who surround them at all times and protect them. Others say, "Hah! Where were my spirit guides when this or that awful thing happened to me?" The nondenominational spiritual teacher White Eagle asserts, "Not one of you stands alone.... ministers of God are by your side; no single detail in your life, not a thought or an action, escapes them." Catholics turn to guardian angels and saints for supernatural help in times of distress. Many other cultures pray to ancestral spirits, whom they believe are always present. The question of why we must undergo tragedy and suffering if we have these invisible guides is confusing. But the angels tell us that they are with us, not to make life free of pain, but to help us face and overcome pain when it comes to us, as it must to all humans.

Have you ever felt the invisible helpers with you? If so, when? How did they manifest their presence? You might want to try contacting the invisible helpers simply by imagining them around you. What do they look like? Can you identify any of them? Let yourself feel their loving, compassionate presence warming and calming you. Ask for any help you need, and see what happens.

An Angelic Reflection: I know that divine aid is always available to me and that it often comes through the vehicle of guardian spirits.

PROVING YOURSELF

An Angel Reminder: When you have to prove yourself to others, you have to prove yourself to yourself.

The need to prove ourselves can be very instructive. When we are challenged to do something, we often amaze ourselves and others by our level of commitment, persistence, and faith. We discover that we can do it, and this discovery leads us to approach other challenges with more courage and confidence. But when we feel compelled to prove ourselves in order to be loved and accepted, it's a different story. Then it seems we are never good enough. Many of us have felt the need to prove ourselves to rejecting parents, or to other people whose love we desperately want, by becoming obsessive achievers. Or we may turn into obsessive pleasers, always trying to prove that we're so good we have to be loved. The angels want us to be able to make the distinction between proving that we can achieve something and proving that we are worthy of love. The former is necessary for the betterment of our spirit and for self-esteem. The latter is completely unnecessary, for in the eyes of God and the angels we are automatically worthy of love, no matter what we have or haven't achieved.

Have you felt the need to prove yourself? In what way? To whom? Do you have to prove yourself to yourself? Do you believe that if you fail you are unworthy of love and respect?

An Angelic Reflection: I strive for achievement and live in contentment.

THE CLAMP OF GUILT

An Angel Reminder: **If you have gotten yourself
in a jam, guilt will not get you out of it.**

Some of us find ourselves in situations that are quite serious, facing problems that require our utmost awareness and energy to solve. Often when we're in such jams, guilt descends on us like a clamp, almost paralyzing us. We hear the voice of guilt say something like, "Here you are again. If you had only stopped while you were ahead and had gotten a new job." Or, "If only you had taken better care of yourself." The clamp tightens if others with their armchair view of our lives offer their judgments of our situation. Often we will meet up with difficult situations, and if we're not careful, guilt will clamp us down every time. The angels want us to use our energy to let go of the clamp and to leave our guilty consciences behind.

When we run into jams—even if we're repeating a lesson in life—it doesn't mean that we are failures. After all, if you look at the lesson with new eyes, you will realize it holds some new circumstance that you would have missed if you had shut down with guilt. Ask the angels for the wisdom that will loosen the strangling effect of guilt. Getting rid of the guilt may be the actual lesson.

An Angelic Reflection: **I don't need to feel guilty when the angels are in my consciousness.**

IMPATIENCE

An Angel Reminder: "Transcendent patience never expects anything."
Chögyam Trungpa

The Tibetan teacher Chögyam Trungpa Rinpoche sees patience not merely as the willingness to wait but as the act of nonexpectation. When we don't expect anything, he explains, we are not impatient. Impatience results when we hold a preconceived plan to which we must adhere at all costs. When something gets in the way of our agenda, we are thrown off course and feel frustrated. We feel we are suffocating with tension, being closed in on, when in reality we are closing in on ourselves; our ego is usurping our spirit. Patience, on the other hand, leads to expansion, of both vision and heart. "Patience feels space," notes Trungpa. "It never fears new situations. . . . Nothing can surprise the bodhisattva because he is aware of the space between the situation and himself."

Do you tend to be impatient? How does impatience affect you? Does it raise your blood pressure? Put you in a fighting mood? Impatience can be useful when something absolutely has to get done. But in the spiritual realms it is a useless pastime, for God is always on schedule. The angels would love to help us adopt an attitude of transcendent patience that keeps us calm and centered no matter what we may encounter.

An Angelic Reflection: I respect the space between myself and my perceptions.

THE WAY THINGS ARE

An Angel Reminder: **The highway of life would be gridlocked if we were all meant to be on the same path.**

At any moment in time, people are experiencing vastly different pieces of life. Some are being born, others are dying. Happy moments are transpiring, tragedies are developing. A wealthy person pushes away the remains of a fifty-dollar dinner while waiting for a fifteen-dollar dessert, as another person starves in poverty searching Dumpsters for an evening meal. And all of these scenes are happening simultaneously. There comes a point in each human life when we have to contemplate the uniqueness of everyone's experiences. Sometimes the urge to take away everyone's suffering comes from a big heart. But it may come also from feeling troubled that people are different and their lessons in life are different. When our urge to help comes from a belief that everyone must think, act, and behave the same way, then we are acting, not out of compassion, but out of a misplaced desire for sameness.

How do we recognize differences between our own and others' experiences and feel okay about them? It takes awareness, hope, being awake, and accepting a higher purpose in life. If you ask the angels for answers to the human mystery, you will find that they will guide you to a sense of peace and comfort in the mystery. The angels do this not by bringing you answers and intricate theories, but by bringing creative ways of responding to life with light in your heart.

An Angelic Reflection: **I will honor the uniqueness of each person's path and practice being open to the mystery.**

EXTENDING OURSELVES

An Angel Reminder: **The more we extend ourselves, the more we grow.**

You may be familiar with the term *life extension*, which we take to mean living longer. But the angels have a different definition. To them, life extension means the extent to which we are willing to extend ourselves to others. A lot of times this isn't easy, especially when we're bogged down and feel that there's barely enough of ourselves to go around. There are times when we need to establish protective boundaries in order to keep ourselves sane and balanced. But there are also plenty of times when it wouldn't hurt us to go out of our way a little more, giving help when it is asked or offering help to people who may be too ashamed or proud to ask for it or simply being there for those who need us, without judging and without expecting anything in return. Sometimes extending ourselves can be a real challenge, like moving back home to care for a sick parent or giving up some of our own dreams so that our children might realize theirs. The more willingly—and wisely—we extend ourselves however, the closer we come to the angels, and the closer we come to being angels ourselves.

What are some ways in which you have extended yourself to others? How have others extended themselves to you? Is it ever hard for you to extend yourself? Hard not to extend yourself? How does extending yourself bring gifts into your life as well as the lives of others? How can you extend yourself right now to someone who could use your help?

An Angelic Reflection: **I am continually stretching my capacity for giving.**

SOAPBOX

An Angel Reminder: 'Tis better to err on
the side of passion than to live in apathy.

One of the wonderful things about London's legendary Hyde Park is its tradition of allowing anybody and everybody the opportunity to air their most impassioned opinions in public. In the old days, self-proclaimed orators would regale and harangue the multitudes from the everyday pulpit, the soapbox. It didn't matter if you were sane or potty; as long as you were in the vicinity you were allowed the privilege of expounding on your views, whatever they might be. The angels like soapboxes because they are a good antidote to apathy. Maybe a lot of soapbox philosophies are out in left field; some may even be dangerous. But the angels would rather we become passionate about something than not care about anything. Besides, the sharing of opinions keeps our thinking mechanism well oiled. The angels certainly don't approve of our always being on a soapbox, trying to shove our ideas down everybody's throat. But they encourage us to care, to be committed to social issues, and, even more important, to get off our soapbox once in a while and actually work for the things we really believe in.

Are you on a soapbox about anything? If you had to pick a cause, what would it be? Do you work actively for your community in any way? You don't have to be in politics or the Peace Corps to uplift the human condition; whether you're a teacher, a writer, an artist, a bank clerk—or even if you have no job or career—there are always outlets for your passions and ways you can make a difference.

An Angelic Reflection: I work actively and passionately to improve my environment.

CONTENTIOUS

An Angel Reminder: **Being contentious will not lead to contentment.**

It is natural to feel contentious once in a while. When we are feeling contentious we are argumentative and want to dispute every opinion. Underlying contention are real feelings of frustration caused by a variety of things. When you notice a bout of contention coming on, take a break and look into the underlying causes. They may not be mysterious; it could be as simple as a phone call that set off a chain of events in your mind. When you follow the chain back to its source, you will see that the problem is not so big. The danger of contentiousness comes when we argue with a friend who doesn't deserve it. Better to address the underlying frustration that to put the friendship at risk.

If you have been contentious lately, think about where the argumentative energy came from. The need to debate and argue is masking something greater. Get underneath your dispute, and stop arguing with life. Do you think the angels are really that impressed when you are beating a dead horse?

An Angelic Reflection: **I seek contentment by dealing with buried feelings instead of becoming contentious.**

HUNGRY GHOSTS

An Angel Reminder: **How do you feed a ghost?**

Buddhists recognize six lower realms of experience, one of which is the realm of the hungry ghosts. This is a metaphor for our state of mind when we are hungering, starving for the bliss that cannot be found in the material world. In the realm of the hungry ghosts we think our hunger will be appeased if we just consume this or that. But just as ghosts can never find satisfaction in the physical dimension, so our soul can never be satisfied with material food. In fact, it can't even digest it. Many people are like hungry ghosts, wandering the Earth in a doomed search for inner peace. They hunger for power, fame, money, or sex instead of true enlightenment, and consequently they never feel full. As Sogyal Rinpoche observes in *The Tibetan Book of Living and Dying,* "The Hungry Ghost Realm exists wherever people, though immensely rich, are never satisfied, craving to take over this company or that one, or endlessly playing out their greed in court cases. Switch on any television channel and you have entered immediately the realm ... of the hungry ghosts." The angels know that the only way to feed a ghost—to feed a spirit—is with the things of the spirit. When we begin to hunger for God, we have a chance of finally feeling full-filled.

Do you know any hungry ghosts? What are they hungry for? Do you ever feel helpless in the face of their hunger, as though you can never satisfy them? Have you ever paid a visit to the Hungry Ghost Realm yourself, or are you possibly in it now? If so, remember that the more things you do to satisfy your spiritual cravings, the less hungry you will be.

An Angelic Reflection: **I look for ways to feed my spirit as well as my body.**

IRRELEVANT

An Angel Reminder: **Relevance is relative.**

To be relevant is to be significant to the matter at hand. Its Latin origin is the word *relevare*, to lift up. Sometimes we lift up to a level of importance something that simply isn't worthy of the attention we are giving it. It is important to stay awake to what is really relevant in our lives. The angels are master teachers in this area. Although significance can be found in many things, think of what is important to you, and ask yourself if it is relevant to your spiritual growth.

As you look at your life, what things appear most important? What do your choices about where you spend your time or money say about what you consider most relevant? Think about what you want to lift up in your life and what you would like to discard. The angels are good at helping you lift up the good.

An Angelic Reflection: **I choose things that are relevant to my highest good.**

ETHERIC REALMS

An Angel Reminder: **We can communicate with the angels by tuning in to the etheric realms.**

Some of us may remember the days when ether was used as an anesthetic. A mask was put over the face, and one immediately lost consciousness, awakening perhaps hours later and feeling as if only an instant had transpired. In the etheric realms time has no meaning as we know it. A minute may seem like eternity and an eternity like a second. The angels reside in the etheric realms, and sometimes it's not a bad idea to "pass out" and join them for a while, setting our earthly concerns aside and feeling the lightness and freedom of spirit they embody. Passing out in this context does not, however, mean losing consciousness or becoming anesthetized. Rather, in passing out of the physical realm we pass into the spiritual realm, where we feel and sense things more, not less, acutely.

Take a trip with your soul into the etheric realms. Breathe deeply, "inspiring" yourself with the pure air of freedom of thought and consciousness. Feel this air filling you as though you were a helium balloon. Feel yourself rising into the air, all your worries, concerns, and limits falling away. You are free now to receive any messages and insights it has to give you. Let it speak to you now in images, thoughts, ideas, colors—in any language it chooses.

An Angelic Reflection: **I draw energy from the refined vibrations of the angels.**

BAD DREAMS

An Angel Reminder: "One trembles to think of that mysterious thing in the soul, which seems to acknowledge no human jurisdiction, but in spite of the individual's own innocent self, will still dream horrid dreams, and mutter unmentionable thoughts."
Herman Melville

We often try hard to get rid of our "bad" thoughts and habits, but just when we think we have overcome them we find they simply have moved into our dreams. It is well known in psychology that if you ignore or deny something negative or uncomfortable, it will gain more strength and eventually pop out in another form, demanding an acknowledgment. A bad dream can be a healing process. It can be our psyche's way of working out the things we are not totally conscious of. The angels are always with us, and they remind us of our innate courage even while we sleep.

When is a bad dream a full-blown nightmare? Do bad dreams always means we are hiding secrets? We are multidimensional in our response to life, including while we sleep. Keeping a dream journal can be very helpful in understanding ourselves and how our unconscious works. You will most likely find that in time the bad dreams are simply interesting—not good or bad.

An Angelic Reflection: The angels give me the courage to know that bad dreams can transform into good insights.

SIMULTANEOUS REALITIES

An Angel Reminder: **Life is multidimensional.**

Life isn't black-and-white, this way and not that way. Have you ever stopped to think that when you're in the midst of unhappiness about one thing, you can be simultaneously happy about another? So, we can't say that we're totally unhappy, because happiness is coexisting with unhappiness. The angels know that we are always experiencing simultaneous realities, even if we're not aware of them. We can move in and out of these realities at will; we don't have to remain stuck in one or another. No one feeling is ever permanent unless we prefer to remain wedded to it—and even then we have to try awfully hard to sing on one emotional note and ignore the chorus of other experiences that make us the complex and fascinating creations that we are.

What simultaneous realities are occurring in your life right now? If you are in pain, stop and think of anything that is good in your life or that brings you joy. Realize that you can experience seemingly contradictory emotions concurrently and that your thoughts are like doors opening onto different rooms. Feel free to go into any room, at any time.

An Angelic Reflection: **I try not to allow any one feeling to determine my perception of reality.**

Turn It into a Game

An Angel Reminder: **We all have a complaint from time to time.**

Have you ever run into someone who upset your balance so much that you had to talk about it extensively? After a while this turns into complaining. When we complain we are expressing pain, dissatisfaction, or grief. If someone or something has upset your life, it usually means you have been tricked. If you have been tricked, it is as if you have been brusquely awakened. The angels see a situation like this as a glorious opportunity for wisdom, but only after some initial complaining sessions. Your process of resetting the balance will first include outrage, so you need a friend or counselor to hear you out. Then you will probably want to complain. The key to not getting stuck in this stage is humor—laughing at ourselves.

If you feel stuck with an outrageous situation and you have some good friends, play a little game called The Complaint Department. Call up a friend, and ask if the complaint department is open. If your friend says yes, then register a formal complaint, being careful not to go on for too long; the angels want you to keep your friends. While complaining, listen to yourself and to your friend, and at some point have a good laugh. If you don't want to do this to your friends, you can do it with the angels by having an imaginary dialogue or writing up a formal complaint.

An Angelic Reflection: **I am fortunate to know the number of the angels' complaint department.**

HILLS

An Angel Reminder: **The higher we climb, the more we see.**

A woman we know has a lovely house with a breathtaking view of the city and the mountains. But the house is on a steep hill, which is very wearing for her when she has to walk her dog. One day she found herself wishing that she lived on a nice, flat street where she could walk the dog without getting tired. But then she realized that if she did she would be giving up her magnificent view, which afforded her a great deal of joy. She saw then that the hill, as difficult as it was to climb, was its own reward. This is a good metaphor for life. Everything is a trade-off; every challenge we face has a benefit and every benefit a challenge. The angels know that nothing is perfect, that we usually don't get a great view without having to trudge our way to the top of the mountain. But the prize isn't just at the top; it's also the strength we gain along the way.

Are there any hills in your life? Are you up to climbing them, or do you look for ways around them? The next time you find yourself avoiding a hill, ask the angels for a good sturdy pair of climbing boots and a helping hand when you get really winded. And remember: when you're out of breath, it's a good time to slow down and admire the view.

An Angelic Reflection: **I appreciate hills because they take me to higher levels of awareness and achievement.**

MERCY

An Angel Reminder: "For Mercy has a
human heart, Pity, a human face."
William Blake

To show mercy is to treat an offender or enemy with compassion, to be kind and forgiving. Society is very unforgiving these days; one rarely hears the word *mercy* used. Instead, we see alleged offenders tried in the kangaroo courts of TV talk shows; the ratings aren't good unless a sensational guilty verdict is reached. Mercy is not sensational for the masses, but it is quite a sensation on the inner planes of heaven. When the angels witness human mercy, they rejoice and bless us.

Dare to be different from most of our society: practice showing mercy to both yourself and others. In what ways are you unmerciful with yourself? Where do you pass verdicts on others instead of extending kindness and forgiveness? In order to have mercy, we must make room for the surrounding circumstances in our own and others' lives. Ask the angels for the courage to be merciful instead of judgmental.

An Angelic Reflection: **I will allow loving-kindness to be my guiding light.**

IF YOUR THOUGHTS
COULD BE HEARD

An Angel Reminder: **"If you could read my mind . . ."**
Gordon Lightfoot

Can you imagine what the world would be like if we had the ability to read everyone's thoughts? Rod Serling could; in a wonderful episode of *The Twilight Zone*, the main character was mysteriously given the ability to hear the thoughts of others. Naturally, the hypocrisy of the human race was instantly exposed. While we might think that our thoughts are private and have no bearing on our interactions, this is not always true. Of course we have thoughts that are no one else's business. But when we are saying one thing and thinking another, we are not living in accordance with our true selves. The angels can hear all our thoughts, and the amazing thing is that they love us in spite of them.

Are there times you're glad your thoughts can't be heard? Remember that you don't have to reveal all of your thoughts all of the time and that thoughts are only thoughts, unless, of course, they're causing you to live a life of hypocrisy instead of integrity. Then you may need to examine your thoughts and decide which ones are crying for expression and which ones could use some changing.

An Angelic Reflection: **I try to think in ways that are helpful, not hurtful.**

WHAT THIS COUNTRY NEEDS IS A CHEAP SHOE

An Angel Reminder: **Cheap is as cheap does.**

We have a problem in this country that is eating away at the soul of our nation like termites bringing down a house. Let's use a shoe company as an example. Executives at this shoe company get the grand idea that they can lay off thousands of workers in the United States, where the shoes are bought. Then they move to another country and hire cheap—almost slave—labor, which gives them a shoe they can sell for considerably less money. But other companies are also doing the same thing, so the workers who are laid off are now in competition with thousands of other unfortunate people needing jobs that don't exist and will not be created. Their entire world has been completely upset, and they have been cast off to fend for themselves. If "we the people" do not have jobs, how can we buy shoes at all? If "we the people" do not have health insurance and benefits for our loved ones, all kinds of problems come forth. Nothing comes cheap. Inexpensive goods and services may signal problems at other levels of our economy.

If top executives gave up a few dollars per hour or one of their outrageous bonuses, not only would they not miss the money, they would be operating within the law of abundance, and it would come back to the company in blessings. What decisions could you make in your life that would help balance the invisible ledger of abundance?

An Angelic Reflection: **I pray for those whose life has been rendered cheap.**

DREAM STEALING

An Angel Reminder: You can't do that!

Let's say someone starts to write a screenplay, gets very excited, and shares the enthusiasm with a friend. This person informs them that at least 43,000 scripts are registered each year and maybe eight get made, and besides, who are they to think that they can write a good script? and what a waste of time! This is an example of the crime of dream stealing. In certain native cultures, one of the worst offenses is dream stealing, which is punishable by banishment from your tribe. Many of us have had the water of our dreams poisoned so often we may unconsciously do it to others. The angels drop their heads when they hear a dream stolen. So what if someone's script never gets picked up and the writer doesn't make a dime? Simply following through on the dream spells success in the eyes of the angels, and many blessings will follow. The angels remind us that *enthusiasm* comes from the Greek *en-theos,* to be filled with God. Let the dreamers dream!

Next time someone comes to you with their heartfelt dream, listen and bless them without judgment or comment. We too often listen to ideas in the context of how much money they will make or cost and how realistic they are. You never know, the eccentric friend telling you of the spaceship they are designing may surprise us all and end up saving the world. If you are cutting short someone's enthusiasm, think about how you are taking God out of their life.

An Angelic Reflection: I welcome enthusiasm as divine inspiration, and I am careful not to burst anyone's bubble.

UNDERMINE

An Angel Reminder: "If schizophrenia is a disease
of the human condition, then polyphrenia—
which is the orchestration of our many selves—is health."
Jean Houston

To undermine something is to weaken it gradually, usually below the level
of awareness. There are many ways we undermine ourselves and our con-
victions. One of them is by listening to some of our inner voices and
ignoring others. Often we are not aware that our intentions and motivations are multifaceted. We may intend to stay on the straight and narrow
path of moderation, but our spirit and soul may be motivated to break
out and dance in the wide open spaces of extravagance. If we do not fight
the fact that within us dwell many voices, we will be healthier in so many
ways. A sure way to drive ourselves crazy is to pay attention to only one
voice and one motivation.

*Strict beliefs lead to restricted experiences. Life is a full experience, and in order to be a
part of it, we must allow our many selves to have a safe outlet for expression. Just because
you listen to a voice doesn't mean you must do what it says. Our good intentions will hold
up better if we invite the angels in to let love lead our way and to help us listen carefully.*

An Angelic Reflection: **The angels help to conduct the orchestra of my
many selves with love.**

RIPTIDE

An Angel Reminder: "**What you resist persists; surrender to the swirl.**"
Ken Kalb

A riptide is a tide that is running against the other tides, creating turbulent waters. It comes from below the surface and suddenly grabs your legs or even your waist. A good swimmer knows that in order to get out of the turbulent swirl of a riptide, you cannot panic and try swimming to shore; you instead must relax and surrender for a moment. Our friend Ken Kalb, also known as the "Dolfunman of Santa Barbara," says that you must do aikido with a riptide and let the power of it release you. So you must wait until the juice is gone, conserving your energy, then swim out under the bottom of the current. Water represents our emotional nature, and emotions can be like currents and waves. Sometimes we can easily swim with emotional currents, until a riptide comes from the depths and we begin to swirl around in an emotional tornado that we cannot control. This is when it is time to surrender and let the angels take over.

When caught in a riptide, don't let it rip you in half. Emotions are dark and scary sometimes, but they can't kill you unless you panic. Sometimes we have to sit in the center of the storm when the unexpected hits and wait until the angels guide us to safety.

An Angelic Reflection: I am always protected; I will always find my way back to peace.

CONSENT

An Angel Reminder: "Remember, no one can make
you feel inferior without your consent."
Eleanor Roosevelt

When we give our consent, it means that we agree with something or
someone; we acquiesce. There are many things we consent to without
thinking them through or having keen awareness of them. Often we are
manipulated into giving our consent to something and then later feel
used when we realize it.

*The angels want to help us know when to give our consent to something. We should guard
our right to agree like we would a precious jewel and think something through before we just
agree to it. Think about what you have consented to lately. How did it turn out? Did you
have any regrets?*

An Angelic Reflection: **The angels remind me that I give consent to my
thoughts, words, and deeds.**

SEEING

An Angel Reminder: "We do a lot of looking . . . through lenses, telescopes, television tubes . . . but we see less and less. Never has it been more urgent to speak of *seeing.*"
Frederick Franck

Sometimes we think we are seeing when we are actually blind to the real wonders around us. We generally take our surroundings for granted, so the trick is to look at things with new eyes, the eyes of someone who has just entered the room for the first time, or perhaps the eyes of a newborn baby. That chair—the mind that designed it, the hands that crafted it, the wood from which it was fashioned, the tree from which the wood came, the seed that grew into the tree, the wind that carried the seed—it is so mysterious, so marvelous! There is also a difference between looking and seeing. Looking objectivizes and separates; seeing dissolves barriers and allows oneness between viewer and object to occur. The angels encourage us to learn to see with both our outer and inner eyes. Then we will be better able to move away from our own little world into the realm of real in-sight.

Practice seeing things as if for the first time—objects, people, animals, trees, and flowers. What do you notice that's new or amazing? Now, practice looking into a confusing situation, past surface glare and into truth. As you open your inner eyes, open your heart as well. Do you feel more a part of the world, no longer blind? Give thanks for this "second sight."

An Angelic Reflection: I see with new eyes and experience a new life.

FILLING UP TIME

An Angel Reminder: "The Wintu Indians have a suffix to refer to alert non-activity, to a silent, non-mobile commitment to awareness; a suffix I found impossible to translate because there is no equivalent concept in American culture."

Dorothy Lee

What if we had been taught as children to sit still and enjoy it? What if we had been shown at an early age that free time could be used to "just be"—to look when there is apparently nothing to see, to listen when there is only silence? Most good little American children have their free time planned out. We have been warned that free time may lead to boredom, so to prevent that we plan something to do in every spare moment. If children are not bombarded by their parents' planning activities and are left to use their free time in their own way, they will do things like sit and look at the sky, let silence comfort them, and not even give a thought to the fear of boredom.

If you have been raised to fear boredom, you may not be comfortable with silences and pauses that naturally happen in life. You may feel anxious to say something when a conversation has reached a natural lull. Start to honor the space between the words, the white paper, the intervals; they are home to the angels. Your special connection with the angels will be profoundly deepened when you learn to listen to the silence, to be in touch with the present moment, and to look at what isn't apparent.

An Angelic Reflection: I will honor the deep silence to make room for the angels.

HELPFUL DISTRACTIONS

An Angel Reminder: **Sometimes distractions lead to new actions.**

Have you ever watched a cranky baby who's about to let the world know about it? It screws up its face and opens its mouth, all set to emit an ear-splitting wail. But there is a blessed couple of seconds in between the discomfort and the howl that can be used to divert the baby. Show it a new toy, distract it, and it will likely forget all about crying. It may even forget why it was going to cry in the first place. Sometimes it's a good idea to use similar distractions in our lives. When we're out of sorts, we don't always have to dwell on our problems. While a good cry can be a great help in times of distress, it isn't always essential. In fact, solutions come, more often than not, when we allow ourselves to forget about the cause of our misery and become involved in something more fascinating. The angels don't want us to go around denying pain. Neither do they advocate putting all of our energy into it. They approve of helpful distractions— activities that give us a burst of enthusiasm and a new perspective just when we need them the most.

What are some helpful distractions you can think of to divert your attention from your woes? Make a list of them. They might include taking a friend out to lunch, going to the gym, starting a new project. If you're currently experiencing a low period, what are some things you could do right this minute that could make you forget about your problems in a healthy way?

An Angelic Reflection: **I acknowledge unhappiness, but I do not dwell on it.**

DIE TO IT OR DIE OF IT

An Angel Reminder: "I know what the great cure is: it is
to give up, to relinquish, to surrender, so that our little hearts
may beat in unison with the great heart of the world."
Henry Miller

There are some stories and situations in our lives that we had better give
up on and let go of, or they will kill us. If we don't die to them, will may die
of them. We may be living in a story of drinking and betrayal (ours or
another's), and it may seem somewhat harmless, but if it goes on it will
destroy us. We may be holding on to a belief that isn't working anymore, but
we won't let it go. At the essence of dying to something is a surrender to
God's will. We are always in the process of surrendering to God's will.
When we are "willing," then we affirm life; when we resist, we affirm death.

*Is there anything in your life that you need to die to and let go of before it turns on you?
If so, ask the angels to help you understand that dying a little each day is better than a
major brush with death.*

An Angelic Reflection: I will learn to live and die each day.

UNSETTLED

An Angel Reminder: "The light of a lamp
does not flicker in a windless place."
The Bhagavad Gita

When we feel unsettled, it's as if every cell in our body is restless. We feel a subtle tug on our being and can't even identify what direction it's coming from or where it wants us to go. Obviously this is not a good state to be in if we have big decisions to make. An unsettled mind can think of only a few possibilities, whereas a love-centered mind is open to all possibilities. When we open to help from the angels, we can let go of the decision making completely, say a little prayer, and know that we are always in good hands.

Next time you feel unsettled, imagine the uproar being gently settled down by the love of the angels. Then give it up. Give up anything that is just too much for you to decide; this is a sign that God wants to speak to your soul and guide you to a place in which you will feel settled and sure that you are taking the right step.

An Angelic Reflection: **I am letting the angels' love settle into my cells.**

KEEP IT SIMPLE

An Angel Reminder: "What you get is a living.
What you give is a life."
Lillian Gish

These days people seem to be increasingly interested in simplifying their lives. Often what they mean is that they would like to change the way they work. Ideally we want our work and our lives to be for a higher purpose. This is attainable if we change the way we think about work and change little things in our lives to make our work more an expression of ourselves. As our work takes on new and higher meaning, we automatically become less concerned with stockpiling the acquisitions that are often used to fill up the empty spaces in our souls. We are less susceptible to distractions or given to clutter. We find that life is simpler simply because we are harnessing, not scattering, our energy for a cause that transcends our grasping egos. We are no longer making a living but giving a life.

If you had to simplify your life, how would you go about it? Do you have to make a certain income in order to support your lifestyle? Are you happy with your job or career, or would you rather be doing something else that might not make as much money but that would bring you more joy? Would you be willing to pare down in order to be happier in your vocation? What do you perceive of as essentials? What do you think you could live without?

An Angelic Reflection: I am willing to simplify my life in order to live more fully in my purpose.

KINDNESS

An Angel Reminder: **Kindness is like a boomerang;
it always comes back to us.**

There's a wonderful children's story by the English author Eleanor Farjeon called "The Kind Farmer." It's about a rich farmer who's a miser. Everyone in his village hates him—everyone except a beautiful woman with a pure heart, who is able to see through the farmer's terror of scarcity to the beautiful soul within him. With her love, the farmer finds that for the first time in his life he wants to give—gifts, trinkets, anything that will bring his beloved joy. When she dies he is devastated. But she leaves him with a small daughter, who becomes the recipient of his now burning need to give. He buys his little girl presents, and when she says "Kind Da!" he is astonished and how good the word *kind* makes him feel. Soon he begins to give to everyone—the poor, the downtrodden—until he is known as the kindest man in the village. When he dies he hasn't a penny to his name, because over the years he gave away all of his money to everyone he encountered who was in need. And miraculously, his destitute little girl is adopted by the whole village, ensuring her welfare forever. The farmer's kindness had become an eternal flame of love; whatever he had given to others was returned to him a thousand times over.

Can you think of times in your life when you performed an act of kindness that came back to you in an unexpected way? Think of some really kind people you know. Aren't they the ones that people speak of lovingly rather than disparagingly? Don't others always seem to want to do something for them? The next time you do a kindness for someone, notice how much closer you feel to the angels, who prize a kind heart above all things.

An Angelic Reflection: **I am kind to others and am treated in kind.**

FADS

An Angel Reminder: **Rebel against the fad.**

How does one resist a fad, when it seems to take over one's sense of reason? Fads really have little to do with good sense. A fad causes people to scramble for little pieces of cloth sewn into animal shapes and stuffed with beans. Skirts changing from floor length to miniskirt length within a year's time can drive anyone crazy. One thing is certain: a fad is passing, a trend stays around a little longer, but real quality is timeless. Think about fashions that are always acceptable, and think about why that is. Think about toys that remain on the shelves year after year: What is it about them that keeps them valuable? Are you timeless, in your style and desires?

Next time you have the urge to get caught up in a fad, regardless of whether it is the latest beanbag, vitamin, dress style, music, or new age event, try resisting it. Refuse to be a part of it, even if it makes sense and you desire it. The angels will love this and guide you into the timeless realm of royal fashions and quality that endures. This way you will be eternally in style and beyond fad land.

An Angelic Reflection: **I shall resist the urge to be "in"; I know what is always in style.**

Do-Nothing Day

An Angel Reminder: "We do without doing
and everything gets done."
Ralph Blum, *The Book of Runes*

Doing nothing has strong negative connotations in our society. When we're not busy we're being lazy, right? Wrong! The angels advocate do-nothing days because they know they will always lead us to eventually do something. On a do-nothing day we can relax, take care of ourselves, and figure out ways to unwind. We are allowed to do things as long as they are want-to's and not have-to's. In the process we are giving our weary brains and bodies a rest, which will refocus us and replenish our energy reserves, preparing us for the work that has to be done.

Do you give yourself do-nothing days? If not, why not plan one for yourself? Pick a day on your calendar, and write "Do Nothing" on it. Make no plans, schedule no activities. Keep the day a blank, and let God and the angels fill it in. You never know where do-nothing days may lead!

An Angelic Reflection: **Every once in a while I allow myself the freedom to be, not do.**

SPIRITUAL ENGAGEMENT

An Angel Reminder: "As you become more intimate with your authentic self—as you recover your true, incandescent identity—there will come a gradual but undeniable physical transformation."
Sarah Ban Breathnach

Becoming engaged in something means you are deeply involved and willing to go beyond the surface intentions and venture into the mystery. We can allow spiritual engagement into the mundane and discover magic in places we would never expect. Take, for example, a mechanic working on a car he or she loves. The love brings in a spiritual frame of mind, and the mechanic will sense what the car needs and will be guided intuitively while fixing it. Most work that we do, regardless of how boring it may seem, can be spiritually engaging if we bring the angels in and work for God. Our relationships become an avenue for spiritual expansion when we realize they are sacred cauldrons of growth.

Spend a day becoming spiritually engaged in all that you do. The angels love to help, so ask them to come along. If it seems difficult, keep trying each day. When even one hour becomes spiritually engaging, you have touched the mystery and will be blessed by it.

An Angelic Reflection: When I am engaged in the spiritual, negative energies do not engage me.

COMING APART

An Angel Reminder: "Come ye apart . . . and rest awhile."
Mark 6:31

It's interesting that we think of coming apart as a process of breakdown and fragmentation, when in the Bible it refers to exactly the opposite: becoming whole through contemplation and reflection. Down deep we all seek peace and freedom from the cares and stresses of the world. This is a basic human need and the angels are happy when we heed it, for it means we are drawing closer to them. In his book *A Place Apart*, Father Basil Pennington, a Trappist monk, speaks of the solitude, the "apartness" of the monastic life, that allows the participant to integrate worldly demands and distractions with his need for God, until "all speaks of God and to God in him." We don't have to be monks to attain this apartness. We can create it in our own lives simply by making the time for it. Daily prayer, daily meditation, even simply reflecting on our lives, conducted at a time and place that we designate as ours, brings us back to our center and unites us with God, so that in coming apart we become whole.

Do you ever feel as though you're coming apart? If so, isn't this the perfect time to really come apart—to retreat and do some real communicating with God?

An Angelic Reflection: I make time to get away and rest with God.

CARRIED AWAY

An Angel Reminder: **Do not put the cart before the horse.**

Enthusiasm is a wonderful thing, for when we're enthused, we feel energized and inspired. But we can get into trouble if we get carried away with our enthusiasm and forget the basic laws of life and the universe. We may fall in love with someone and start to make big sweeping plans before we really have any idea who this person is. We may get a great idea to start a business, one we feel God has directed us into, but we neglect all the tiny, tedious steps that are required before the doors open. Most things in life have a natural process and progression to them. It is great to be enthusiastic, and greater still to mix it in with some good ol' fashioned practicality.

Remember that you can fill the cart with lots of wonderful things, but if the horse is not there to pull it, you won't get very far. Think of the angels as the force that will guide the cart. Next time you get carried away, let the angels land you safely behind them, and they will pull you in the right direction.

An Angelic Reflection: **I will ground my enthusiasm and fly to great heights.**

DO THE RIGHT THING

An Angel Reminder: "Most people know what the right thing is. It's the doing that gives them trouble."

Harry S. Truman

Have you ever wondered why it's sometimes so hard to do the right thing? Sometimes it's because we may want to do the right thing but refrain out of legitimate fear for our safety and the safety of those close to us. But, in the above quote, Harry Truman was referring primarily to the little ways in which we let wrongs pile up. We lie, we avoid, we don't take responsibility, we don't help others when we should. We shirk our work, we substitute criticism for compassion. Yes, we are human, with all the frailty that entails. But we can always choose to get back in touch with our conscience. Perhaps the thing for which Harry Truman will be most fondly remembered was his integrity, his refusal to act in any way that separated him from his conscience. This certainly created many difficulties for him, but, as he put it, as long as he knew he'd done the right thing he could always sleep at night, no matter what people thought of him.

Has it ever been hard for you to do the right thing? Have you ever been sorry you did the right thing? List some right things that are easy for you to do and some that aren't. Ask the angels to help you do the right thing at the right time.

An Angelic Reflection: I will let my conscience be my guide.

Is There an Answer?

An Angel Reminder: "It is enough if one tries merely to comprehend a little of this mystery every day. Never lose a holy curiosity."
Albert Einstein

It is best to have more questions than answers. This keeps your mind fresh and hungry for life's experiences. Answers do not really satisfy for long, because the information held in an answer is incomplete and has a limited life span. Holding on to answers is like keeping bread for too long; it gets stale, and if you try to eat it you may become ill. The way to get more information is not to be afraid to question. Allow fresh answers to pour into your life, and allow your answers to lead to more questions. Keep the energy flowing, and you won't have to deal with stale beliefs.

Don't second-guess God and the angels, and don't answer their questions. If there are certain things you don't understand, don't rush to an answer but instead explore the mystery. Keep questioning, questing, and requesting. What is your personal life question (quest-I-am-on)?

An Angelic Reflection: **Answers may feed the mind, but I will ask the angels to fill my soul with open-ended questions.**

AFFIRMATIVE ACTION

An Angel Reminder: **Affirmation must be acted
upon if it is to become reality.**

The power of affirmations is not a new concept. The idea is that if we affirm something long enough it will manifest, because the way we think ultimately determines what we attract. It's great to believe in affirmations, stating what we want in life. But the angels know we have to take a little affirmative action if we want those affirmations to come true. Often affirmative action involves making actual changes in our behavior. Most of the time these changes do not require huge leaps in consciousness. More often than not, the issues that catch us up are amazingly uncomplicated. Some people have trouble returning phone calls. Others can't bring themselves to manage money and pay bills. Others can't say no when they have to, and still others can't say yes to the possibilities that are held out to them. These may seem like little things, but when we want to create large-scale success, we have to change the little ingrained behaviors, which have the nasty habit of tripping us up. Otherwise we will always have difficulty transforming our affirmations into reality.

Do you enjoy affirmations? What kinds of things do you affirm about yourself and your life? Do you take affirmative actions to go along with your affirmations? If there's anything you'd like to affirm right now, do so. Then begin to think of some actions you could take or behaviors you could change that would help your affirmations to materialize.

An Angelic Reflection: **I take actions that create a positive future for me.**

ANARCHY

An Angel Reminder: "Lord, make me an instrument of your peace. / Where there is hatred let me sow love."

The Peace Prayer

Many people today fear anarchy. They are talking about what they will do when the approaching millennial chaos, disorder, and lawless confusion take over the land and marauding mobs rule. Some want to dig up roads so that the bad people can't get to the good ones. Guns are being stockpiled along with grains. One thing is blatantly left out of these conversations, and that is love; when fear is the focus, love is forgotten. Our fear of anarchy leads to reacting with our survival instinct instead of our spiritual instinct. So you live another year with all your supplies, what would that year be like trembling in fear that someone is always on the horizon getting close to your goods? Stockpile love, and the angels will feed you and you will feed others.

God reminds us that love is our only chance to heal the world. So the best choice, if anarchy rules, is to be in love. Send out a signal of love, and if you die in the process, at least you will go in a moment of love, and love will send you into the arms of the angels.

An Angelic Reflection: **I will sow love, even in the face of danger or death.**

ALL GOOD THINGS COME FROM GOD

An Angel Reminder: **Good, bad, different, same are only human projections.**

We have been told that all good things come from God. When good things happen, when wonderful chemistry sparks between us and another, it may be difficult to remember that what is happening is a gift from God, not the other person. Our human tendency is to capture and possess the moment and make it last forever. It will last forever only if we were fully present during our beautiful moments, knowing that all of the light comes from God. There is no possessing God. When wonderful things happen it is a matter of grace—not to be expected, possessed, captured, forced, created. It is a momentary blessing with the signature of gratitude left behind in our heart.

The angels create beautiful moments for us to remind us how much God loves us and to remind us whence we came. Beauty, love, and grace are not given to us because we are more special than the next person. When your life has been touched by the angels' divine gifts from God, just be present, and it will change the inner chemistry of your being. Never brag about a divine moment, or it will be contaminated. The best response is deep gratitude.

An Angelic Reflection: **Thank you angels for gracing me with your touch.**

TORN-UP SOUL

An Angel Reminder: "Call the world if you please 'The vale of Soul-making.' Then you will find out the use of the world."
John Keats

Have you ever felt like your soul has been torn up into pieces? Anguish comes in waves crashing down on our hopes and dreams, leaving fragments of sadness and doom. In this space we cannot imagine that anything good is at hand, yet the angels look at us and see tilled fertile ground ready to be planted with the seeds of hope and faith. Pretty soon we start to feel the seeds growing in our soul. The lights come up, and life looks different. The angels are always near planting positive seeds. Your job is to know this. When you feel like your life has been torn apart, let hope give you great imaginings of blessings to come.

When our soul is torn and tattered, we feel confused and helpless. It is okay to feel helpless from time to time, but it is difficult for anything new to happen if we stay helpless. Remember that while our soul is suffering, our spirit still says, "Go for it, start anew." And our heart says, "Don't worry; the suffering means you have loved, and love is never lost." When one part of you is lost and helpless, let the other parts join with the angels and take you flying.

An Angelic Reflection: I am a fertile soul, cultivated with love.

ADVERSITY

An Angel Reminder: **To the angels, adversity is a creative challenge.**

Many times what seems like a frustration or a tragedy is a chance for new life. It helps to view adversity not as an affliction but as a chance to discover our creative power, our gifts of ingenuity and inventiveness. Think about it. You'd get pretty fat and lazy if you didn't have any hurdles to jump. When we take the right attitude, adversity can mold us into lean and mean machines, sure of our strength, confident in our power to meet challenges and turn them into opportunities. We become wise warriors, learning when to advance and when to retreat, attuned to the rhythms of the moment. When we conquer adversity, we discover the depths of courage within us. So we are better able to trust ourselves and to become masters instead of victims of our fate.

If you are encountering adversity, think about why this particular challenge is present in your life. Did you create it? Did it happen to you through no fault of your own? Remember, there is no situation that cannot be transformed. What talents can you put into use to meet and change this one? What resources do you have, in terms of brains, people, faith, persistence? Be creative!

An Angelic Reflection: **I use opposition to discover new energy and purpose.**

WAYS TO STAY SANE

An Angel Reminder: **It takes courage to stay sane.**

The angels have a few suggestions for keeping our sanity: Don't care if others are telling you the truth. You can never know. Don't compete with passive aggression. Stop second-guessing others' motives. Know that people play little games, and you may be an unwitting loser in their game, and there is nothing you can do about it. Stop worrying so much about your loved ones; it isn't necessary, for the angels are in charge of worrying about them. Know that power and love don't go together, so if you are in a power struggle in a love relationship, it's a signal that love is missing.

Take care of yourself, and stop caring about what you will never control.

An Angelic Reflection: **I am safe and sane.**

POWERFUL RESOLVE

An Angel Reminder: "Life serves up plenty of opposition to maintaining an inner life. Holding onto a vision calls for powerful resolve. Still, if we are dedicated, the vitality of the soul somehow manages to endure through many dangers. This survival sometimes involves seemingly miraculous assistance."

Jonathan Young

To resolve means to solve or settle doubts, to make a firm decision, or to state formally in a resolution, like we do with our New Year's resolutions. To resolve to do something indicates that one has great determination. *Resolve* comes from the Latin *resolvere,* meaning "to untie." To have resolve, we must be willing to disentangle and free ourselves from forces that oppose our decision, especially when navigating in the realm of the angels and the mystery.

Strengthen your resolve with the angels. Make a firm decision to be true to your own vision. You don't have to wait for New Year's Eve to make your resolutions. Begin them now, and periodically update them with the angels.

An Angelic Reflection: With the angels I have powerful resolve.

To Guard, Not to Own

An Angel Reminder: The angels guard; they don't possess.

Most of us believe in the concept of ownership. Ownership is our right; what we have defines who we are. But ownership is actually the most destructive of all illusions, for it is at the root of most of life's problems. Envy, oppression, depression, arrogance, greed—these are just some of the unhealthy outgrowths of the need to own or possess someone or something. Native Americans, on the other hand, believe that we do not own anything but are merely guardians of the property of the Creator. And as guardians, we have the duty of protecting and preserving the Earth and its contents for future generations. It is interesting that the image of the guardian angel is so prevalent in religion—an angel that does not own or control us but rather serves as our guide and protector. In this way we are never beholden to him or her but instead are free to be and grow at our own pace, in our own way.

What do you think you own? Your house? Your land? Your car? Your children? Imagine for a moment that you don't own anything—that all that you have has only been entrusted to you for safekeeping. How would your perceptions change? Would you begin to value more the things that you have, to take better care of them because they belong to some-one else? Would you cease to equate your worth with your possessions because you no longer have possessions? Would you feel more of a sense of purpose if you knew that your guardianship would benefit the Earth and the generations to come?

An Angelic Reflection: I serve God, not my ego.

DENY, DENY, DENY

An Angel Reminder: "Hence with denial vain, and coy excuse."
Milton

Denial will not rescue us from trouble. It's the other way around. Denial will catch up with us and make us look at every little detail of harm that our little fling with it caused. Being in denial is like putting your hands over your eyes and believing that the person standing in front of you can't see you, because you have blocked your own view. Someone who is really good at denial can convince the person looking at them that they aren't really seeing them. There is nothing funny about denial, and no human is exempt from it. When we slip into denial, we are inviting all the floating two-by-fours to knock us over the head.

Do you ever get the urge to outright deny something you did? Have you ever been a victim of someone else's denial and it caused great problems in your life? Denial is tricky, and the angels are alerted each time it enters our consciousness. Be on alert to denial, and you won't get knocked out.

An Angelic Reflection: **I will not deny my denial.**

AUGUST 24

How Did I Get Here?

An Angel Reminder: "One doesn't discover new lands without consenting to lose sight of the shore for a very long time."
André Gide

When it is time to make a major change in our lives or consciousness, everything becomes unfamiliar for a while. You may start to feel like a stranger in a strange land. Sometimes our reality changes on a dime and leaves us reeling. We may try to jump back into the previous reality and realize that we can't find the door; it is forever gone. Don't worry, no one "slipped you a Mickey"; it's just the angels readjusting your awareness level.

When you have lost the door of perception, be patient. A new door will appear as soon as you let go of the search. When you walk through this new door you will feel safer and stronger, because you know the angels brought you to it.

An Angelic Reflection: I am a stranger, and this is a strange and beautiful universe.

SKIPPING TOWN

An Angel Reminder: **There are two things we can't run from: our shadow and our conscience.**

Our culture is full of stories about deadbeat dads who skip town or husbands and wives who run off with their lovers or scam artists whose victims discover a disconnected phone number when they try to collect on what was promised to them. But there are other less obvious and dramatic ways of skipping town. We might keep our voice mail on to avoid talking to someone we are having trouble confronting. We might live in denial, refusing to see a problem or admit our responsibility in its evolution. Skipping town might seem like the easy way out, but in the long run it's easier to confront our issues and our mistakes. When we skip town we will always be haunted by unfinished business. When we face up to things, we are rewarded with a clean slate, an unblemished future, and the chance to live in the free state of honesty rather than the police state of denial.

Have you ever skipped town? If so, how, and in what context? How did it make you feel? Did you ever come back to make things right? Is there a chance that you could still do so? If you've ever regretted skipping town, try putting your feelings, regrets, apologies, or hopes on paper. If you abandoned someone, write that person a letter. If you ran from misfortune or opportunity, write yourself a letter of forgiveness. Then sit with what you have written and see if any changes in your life take place.

An Angelic Reflection: **I face up to my responsibilities.**

CATCH UP

An Angel Reminder: "When the body is finally listened to, it becomes eloquent. It's like changing a fiddle into a Stradivarius."
Marion Woodman

A large percentage of prosperous people are spending less time sleeping, eating, and attending to their children and relationships, and they are reporting more stress. Jungian analyst Marion Woodman says that it would take most of the people she sees three months "with nothing to do" simply to catch up with themselves. One way or another we will get that time—dead or alive, sick or well. What does Woodman mean by "doing nothing," when most of us may think we need three months of *work* to catch up with ourselves? What would doing nothing look like? If you found yourself with no list of phone calls to return, all your bills paid, your laundry current, no stack of books to read, all the little things taken care of, what would you do? How would you spend your "free" time? A lot of us don't know and don't really think it through. We may say, "If I had time I would . . . ," yet when we say that we know that we may never see the day. We can certainly have more of choice in rejoining ourselves. The angels guide us to catch up with ourselves *along the way.*

We can enjoy our journey in life more by taking baby steps to get small things done instead of constantly having to leap over hurdles. We can redefine our goals so that they are the process of our life instead of a destination. The angels help us best when we allow life to unfold according to our own rhythm.

An Angelic Reflection: I will keep up with my own timing.

TEN STUPID WAYS TO POLLUTE THE SPIRITUAL ENVIRONMENT

An Angel Reminder: **Spiritual air needs cleaning too.**

Human beings are very adept at the art of polluting. From creating a cloud of cigarette smoke to leaving behind toxic waste, we are notoriously unconcerned about what we're doing to the Earth and how it affects the physical and emotional health of all living creatures. The spiritual environment is equally susceptible to pollution. Here are ten common ways to pollute the spiritual atmosphere:

1. Talk about fearful, tragic things relentlessly.
2. Report awful statistics to those in need of hope.
3. Bore others with an insatiable need for attention.
4. Indulge in envy or jealousy.
5. Pity yourself in front of others.
6. Refuse to find humor in anything.
7. Suppress inspiration.
8. Steal a dream.
9. Put other people down.
10. Act anxious and focus on time when you are with someone.

You probably can think of many more ways to pollute the spiritual atmosphere. Make your own list of some pollutants that you find particularly irritating. Who do you know is guilty of spiritual pollution? Do you ever do it yourself without realizing it?

An Angelic Reflection: **I am an active member of the Spiritual Environmental Protection Agency.**

MAKING THE MOST OF EXPERIENCE

An Angel Reminder: **Over the hill there just may be the promised land.**

Being "over the hill" is regarded with horror in our society. What a sad state of affairs this is, when we cannot appreciate the gifts that come with advancing years, when we cannot walk with pride and purpose toward our final destination. The angels don't want us simply to age gracefully, however; they want us to make the most of age. As we grow older we are able to understand and appreciate things we couldn't when we were younger. We have much we can give in terms of wisdom and empathy, and we hopefully have more time to spend with and on others. Above all, we don't have to buy into myths about aging. When, at the age of seventy-seven, John Glenn became the oldest man in space, he proved that many of our prevailing beliefs about age are hogwash. The angels salute Glenn and the many other older people who know what they can be. These pioneers are living testimony to the joyful truth that we are never too old to dream and to make our dreams come true.

Do you dread getting older? If so, what do you fear most? Illness and incapacitation? Loss of attractiveness and love? Loneliness? Senility? Death? Write down some of your beliefs and fears about aging. Now think of some of the good things that come with age and some of the ways you are happier now that you are older. Visualize yourself as radiant and healthy at an older age, still ready to conquer new vistas and grateful for the added years God has given you.

An Angelic Reflection: **I look at age as a gift, not a curse.**

HOW ARE YOU TODAY?

An Angel Reminder: **If you don't care about
the answer, don't ask the question.**

There's probably not a soul in America who doesn't break out in hives at
the sound of that brash disembodied voice at the other end of the phone,
jolting us from sleep or interrupting our dinner with the loaded query,
"And how are *you* today?" This is the rallying cry of the telemarketers,
who invade our privacy and make otherwise decent, kind, and law-abiding
citizens want to commit mass murder by phone. We have the right not to
be asked how we are by perfect strangers who are merely using it as the prelude to a sales pitch. The angels prefer that when we ask someone, "How
are you today?" we truly care about their response. The angels' favorite
answer to the telemarketers' favorite question is, "Do you *really* care?"

*Have you ever asked a question without really caring about the response? The next time
you find yourself doing this, think about how you feel when the telemarketers come calling.
And the next time you find yourself harassed by the question, "And how are you today?"
be creative. Tell the telemarketer that you're dying and see what happens. Ask, "Do you
really care?" and see what transpires. Forcing them to acknowledge your personhood is a
sure way to either cut the conversation short or reconnect them to their own humanity.*

An Angelic Reflection: **I am sincere in my concern for others.**

JEALOUSY

An Angel Reminder: "If you are jealous, for example, you will find that jealousy is what brings to the surface in your partner an aspect that needs to be healed, and that aspect is mirrored in yourself."

Gary Zukav

Jealousy, at its heart, is an intense fear. It is the fear of losing something to another, and it is most prominent when we fear losing someone's love and affection. Sometimes the fear is imagined. We see our lover talking to an eligible person, and we think that our lover is going to leave us and give their love to this new person, when all they were doing is exchanging boring conversation. Other times we give in to jealousy because someone else has been encouraging our jealous reaction by flirting or giving something to someone that was meant for us. Jealousy is not fun for either party. It can start as a game and end as a tragedy.

If you feel jealous often, you need to look at the situation from all directions. Ask the angels to help you with new insight. It could be that a certain person is spending more time than you would imagine trying to make you jealous. Maybe such a person really needs to know he or she is loved. Otherwise, step away from a situation that is causing jealously and then after a few days look back and get some new information.

An Angelic Reflection: The angels remind us that fear and jealousy exist in our minds.

STRENGTH

An Angel Reminder: "Strength, when life's surges rudest roll."
Schiller, *Hope, Faith, and Love*

Strength isn't simply something we're born with. Just as we can develop our physical muscles, so we can find many ways to boost our spiritual and psychological stamina. Everyone has a different way of finding strength in difficult times. For some, strength comes from reading the Bible and praying. For others, a long walk in nature is a source of strength. Some of us find strength in numbers, in the form of twelve-step programs or support groups. Others may discover that their strength comes from sitting with themselves in the silence of reflection or meditation. There are probably as many sources of strength as there are personalities to go around. It's up to us to discover what works best for us—what gives us the courage and commitment to forge ahead when things are definitely not going our way. The bottom line is that wherever we turn for strength, it's ultimately inside of us, a natural resource that's always on emergency call. It may take a little digging to uncover it, but never fear—it's there.

What are your sources of strength? Are there people who particularly inspire and support you? Do you find strength in action? Strength in reflection? You might want to make a list of the "strength sources" that you can turn to for comfort when you're feeling the need of some bolstering up.

An Angelic Reflection: I have many places I can turn to for strength.

THE ANGELS HAVE IT BETTER

An Angel Reminder: "All of the angels are amazed at
humans, who through their holy works appear clothed
with an incredibly beautiful garment."
Hildegard of Bingen

Angels are pure spirit and light. Wouldn't it be great to appear anywhere
in an instant and send light everywhere? We would be free of these
weighty bodies that cause us so much pain and keep us tied to the Earth
realm. Life would go on forever if we were angel, and, best of all, we
would truly know God's thoughts because we would *be* God's thoughts.
But look at what we would miss if we were angels: the chance to create
art in physical form, the chance to hug a loved one and to transmit love
physically to others. These are just a few of the things angels, who don't
have earthly bodies, don't experience as deeply as do human beings.

*It is tempting to imagine that if we were an angel we wouldn't have all these earthly prob-
lems to deal with. But Hildegard of Bingen saw human bodies from the perspective of the
angels, and she said we were clothed in "an incredibly beautiful garment." Next time you
get a bout of angel envy, take a moment and connect with something human. Try sending
love in a human way—through your hands, your arms, your "holy works."*

An Angelic Reflection: I know deep in my heart how truly amazing
human life is.

YOUR BELOVED

An Angel Reminder: "When two people feel an unconditional attraction to each other and are ready to sacrifice for one another, they are truly in love."
Paramahansa Yogananda

How often we dream of a beloved who can fulfill all our needs, who will sweep us up and away onto a cloud of bliss! But true love is not simply mad passion or romantic ecstasy. Rather, it is the willingness—the desire—to sacrifice for the beloved, in the highest spirit of unconditional love. Our true beloved means more to us than ourselves, and giving joy to him or her brings us so much joy in return that it becomes a high far more potent than any drug-induced or fantasy-propelled euphoria. Our beloved brings out the best in us—the noblest aspects of our being or, to use a phrase of Abraham Lincoln's, "the better angels of our nature." We are beloved by the angels, who give to us wholly and unstintingly, and when we give of ourselves in the same way we are as close as we will ever be to the angelic realms.

If you are in a love relationship, can you say that your partner is your true beloved? Is he or she unconditionally loving and supportive, willing to make sacrifices for your happiness? Are you the same way? If you can say that you have this kind of a relationship, consider yourself blessed beyond measure. If you are searching for your true beloved, begin to cultivate the qualities of unconditional love and compassion within you, and chances are you will draw someone of like qualities to you.

An Angelic Reflection: I give love from the depths of my heart and the heights of my consciousness, and I deserve to be loved in the same way.

CONSISTENCY IS STIFLING

An Angel Reminder: "A foolish consistency is the hobgoblin of little minds, adored by little statesmen and philosophers and divines. With consistency a great soul has simply nothing to do. . . . Speak what you think today in hard words and tomorrow speak what tomorrow thinks in hard words again, though it contradict everything you said today."

Ralph Waldo Emerson

Are you ever worried that if you don't appear to be the same person today—with the same beliefs, desires, and thoughts as you were yesterday—that you are somehow being untrue? Have you ever realized that you are not the same person as you were yesterday and that this is okay? It may not be okay with the people around you, though. If you change your thoughts or desires, they may remind you, "But yesterday you said . . ." Yes, and that was yesterday. We often think that in order to be committed we have to feel the same about the commitment every day. A real commitment is based on something deeper: love. Love is not what we say; it is what we do and how we behave.

The angels remind us that we can love and change at the same time. The angels don't want us to be tortured with hobgoblins and small minds.

An Angelic Reflection: I will speak for today and love forever.

LECTURES

An Angel Reminder: **Lectures belong in the classroom.**

Lectures are, theoretically, discourses given by those in the know to those in the dark. But when we lecture someone else, or have one directed at us, lectures can be downright obnoxious. Now and again you may feel the need to lecture a friend or loved one about their lifestyle, health, or choices they have made. You may feel that your lecture stems from love, from a genuine desire to help the other person, and it very well may. Unfortunately, however, it seems to be a fact of human nature that people respond much better to being listened to than being lectured to. Very few of us appreciate being told what to do, and even fewer are apt to change as a result. The angels are not big on lectures, but they are big on understanding. When we really want to help someone, we will listen to them, meet them where they're at, and ask key questions that may assist them in achieving clarity about their situation and discovering their own way of dealing with their situation.

Are you ever tempted to lecture anybody? Are there people who like to lecture you? Imagine the angels giving you a lecture on your life. What would they say, and how would they say it? Is this a lecture you would resent, or one you could learn from? If you really want to help someone else, what angelic elements could you incorporate into your lecture?

An Angelic Reflection: **I respond to the true needs of others, not to my idea of what their needs should be.**

Preparing for Doomsday

An Angel Reminder: "If we're going to be eating each other, we'd better stock up on marinade, along with the guns."
Tony Gwilliam

Every age has had its doomsday prophecies. But our current one seems to rate particularly high on the hysteria scale. Killer viruses, earthquakes that will sever the coasts from the continents, the collapse of the global economy, not to mention a little nuclear holocaust and a scuffle with the Antichrist thrown in for some real excitement—everywhere we turn, it seems, Armageddon beckons. This may be true; who knows? But if the end of the world really is near, what are you going to do about it? Where are you going to escape? Since it is highly doubtful that you will be able to change the course of events, the angels suggest that you prepare accordingly. Strive for excellence, live an honorable life, tell those you love that you love them, and enjoy every breath you take from here on in. Then when it's over, it's over. And you'll be able to say of your life: I gave it all I had, and I welcomed all it had to give.

If you are concerned about doomsday, start keeping a doomsday journal. Start with something like "365 days left 'til doomsday." Then record what you're doing every day in preparation for the final countdown. Make it as humorous as possible. Pretty soon you may realize that whether or not doomsday is up ahead, you still have every day ahead of you to live however you wish to live it.

An Angelic Reflection: I know the best way to prepare for the future is to live in the now.

LABOR DAY

An Angel Reminder: **We know satisfaction through the fruits of our labor.**

Labor Day is a holiday honoring the working person, which makes it a good day to reflect upon the nature of work. Labor generally has negative connotations, referring to toil or physical exertion or a burden. But it also means "to cultivate or till." Thus, labor involves effort—but it is not effort without reward. When we labor over something we give it our full attention, even passion, such as a labor of love. The labor of childbirth is the supreme labor of love. Through the painful work of giving birth, we get to a place of unparalleled joy. Labor makes us strong, physically, mentally, and spiritually. It hardens us, makes us resilient, gives us a sense of satisfaction in what we can do. The angels are firm believers in the benefits of hard work, which helps us to stay healthy and active and encourages us to push ourselves past what we thought were our limits. When we achieve something through the sweat of our brows and the work of our own hands, it acquires a meaning far more precious than if it had been handed to us on a silver platter.

What have you been laboring at lately? Are any of your labors labors of love? Do you dread or embrace your work? Is it something you have to do to make a living, or does it enrich your life and strengthen you? Today, explore the role work plays in your life, and think of ways you can make it more rewarding.

An Angelic Reflection: **I labor to do the best and highest work I can.**

DON'T RETIRE

An Angel Reminder: **Retire your retirement.**

It is time to be free of the idea that aging is bad and that when we reach retirement we have to follow a certain path. In the usual story of aging, our sexuality will end, our minds will become dull, our bodies will totally give out on us, we will not be beautiful anymore, and we may end up in a nursing home. That is a very sad story, the angels don't like it, and it does not have to be true. *Retirement* is one of the worst word tricks invented. It means to withdraw, depart, resign, and remove from a career. Of course we change as we age, but that doesn't mean we need to withdraw from life. The changes can be beautiful if we accept them and do our best.

Only God knows when we depart from life. If we are going to invent an age marker for such a negative idea like retirement, we are cheating ourselves out of the best part of life. Have you thought about retiring lately? If so, rethink it.

An Angelic Reflection: **I shall not retire; I shall remain engaged with life.**

STUDY VERSUS EXPERIENCE

An Angel Reminder: "When the anthropologist
arrives, the gods depart."
Haitian proverb

Most of us were taught how to study by mentally going over something.
Few of us were taught to study with the heart, soul, body, and spirit. The
dictionary tells us that *to study* means "to apply one's mind purposefully in
order to gain knowledge or understanding"; "to examine closely"; "to
inquire into, investigate"; and "to scrutinize." Where does our mental
knowledge take us? The angels ask that we study with our hearts and
souls as well as our minds, so that we can achieve real learning, which is
compassion.

*Next time you need to study something, try a different approach. First ask the angels to be
your study guides, then begin by just sitting quietly and allowing the new subject to gently
enter your thoughts. Pay attention to any images that come up, especially if they don't seem
related; just let them be for now. Next, check in with how the images feel, and then ask the
images what they can tell you. Respect your subject and, before dissecting it analytically,
take time to live with your subject in its wholeness.*

An Angelic Reflection: I have a new studio with the angels, it is everywhere I go.

CRITICAL JUNCTURES

An Angel Reminder: **When you feel like the whole world is on your case, watch out, there will be people adding to the caseload.**

One of our worst fears is the criticism of others. For example, we may worry about our looks, weight, age, or energy level, and we get confused and think that these things represent who we "really" are, so we want them to be perfect. But, since we're human, we're just not perfect, so we start to feel vulnerable. Well, just when we're feeling weak and fragile, someone may come along and give us "a talking to" about our weight, looks, or energy level. We wouldn't take their criticism so seriously if we hadn't already directed the same barbs at ourselves. This is when our sense of humor and humility are the only saving graces. The angels know we are a lot more than our looks or our energy level, and they ask us to have the same loving perspective on ourselves. Then when others criticize, we'll be able to smile and say, "Thank the angels I don't believe *that* one!"

In spiritual perspective, we know that our looks, our job, and all outward things fall away. If we know who we are on the inside, we will attract to us those who know themselves and don't need to project their weaknesses onto us. Next time someone criticizes you, tune into the angels' view of you; you will be stronger when you keep the higher perspective.

An Angelic Reflection: **I will listen to the angels, who speak in love, not to those who criticize.**

LIVING WELL

An Angel Reminder: **Living well means making the most out of life, no matter what the circumstances.**

The saying "Living well is the best revenge" is accurate up to a point. Doing ourselves good is certainly much more productive than doing or dreaming about doing harm to someone else. But "living well" in this context usually refers to being wealthy and successful and enjoying the material comforts these things can bring us. To the angels, however, living well means something else entirely: making the most of our lives and the moment, spreading the spirit of hope and inspiration wherever we go. When we live well we feel alive and well. Our energy levels are high; we enjoy getting up, we feel a sense of gratitude and purpose. The angels remind us that any of us can live well, at any time. We don't have to be rich, or even without troubles. All we have to do is draw from all the exciting possibilities for experiencing aliveness that the present continually affords us.

Are you living well? If not, why not? Do you make the mistake of thinking that you have to be in perfect health to live well? If so, think about people like Christopher Reeve, one of the best examples of someone who, although paralyzed and unable to exist without a respirator, still manages to live a life full of purpose and meaning as an artist, activist, and human being. If he can live well, can you, too?

An Angelic Reflection: **I know that living well is a matter of attitude rather than circumstance.**

THE LITTLE SELF

An Angel Reminder: **We have two selves. One is little and one is big.**

All spiritual disciplines address the struggle between the human and divine forces that is at the core of our earthly experience. We were made as both physical and metaphysical entities, which can create confusion and unhappiness until we learn how to balance these two seemingly divergent aspects of our being and fuse them into one harmonious partnership. The angels remind us that when we are assailed by negative thoughts and less-than-honorable impulses, this is our little self at work. They suggest that we go into our big self—the higher consciousness that transcends the petty human plane—and take our little self by the hand, listening to it, talking to it, and guiding it to a higher level of wisdom and compassion. Every one of us, after all, is nothing more than a soul waiting to be noticed and loved.

The next time you get bogged down by fears, doubts, and other uncomfortable and unproductive feelings, try this exercise. Close your eyes, breathe deeply, and imagine yourself leaving your body and rising up, up above it. As you're floating on the ceiling, imagine your soul expanding until it fills the room, the sky, the universe. From this infinite perch, look down at your "little" self. What is it saying and doing? How do its problems and insecurities measure up on the grand scale of cosmic importance? When you're ready, slowly float back into your body. Do you have a new perspective on your problems? Wait and see if solutions suddenly seem to present themselves.

An Angelic Reflection: **I know that within my big self are the answers to all the problems my little self has created.**

GOD NEEDS LOVE, TOO

An Angel Reminder: "Bless the Lord, O my soul: and all that is within me, bless His holy name."
Psalm 103:1

We are very good at expecting to be loved by God, but how well are we loving God back? Do you stop during your day and think about how much you love God? The angels praise God in all that they do. How do we praise God? As humans, we have many creative ways to show God our love. We can create art, beauty, and music. We can parent well or inspire others with a smile or moment of kindness. All of this lets God know our love and devotion. When we acknowledge God in all that we do, no matter what happens God will bless us with the strength to unfold in grace.

Take today and be in love with God. However that moves you, go with it. Ask the angels for a good example of God's love for you. Say "I love you, God" at least three times today.

An Angelic Reflection: Let all within me bless God's holy name.

ARTFUL DREAMING

An Angel Reminder: **Along the winding avenues of
our dreams we journey toward consciousness.**

What is a dream? It's an experience we have while we're sleeping, but it's
also a goal we aspire to, a strong and sometimes overwhelming desire
whose siren call often leads us to higher places. Artful dreaming is the art
of making the most of our dreams—taking them out of the unconscious and into the conscious and learning from them. This can also be
called creative dreaming—creating a new reality from our dreams. The
artful dreamer recognizes the value in recording dreams, in daydreaming,
and in paying attention to visions. Angels and other spirits can speak to
us through our night and day dreams, so it is very important to remember, value, and listen to them. Otherwise we may be missing messages and
insights that could transform our lives.

*What are your dreams, in terms of goals, aspirations, or wishes? What do they tell you
about yourself? Do you think sleep-time dreams are "just dreams" and have no connection
to reality? Do you think daydreaming is silly and unproductive? Try remembering your
night dreams. Write them down if you like. Let them work on you. At the same time, pay
close attention to your daydreams, as they may be vitally linked to the needs of your soul.*

An Angelic Reflection: **I am not afraid to be guided by my dreams.**

ATTRACTING WHAT WE DON'T WANT

An Angel Reminder: **Think and ye shall create.**

Mary Beth remembers an old woman she once knew who hated animals. She kept an arsenal of weaponry by her door to fend off the ever-present enemy and could often be seen shaking a broom or a cane menacingly in the air and yelling, "Get away, now!" to any cat or dog walking down the street. And what do you know? Every cat and dog in the neighborhood seemed to gravitate to her house, rolling teasingly on her porch or picking her lawn as the perfect spot to do their business. The experience of attracting what we don't want is not as mysterious as we might think. Life consists of energy fields and vibrations, and we are powerful magnets. Our thoughts and fears have far more power than we can imagine to create our reality. The angels remind us that when we focus our energies on life-affirming ideas and solutions rather than those that make us angry or fearful, we are sure to attract the people and situations that we really want.

Examine your energy field right now. How does it feel? Strong? Weak? Positive? Negative? As you move through the day, take note of how different people affect your energy field. Do you feel high around certain individuals and low around others? Visualize strengthening your energy field by relaxing and breathing deeply, exhaling your fears and negative thoughts, and inhaling a powerful light that protects your energy field at all times.

An Angelic Reflection: **My thoughts are as powerful as my deeds.**

NOT WORKING OUT

An Angel Reminder: **When trying becomes trying, let it go.**

When something isn't working out in our lives, we often refuse to face it. Instead, we resist the truth and beat our heads against the wall. But this only gives us a headache. The angels remind us that if something isn't working out, there's usually a good reason. If it's a project, perhaps the timing is wrong. If it's the deal on the house of your dreams, another will come along that's better suited to your needs. If it's a love relationship, then maybe this just isn't the person for you; if it's not working out now, how could it possibly work out in a marriage? Sometimes we know the reason something isn't working out, and sometimes we don't. These are the times we have to trust in the wisdom of the universe and the blessings of the unknown to bring us the right thing at the right time.

Can you recall things that didn't work out in your life even though you wanted them to? Did something more appropriate eventually take their place? If something isn't working out for you right now, can you think of any reasons why this might be? Are you trying to hold on to something that isn't good for you or that isn't right for you at the present time? Remember that you may not be able to know all the reasons something isn't working out, so the best thing is to let go and let the angels lead you to a better place.

An Angelic Reflection: **I put my trust in the perfect timing of the universe.**

NEVER

An Angel Reminder: Never is clever.

Have you ever said "I'll never" and found that soon you were doing what you said you never would do again? What power the word *never* has. It is a strong word; it means at no time, ever again, on no occasion, not ever, in no way. It is quite amusing that we would have a word like this, for we can't stay true to its meaning. We just don't know what the future may ask of us. Often we use the word in relation to something precisely because we are not yet finished with that something. The angels ask us to have the courage to look at the reason we feel the need to say "never."

Next time you hear yourself say "I will never," take the next moment and ponder the fact that you may have just called forth the "never situation" for another round. If you can find the humor in our use of this word, then you can laugh at yourself when you say "never" and then find yourself the next day doing just the opposite. The great thing is that we never run out of God's blessings.

An Angelic Reflection: I will never, ever again, in any way, take the word *never* for granted.

DO IT WITH LOVE

An Angel Reminder: **Love transforms work into prayer.**

In his book *The Sri Chinmoy Family Vegetarian Cookbook,* the Indian spiritual leader Sri Chinmoy speaks of the importance of cooking with "cleanliness, purity, and good feelings towards the pots and pans." The reason behind this is that "food is life, and life is God." Therefore, we should both cook and eat our food with higher consciousness and in the spirit of love and gratitude, so that these vibrations will be digested with the food. When we perform any activity in the spirit of love and gratitude, it changes the vibrations around us. We can vacuum with love. We can wash our car with love. We can go to work with love. And suddenly, things we weren't in the mood to do become acts of devotion. Our home becomes a nucleus of love. Our car runs smoothly and happily. Our work environment becomes calmer and happier. It is truly amazing how a simple shift in attitude can alter our entire life. But the angels say, sometimes the simplest changes have the most profound effects.

Imagine changing your life so that every activity is performed with love. Can you imagine doing the laundry with love? How about a term paper? Taking out the trash? List some of the activities you do at best grudgingly. Tomorrow, do one of them with love and gratitude, and note how you feel. Also be aware of any effects you might have on others as you perform your duty in a state of higher consciousness.

An Angelic Reflection: **Even if I can't always do what I love, I love what I do.**

AMUSED

An Angel Reminder: Life is one big amusement park, complete with joy rides, houses made of mirrors, and scary roller-coasters.

To be amused, one must be awake to and aware of the irony of life. When we are amused by something, elements of awe, entertainment, and humor are at hand. Being amused by life gives us an attitude of detaching from the ultraserious. The art of being amused by life and by ourselves means we have to slow down, get to know the inner council we travel with, and learn to talk to ourselves in the manner of detached observers. If we run around harried, worried, and anxious, we will miss the ever-present amusement the angels guide us to see.

Understanding that our muse is a very playful character who often tricks us into staying on track means we won't feel mocked when life plays tricks on us. We can say, "Well, this is amusing," whenever life brings us a surprise.

An Angelic Reflection: I will find the amusement and humor that are always at hand on the journey of life.

THE MYSTERY OF LONGEVITY

An Angel Reminder: "Life is short; live it up."
Nikita Khrushchev

Here's a mystery for you. What about all those octogenarians, nonagenarians, and centenarians who never gave a hoot about their diets, never joined a gym, never took a vitamin—and are still going strong? There's the famous potter Beatrice Wood, who died at 105 and was still working up until the end. She attributed her awesome years to "plenty of chocolate, butter, and young men." There was the great pianist Arthur Rubinstein, who lived to 104 and was a notorious smoker of cigars and lover of alcohol and rich pastries. And then there was the incredible old Frenchwoman who celebrated her 127th birthday a few years back with a huge meal of pâté, roast duck, and wine. The angels don't advocate going overboard and purposely living in a way that will endanger our health. On the other hand, they remind us that longevity and good health are ultimately mysteries that we will never be able to fully understand. The trick is to take on life as enthusiastically, youthfully, and productively as possible so that when our time is up we can depart knowing we really lived.

Are you worried about how long you will live? If so, it's better to start concentrating on how well you will live, from the standpoint of enjoying what you're doing, making the most of the day, and feeling healthy and in good spirits.

An Angelic Reflection: **I concentrate more on living the moment than living forever.**

YOU CAN'T HAVE DAY WITHOUT NIGHT

An Angel Reminder: "One does not become enlightened by imagining figures of light but by making the darkness conscious."

C. G. Jung

Jung's quote points out something very important for anyone sincerely seeking transformation. We live in a physical world of polar opposites; when we deny the realities of our world and its law, we miss enlightenment. Enlightenment means the combining of wisdom and compassion. Wisdom comes from knowing—and from the darkness of not knowing. Some people are so happy to realize the goodness of angels and get so carried away with the angelic force that they want to become angels. They want the light of the angels—and they try to avoid the darkness that also accompanies our journey here on Earth. Humans have the light inside them, but we live in a world of day and night, light and dark, yin and yang. Bringing our darkness to consciousness means accepting the darkness and loving ourselves through the process of bringing it to the light.

When we make the conscious decision to bring qualities of the Divine into our awareness and to practice loving God, the opposites of these qualities often crop up and demand attention. How can you "make the darkness conscious" today?

An Angelic Reflection: In my life, light and dark are equally important on the road to enlightenment.

JOB HELL

An Angel Reminder: **It's our job to work in our soul's best interest.**

Job hell is, unfortunately, not an unfamiliar place to many of us. Job hell can take many forms: boring or unfulfilling work, backbiting co-workers, inept—or even psychotic—supervisors, miserly employers, unreasonable workloads. These are just a few of the nightmares that most of us, at some time or another, have experienced in our noble attempts at an honest living. There are lots of reasons people stay in job hell, but most of them don't hold up to the light of rationality. "I'll never find another job that pays this well. . . ." "I've got a family to support. . . ." "I'm too old to get hired someplace else. . . ." "If I left this job, what would I do?" Do any of these excuses sound familiar? If so, contact the Angel Placement Agency immediately! God definitely does not want you in job hell. For every negative reason you have devised to keep you there, there is a positive counterreason to get you out of it. The Angel Placement Agency operates on the principle that it's never to late to (1) find meaningful employment; (2) change careers; and (3) be happy. It's only our own beliefs that either block or open the door to our fulfillment.

Are you in job hell? If so, how did you get there? What are the things about your job that make it unfulfilling? Do you have excuses that keep you in job hell? Write them down and then challenge them. Ask the angels to help you plan a definite strategy that will enable you to find the work you're meant to be doing. Know that there is always a way out of job hell, and listen for divine direction. It will come.

An Angelic Reflection: **I deserve a job that is creative and fulfilling, and I know that the angels will help me create this situation for myself.**

FROWNING

An Angel Reminder: " If you just light up your face with gladness, hide every trace of sadness. Although a tear may be ever, ever so near. That's the time you must keep on trying, smile what's the use of crying, you'll find that life is still worthwhile if you just smile, come on and smile."
Charlie Chaplin, John Turner, Geoffrey Parsons

Think about a human face for a moment. Think about how much information you can acquire from a facial expression. *Frown* is one of those words that sounds like it looks. When someone is frowning, we get the message that they are not comfortable being in their bodies. Take a moment and purposely frown. As you are frowning, get into the feelings of a frown. Think about someone you know who may frown a lot. What are they usually going through? Now change your countenance to a smile, a real one. Let it go! A smile brings about a completely different experience. A smile signals that things are right in the moment and that the soul and spirit are shining out through the face. The angels make us smile.

One great thing about a face is that it is easy to change expressions. Even when one is sad and crying, a smile can emerge. We are not static beings; we can have many feelings going on simultaneously. Next time you find yourself down and frowning, lift up your face and smile. Even if there is nothing to smile about, try doing it anyway. Think about the angels and make yourself smile at least once an hour, and it will change your life.

An Angelic Reflection: I will light up my face with angel love.

FLATTENED OUT

An Angel Reminder: "First of all, I would like to make one thing quite clear; I never explain anything."
Mary Poppins

So much of life is mysterious, and parts of the mystery will not be known to us while we reside in our human temple here on Earth. This is hard to accept, so we go looking for ways to explain everything with words. Words have their uses but also their limits. Are words necessary for the language of the soul and spirit? Do words speak to our hearts, or is it some other quality of communication that brings us knowing in our hearts? If everything were explained, wonder would vanish. We would be able to see ahead, and life would be flat, explained, and unchallenging.

Take a day and refuse to explain yourself. If you are late somewhere, just be late. If you buy something you can't afford, don't come up with a reason. If you feel like saying something off the wall, do it and let it be. The angels will love this, and pretty soon magic will follow you everywhere you go.

An Angelic Reflection: **I have no need to explain myself or flatten out the beautiful peaks of life.**

FLIPPING COINS

An Angel Reminder: **God does not play dice.**

Our ancestors in the ancient world consulted the gods when they faced major decisions. If a dispute could not be resolved, then it, too, was placed before the gods. We applaud their spirit in consulting a higher realm for answers to life's pressing problems. The only problem came when these people wanted an unequivocal yes or no. They tried to squeeze divine wisdom into black-and-white answers, the kind you get from flipping a coin. Julius Caesar established the practice of flipping a coin for heads or tails, since his head was on one side of every Roman coin. If the coin landed heads up, it was as if the emperor himself had agreed with a particular decision. You can see the problem right away: now people were consulting the emperor rather than divine wisdom. Heads-or-tails thinking is a sure sign that God is not in the process.

Think about a major life decision you have had to make, such as marriage. What if you had decided it through a coin flip? Would you ever feel right about it? When we open to the angels, we are no longer satisfied with yes-or-no answers. The next time you have to make a big decision, consider more than yes or no. Ask the angels for the courage to see a larger picture.

An Angelic Reflection: **There are no heads or tails to show me the way.**

ORDINARY

An Angel Reminder: "A philosopher never quite gets used to the world. To him or her, the world continues to seem a bit unreasonable—bewildering, even enigmatic. Philosophers and small children thus have an important faculty in common."

Jostein Gaardner, *Sophie's World*

One of the most important ways to keep life fresh is to keep wonder alive and embrace the ordinary as it truly is: extraordinary. The extraordinary is often hidden, and noticing the wondrous things hidden in the ordinary requires a special awareness. When we are blessed with an extraordinary experience, there is a natural tendency to be greedy for more or to venture down paths that we are sure will bring us greater experiences. But if you practice letting the angels into your heart, they will show you how to see the ordinary with new eyes, and once again you will be like a little child finding magic in so many things.

If you feel you have lost your capacity for wonder, ask the angels to help you really live in the miracle of nature, humanity, love, mystery, and the vast imagination of God. You don't need mind-altering drugs, alcohol, or any other chemical to change your perception—only the willingness to invite in the angels.

An Angelic Reflection: I am not so ordinary, and my world is a magical vista full of wonder and God.

Spiritual Tank-Up

An Angel Reminder: **We often pay more attention to our car's gas tank than we do to our own.**

When our life starts to chug and sputter and we feel like we're running out of gas, it might be time for a spiritual tank-up. As a car just won't run without gas, so we can't move smoothly ahead if we're being deprived of necessary fuel. The soul runs on many sources of fuel; love, compassion, joyful work, and faith are just a few of the things that get us from here to there on life's long highway. And, like a car, the soul doesn't do well on cheap gas. When we are living empty or unfulfilling lives, when we mistake material for spiritual comfort, or when we are in denial to our true selves, our souls suffer accordingly. The angels prefer that we give our soul premium gas, in the form of life-affirming and nourishing activities that feed the spirit as well as the body.

If you're low on enthusiasm, if your get-up-and-go just got up and went, check your spiritual gas gauge. Is it half full? A quarter full? Empty? What sort of fuel do you usually put into it? If it's the cheaper variety, you're probably starving your soul. Imagine yourself pulling into the Angel Gas Station, getting a fill-up, and roaring off with renewed energy and sense of purpose.

An Angelic Reflection: **I take care of my spiritual health.**

POWER VERSUS LOVE

An Angel Reminder: **Power and love are like
oil and water; they don't mix.**

Too often human beings mistake power for love. When we try to run
someone else's life because we think we love them and know what's best
for them, we are not being loving, we are being domineering. When we
use money or influence to try to buy love, we are getting servitude, not
devotion. Some people, of course, prefer to give their power over to others, to abdicate the throne of responsibility because they don't trust in
their own ability to make decisions for themselves. This is common in
many relationships; those to whom the power is relinquished may honestly believe that they are acting in accordance with the other's wishes,
that dominance is love. But the angels know that real love does not seek
power; it seeks only the true happiness of the beloved. When we really
love someone, we want them to realize their potential and be responsible
to themselves, not to us.

*Have you had or are you currently involved in any relationships that involve power play-
ing? Do you give your power over to anyone? If so, why? Do you try to control those that
you love in any way? Realize that you neither have to give away nor take power in order
to be loved.*

An Angelic Reflection: **I am the co-worker, not the manager, of those I love.**

OUT OF TUNE

An Angel Reminder: **If we are out of tune with our inner music, we are not in harmony with the universe.**

In its most basic form, music is the link connecting the human voice to the ear of God. Different cultural myths say the world was formed through sound and that music thus echoes the voice of the Creator. Every religion and spiritual tradition has its hymns and songs of praise to the Divine; the angels are usually depicted as singing praises to the glory of God in vast celestial choirs or as playing harps or lyres. The monks of the Tibetan Tantric Choir perform concerts all over the world in which they chant for world peace. The angels encourage us to bring music into our lives and to express our own inner music, for this naturally puts us in tune with God and the "muse" within us. When we allow ourselves to be guided by the muse, defined as "the spirit or power regarded as inspiring and watching over poets, musicians and artists," our own spirit is connected to the higher vibrations and we are able to contribute more fully to the spiritual elevation of the universe.

To achieve harmony in our lives we need to be aware of the people and things to which we instinctively resonate and those that cause discord. With whom do you feel in harmony? With whom are you out of tune? Do you listen to the song of your soul, or are you dancing to someone else's tune? Do you honor your creative needs and heed your creative impulses? Music is a powerful healing force; you might try listening more to your favorite music, moving and singing with it, or taking up an instrument in order to bring vitality and harmony back into your life and give you a spiritually expressive outlet.

An Angelic Reflection: **I am in tune with the vibrations of the angels.**

NOT FAIR

An Angel Reminder: "We need less 'knowing' about how
life should be and more openness to its mystery."
Jack Kornfield, *A Path with Heart*

President Jimmy Carter once proclaimed, "Life isn't fair." Coming from a
president, this statement makes an indelible impression. Life *isn't* fair.
This is sad, but where did we get the notion that it should be fair? Is it
fair for all of us to live under someone else's perception of fair? When
thinking about what life is, forget the issue of fairness. Remember you
have accepted that there is a bigger picture in the universe, a divine intelligence that reminds our hearts that we are not alone and that there is no
big dice game being played at our expense. If fairness exists, it resides in
the mystery. Although we may never really understand *why* good things
happen to bad people (and vice versa), we must accept that "good" is a
judgment we make, and there is always much more to the picture than the
limiting information that our physical bodies and minds can perceive.

*If you get stuck in the tangled mess of needing fairness, you will drive yourself crazy. Stop
waiting for things to be fair. Accept the things that happen to you and others; they are done,
and you can't change them. Then find ways to heal. Cultivating the quality of compassion
is the best way to start the healing process and move into surprising places. Life is not fair,
and God does work in mysterious ways.*

An Angelic Reflection: I will let go of fairness and let God lead me to
acceptance and love.

TRANSFORMATION

An Angel Reminder: **Transformation is change. Life is change. Transformation is life.**

Transformation is the central theme of mythology. Beings are always changing shape, and heroes are undergoing inner transformations through rites of passage and trials of purification. The message of myth is that transformation is both painful and magical, that if we are brave enough to search for our real self, we will be rewarded with mysterious aid from supernatural realms and will discover a magical power within us to transform our lives. While we often fear change, the angels assure us that it is not only beneficial but inevitable. Nothing is stationary; even though things may seem the same day in and day out, they are constantly undergoing changes in atomic structure and energy shifts. If we long to transform our lives but are afraid of the unknown, the angels ask us to turn our fears over to them, to trust more in divine direction and protection and the natural life process.

There may be important changes occurring or about to occur in your life. You may be aware of some of them; others may be transpiring on an unconscious level. And others may be just around the corner. Be on the lookout for opportunities for transformation. If you feel stuck in any way, let the angels assist you in letting go of any fears you may have about change.

An Angelic Reflection: **I love life in all its changing forms and take advantage of its potential for newness.**

ROLE MODELS

An Angel Reminder: **If we are living a lie,
how can we uphold the truth?**

Role models are a vital part of life. We all need people to inspire us, to give us hope, courage, and a vision to which we can aspire. The angels are asking, what kind of role models do we have today? Who are the people of integrity and bravery to whom we can look for inspiration and direction? One of the most serious problems in our society is the way in which we have blurred the line between work and personal integrity. We say, as long as someone's doing their job, what do we care what they do with their personal life? The angels care. To use a pointed example, a president who cheats on his wife and lies to his family and the country may be a good leader in terms of doing his job, but he's a pretty dismal role model in the angels' eyes. Our leaders have a responsibility to our youth and all of us to practice a life in which their personal and political selves are in alignment with the basic principles of integrity. And similarly, the angels expect each and every one of us not only to seek out role models of integrity, but to be good role models to others. This is the only way right conduct can be taught and preserved—through our actions as well as our words.

Who are your role models, the people who have most influenced you? Why did you choose them? What kind of role model would you like to be? You have the power to inspire others. Do you use it?

An Angelic Reflection: **I am conscious of my responsibility to set an example of integrity for others.**

STAY OUT OF YOUR OWN BUSINESS

An Angel Reminder: **It's all God's business.**

We have most likely heard someone say, "Mind your own business," or "Stay out of my business." But sometimes the angels would like to say to us, Stay out of your own business. What they mean is, Stop taking yourself and your business so seriously. What do you consider your business? We may be giving advice to others, offering our opinions without thinking, and all of this just takes us further away from looking at our own lives and knowing better what to do with the business we have going. If the people around you are doing things you don't agree with, to the point that you make it too much of your business, pay attention and then ask yourself, What is really my business? Be brave enough to take an honest look.

When the angels give us the message to stay out of our own business, they are reminding us to let it be and to let them take care of things that are way out of our control. By letting go of all this business, we can return to simplicity, and we can be at peace no matter what all the neighbors are doing.

An Angelic Reflection: **I will get past business and go to love.**

OCTOBER 3

LESS IS MORE

An Angel Reminder: **We need more reverence.**

Often we think that the reason we are not happy is because we need more—more money, more things, and more love. By wanting more we lose the opportunity to enjoy and honor what we have. Sure, it is human instinct to want more out of life, but that instinct flows in mistaken directions in our society. We are bombarded by messages telling us we need more *things*. So think of what you really do need. More material things? Not likely, if you are living now without them. The main thing you need is *less*, so you can enjoy what you have *more*.

When you let go of the need for more, the angels will put you in line for a grant from heaven. To receive this grant is to be blessed beyond compare by the simple things that are all around you right now. You will catch more easily the overflowing messages the angels transmit, and good things will come your way because you can be entrusted to be reverent.

An Angelic Reflection: **I have a special grant from heaven.**

REBELLION AGAINST GOD

An Angel Reminder: **When we rebel against God,
we are rebelling against the good within us.**

In Judaism, the rabbis define sin as "rebellion against God." This means, essentially, willful disobedience to the teachings of right conduct as outlined in the Torah. Life consists of strict moral and ethical precepts that, when adhered to, assure harmony on Earth. When one deviates from these guidelines, one threatens the health, possibly the survival, of the community and upsets the divine order. Sometimes we are tempted to rebel against God when, for instance, we suffer a tragedy. We say, "How could God have allowed this? I don't believe in him anymore!" This is not sin but valid human anguish, which God knows must be expressed before healing can take place. The more complex form of rebellion against God involves acting in ways that do not promote the godly values of love, compassion, honesty, and decency. Then we are not merely angry at a seemingly arbitrary external power; we are rejecting the godlike aspects of our own beings. We become separated from ourselves, unwhole, which is the core definition of the word *unholy.* The angels are agents of wholeness and holiness, here to remind us of the higher consciousness that unites us to God and our own souls.

How do you define sin? What are the worst sins you can think of? The worst you yourself have committed? Think about how much closer to God you feel when you are acting from your higher self—God being the unifying force of love and compassion that holds all life together.

An Angelic Reflection: **I try to live, not the good life, but a good life.**

ADVENTURE

An Angel Reminder: "Either life is a tremendous
adventure or it is nothing."
I. A. R. Wylie

When we think of adventure, the most common images that come to mind are of bold, wild escapades in distant lands—pioneers discovering and conquering new worlds, restless young men going off to war, travelers seeking out new places and new experiences. But adventure doesn't have to involve going to a new locale. An adventure is a journey into the unknown, and since the future is unknown to us, every day is a possible adventure. The way to make it so is to adopt an attitude of expectation, to rise in the morning and greet each day as though it were the next stop on a world cruise, holding who knows what unexpected delights—and maybe even a miracle or two.

Have you had any adventures lately? What, to you, would constitute an adventure? How do you feel about the unknown? Scared? Cautious? Passionately curious? If you are of an adventurous spirit, pretend you're going on a big adventure tomorrow. When you wake up in the morning, prepare yourself for a day of surprise, excitement, mystery. Make sure to write down the adventurous things that happen to you that day.

An Angelic Reflection: I am an explorer of life.

Mutual Dependence

An Angel Reminder: **It takes two to tango.**

In a deeply loving relationship, the partners are mutually dependent on each other. A certain amount of dependence on a loved one is necessary; otherwise the relationship is boring and superficial. A society like ours, which prizes individualism and pulling yourself up by your bootstraps, also looks suspiciously on dependence on others. Well, what is so bad about it? When we depend on others, we can be disappointed and get hurt. Is that the end of the world? Is it always true that with dependence comes pain? Learning to need others and to accept our need for them probably will raise some fear because we will be allowing ourselves to be vulnerable. But it is not possible to be truly intimate without being vulnerable. A deeper problem arises when one person is vulnerable and willing to depend on the other, but the other person does not reciprocate. Mutual dependence is one key to growing closer in a friendship or relationship. If either person is trying to have a healthy relationship by avoiding dependence, you will not grow closer. One-sided dependence is not a good foundation, but two people needing and depending on each other is the stuff of vital intimacy.

The angels want to remind us that we are not loners by nature. Human interconnectedness can be miraculous, and we do need each other. In order to truly love, we must care deeply about others. So what is the worst thing that can happen if you get attached to someone? And, what if that happens?

An Angelic Reflection: **I will follow my heart away from fear, into the rapture of deep love.**

THE SNAKE IN THE BRUSH

An Angel Reminder: **Whatever is repressed must eventually be addressed.**

A friend of ours recalled an incident from her childhood that had, to her, great symbolic significance. A man who was working on their property came upon a snake. Instead of allowing the snake to be and simply walking away from it, the worker chose to torment it, throwing things at it until it slithered into some brush for cover. Later that day, our friend's father came home and went out into the yard. Not knowing about the snake, he began raking near the brush. The snake, still enraged, popped out and bit her father, who almost died as a result. The moral of this story, says our friend, is that when we repress or oppress the snake within us, it is going to have its revenge. Those fears and scary feelings and impulses that we deny or deride have the nasty habit of rising up and biting us when we least expect it. The angels caution us to express, not repress, our feelings; to get them out into the open so that they can be dealt with and will cease to stalk us.

Are there feelings that you're repressing or just not dealing with? Why? Do you think these feelings will go away if you ignore or belittle them? Or will they make themselves heard no matter how hard you try to deny them? The angels suggest that when we have uncomfortable feelings that we want to bury, we allow them to make themselves known, and we let them speak to us. You might try dialoguing with feelings of fear, guilt, or shame and writing down your conversation. It will certainly be instructive.

An Angelic Reflection: **I do not disown my feelings, no matter how frightening they might be.**

TUNE IN FOR THE LATEST BODY COUNT

An Angel Reminder: **Watched by an angel.**

What if you were an angel watching TV for the first time? If you were channel surfing, what would you notice prevails on the tube? Have you ever noticed that most of our prime-time TV dramas center around death by way of murder? Have you realized that most news programming, especially local news, is little more than a body count of recent tragic deaths? And those TV shows that are not based on murder or death are based on betrayal, like soap operas. The shows that are billed as comedies portray exaggerated, inane behavior that we don't want to admit is going on. So what do you think the angels would say about our TV programming and its reflection of the collective consciousness? Is human life really like it is portrayed on TV?

Think about the last time you watched something truly edifying and inspirational on TV. How often does it occur, and how easy is it to find? Next time you watch TV, pretend you are an angel. When a body count is happening, pray that God watches over the souls as they make their passage. Take a new look at what you spend a lot of time looking at.

An Angelic Reflection: **I will pay more attention to the angels' view of our world.**

FORMULAS

An Angel Reminder: **You don't get something for nothing.**

Our pop-psych world of one-minute fixes and one-line spiritual rules is not helping us create solid foundations. If we believe that true spiritual success comes easily and effortlessly, we may miss opportunities to hone our skills and discover parts of ourselves we will need when we are successful. Effort and hard work allow us to ground our experiences and lessons in the reality of experience. Then we have strong cornerstones. Explore ideas, listen to people's stories of how they "made it," and remember real life isn't a formula.

The angels want us to be careful of other people's formulas and blueprints for success. It never hurts to study formulas for success as long as you don't try to copy them literally. If we try to force situations to obey these formulas, we will not be true to the moment, which may require a different strategy. Next time you are tempted to follow a formula, stop a minute and ask what this moment requires.

An Angelic Reflection: **My life is not formulaic.**

MORALITY WITHOUT GUILT

An Angel Reminder:

Watch your thoughts; they become words.
Watch your words; they become actions.
Watch your actions; they become habits.
Watch your habits; they become your character.
Watch your character; it becomes your destiny.
                                        Frank Outlaw

Morality is inner discernment of what is right or wrong, based on what is right action for the whole according to each situation. Morality is not about adopting behaviors that please others and then doing the opposite when they are not looking. Too many of us have experienced morality as guilt-tripping, for many people use morality to control the behavior of others. Armchair moralists write books in which they scold children by saying that the friends you have will depend on your moral virtues. They are saying, basically, that you better follow our rules, or you will have only "losers" for friends. The angels point out, however, that the "losers" are often the most fun, and if you have the courage to depart from guilt-tripping morality, the losers may turn out to be the winners.

With the angels' help, being virtuous and moral become creative, not guilt-ridden, endeavors. True morality allows a deep respect for others and is not based on judgment and punishment. This kind of morality comes through spiritual integration. Practice respect for others, no matter what they look like on the outside, and you will become spiritually aligned in your thoughts, words, and deeds.

An Angelic Reflection: I will discover more about virtue each day and practice with the angels.

ETHICS

An Angel Reminder: "When a man appears before the Throne of Judgment, the first question he is asked is not, 'Have you believed in God' or 'Have you prayed or performed ritual acts,' but 'Have you dealt honorably and faithfully in all your dealings with your fellow man?'"

The Talmud

These days it seems that ethics gains little respect in our society. This probably comes as no surprise to most of us, saturated as we are by media whose motive seems to be greed, not ethics. All around us we see unethical behavior being rewarded. Murderers make multimillion-dollar book deals. Lawyers make their careers defending the obviously guilty. The expression "The truth shall make you free" is little followed, referring as it does to inner freedom more than external prosperity. Today's philosophy, by contrast, seems to be "The truth might make you free, but it sure won't make you any money." As long as we worship the gods of money and power, ethics will take a backseat in our lives. But the angels warn us that when we stand before our true God and are unable to answer yes to the question of whether or not we have lived an ethical life, our false gods will betray us on the spot.

Can you recall instances in your life when you were the victim of unethical behavior? How ethical are you in your everyday dealings? If you've never stopped to think about this, you might try keeping an Ethics Record for a day or two, in which you observe just how you interact with others from an ethical standpoint.

An Angelic Reflection: I deal with others as honestly and honorably as possible.

GUESSWORK

An Angel Reminder: "*Be impeccable with your word.*
**This is the first agreement that you should make if
you want to be free, if you want to be happy, if you want
to transcend the level of existence that is hell.*"
Don Miguel Ruiz

Do you ever get the feeling that everybody is lying, even when they don't really have to? Have you ever found yourself guessing what someone was really doing, after they told you what they wanted you to think they were doing? A lot of energy can be spent trying to figure out what is true. And, unfortunately, one thing *is* true: a lot of lies are told with the good intention of saving someone from being hurt by the truth. The fact remains that the truth shall set you free. This means that our little lies, even when told to save someone from hurt feelings, will enslave us. We can blame it on others and say, "Oh they just wouldn't understand and it would hurt them." But once we choose a pattern of guesswork, we can be sure others will practice it with us, too.

Think about the guesswork you have done in your relationships. If you are brave enough to try something really interesting, begin to tell the truth, even if you risk losing something dear. You may find that not only will you not lose anything, God and the angels will bring you a blessing.

An Angelic Reflection: **My life's work is not a guessing game.**

DETACHMENT

An Angel Reminder: "Letting go and letting God"
does not mean detaching from the human experience.

One of the supposed highest states of spiritual awareness is detachment
or nonattachment. The angels don't agree. When we find children who
are detached we are frightened; it just isn't right. When the angels inspire
us to transcend our worries, they don't mean for us to transcend the
beauty of the world and its people. Humans are clever in avoiding pain,
and detaching is one common method of getting out of the daily soup.
However, if we force ourselves to detach from situations that cause us
pain, we create a new pain much greater and a level of self-centeredness
that robs us.

*If you detach from feelings, relationships, dreams, and raw creativity, there will be no pro-
tection; the angels will have nothing to do. On the other hand, if you attach yourself to the
painful beauty of life, the angels will know just what to do.*

An Angelic Reflection: I am attached and connected to life.

HEMMED IN

An Angel Reminder: **Your spirit is always free.**

We all want to be free. But often we find ourselves feeling hemmed in, constricted and restricted by situations that limit our ability to be who and what we feel we are or should be. This is when we need to remember that there is a place of freedom in all of us that can't be taken away and that is always there for us to return to. The angels define this place as the "state of mind," and they remind us that no matter what our circumstances, this is our state of origin and destination. We may believe that our jobs or our marriages or our families or our invalid parents or bad luck are reasons that we can't be free. But the fact is that we can be free anywhere, under any conditions, once we understand that our minds and our spirits have the ability to roam the universe unfettered. Our spirits are not impressed with physical limitations; the mind can soar to any world, and the spirit can pass through any wall.

Write down some of the beliefs that make up your own personal view of freedom. Is there anything that is inhibiting your sense of freedom in any of these areas? Usually fear and worry are the demagogues that take away our sense of freedom. What fears and worries might be making you feel hemmed in right now? Try sitting quietly and letting your mind and spirit take you to a place free of all apprehension, a place where the angels are waiting to help you relax and trust in your inherent power to make yourself free.

An Angelic Reflection: **I know that freedom is not so much a right as a creative challenge.**

THAT'S LIFE

An Angel Reminder: "What's life? A magazine. How much is it?
Twenty-five cents. Aw, gee, I only have twenty-four cents.
Well, that's life. What's life? A magazine . . ."

Some things just are. If we try to change them or spend our time wishing we could, we only get frustrated and disillusioned. You wish you were six feet tall instead of five-foot-six. You wish you could carry a tune. You wish you had a million bucks. You wish your parents were sane. Well, you're as tall as you're going to be, you're tone deaf, you bank account's where it is, your parents are who they are, and that's life. When we sit around moaning about what we don't have, we find ourselves in the continuous loop of the above little ditty, doomed to repeat it over and over until our life becomes like a room of mirrors in which we are endlessly reflected in all our boring discontent. The angels remind us that sometimes we just have to accept things for what they are so that we are free to go about the real business of living. Then our circumstances are not crosses to bear but simply facts of life that will cease to concern us once we realize that we have neither the power nor the business trying to change them.

An Angelic Reflection: **Anything I can't change I move beyond.**

UNCERTAINTY

An Angel Reminder: **Life is certainly uncertain.**

It helps to know where we're going, to set goals, to have a sense of purpose. After all, nobody really wants to waffle their way through life. But there are times when we hit a fog bank and realize that we don't know where the hell we are. These are truly scary moments. Will we make it through? Can we pull over? Or are we going to crash? This is when the angels remind us that sometimes uncertainty can be a real blessing. It can propel us in new directions. It can make us take risks and live more radically, more intensely. Uncertainty can turn us in the direction of our spiritual selves; so often it is a security crisis in our lives that brings us to spiritual awakening and, eventually, to deeper satisfaction. Uncertainty may force us to face our fragility, giving us the opportunity to release our illusions of control, to face life naked but free. The angels know that uncertainty is the prelude to discovery, and discovery is the prelude to growth. They also know that God likes to rattle us a little, perhaps because the noise reminds us of his or her presence.

Are there things in your life that you're uncertain about? How does this make you feel? Nervous? Frustrated? Curious? What would you like to be more certain of? What happens when you let go of your need to be certain?

An Angelic Reflection: **I have the courage to let go of the need to always know where I'm going and why.**

DIVINE NATURE

An Angel Reminder: "In my view, human and divine are not opposites. The more fully human one becomes, the more he or she exhibits characteristics, qualities, and behaviors suggestive of something other worldly or divine. All forms of dishonesty, evil, depravity, and vice are not expressions of one's human nature, but distortions or perversions of human nature."

Harold D. Jester

Think about the idea of human nature for a minute. What are some of the first things you think of? Your thoughts most likely depend on what recent experiences you have had with humans. Our thoughts about human nature are influenced by programming over the years, what we have come to expect from other people. The above quote reminds us that our human nature is divine and that we can be more fully divine by being more fully human.

The angels are our cocreative partners in life. We allow them to work more deeply in our lives when we develop qualities and attitudes that are like the angel nature. Think of which qualities characterize the angels: love, peace, gratitude, humor, joy, compassion. These are qualities that will bring out our divine nature.

An Angelic Reflection: I am divine in thought, word, and deed.

WRESTLING

An Angel Reminder: "**Your struggles themselves do not create karma or determine the way that you will evolve, only your responses to them.**"
Gary Zukav

Wrestling is a popular sport these days. Pro wrestling is doing great, and at the personal level, we seem to wrestle with life decisions at least once a day. The most famous angel-related story of wrestling is the story of Jacob, who wrestled all night with an angel, eventually dislocating his thigh. Finally the angel said, "Let me go, for the dawn is breaking." Jacob responded, "I will not let you go unless you bless me" (Genesis 32:26). The struggle then was over, and Jacob was renamed Israel, which means "one who yearns to go straight to God." Jacob is in each of us as the force pulling us to God. When we wrestle with life, we can ask for a blessing from the angel, as Jacob did.

When we recognize Jacob within us, we realize that we are connected to God and that we will not be defeated when we wrestle. No matter what is going on in your life, no matter how difficult the wrestling match is, if you use your free will for God's will, you will be blessed. Remember your own Jacob, and know that your real destiny is to go straight to God.

An Angelic Reflection: **When life is a wrestling match, I am yearning for unity with God.**

NO TRESPASSING

An Angel Reminder: "No master, no psychic, no god can enter our inner gate if we choose not to let them in."
Deng Ming-Dao

In the above quote the word *choose* is key. The only way the inner sanctuary of our mind can be corrupted is if we choose to let it be influenced that way. If we don't have our own thoughts, or if we fear we are not good enough, there are plenty of demons ready to agree with us. When we are feeling weak, the demons create lots of deception to fuel our feelings of inadequacy. We let it happen, forgetting we chose to let those destructive thoughts in. When we are feeling weak, we may not need to let in yet another voice; we may need instead to listen to our own.

We are blessed with a great gift: the private world of our mind. Treat your mind like a sanctuary, and when advice you receive doesn't feel right, don't be influenced by it. Ask the angels to guard your inner gate, and then you do your part to not let deceiving information in.

An Angelic Reflection: I will be very careful with who and what gets past my inner gate.

LET IT HAPPEN!

An Angel Reminder: "So you must not be frightened, dear Mr. Kappus, if a sadness rises up before you larger than any you have ever seen; if a restiveness, like light and cloud shadows, passes over your hands and all that you do. You must think that something is happening with you, that life has not forgotten you, that it holds you in its hand; it will not let you fall."
Rainer Maria Rilke, *Letters to a Young Poet*

Many times we have frightening or disturbing feelings that we fight to avoid or eradicate. With the supreme wisdom of the poet, Rainer Maria Rilke knew that every emotion or sensation we experience as humans has the power to lead us to where we were not planning on going, even to transform us into new, stronger, and more creative beings. This is good to remember when we are going through painful times. Even if there seems to be no good reason to be suffering, we can let the suffering take us to a new place. The angels ask us not to avoid uncomfortable feelings or to distract ourselves from them, but rather to have the courage to meet them head-on and let them lead us on a journey whose destination, though seemingly unknown, is surely known to the soul.

The next time you have a frightening or disturbing feeling, try taking Rilke's advice and let the feeling take you where it will, without attempting to block or eradicate it. As Rilke reminded his young poet friend, "Remember that sickness is the means by which the organism frees itself of foreign matter; so one must just help it to be sick . . . for that is progress."

An Angelic Reflection: I know that sadness is often a prelude to transition and transformation.

BAD PROCLAMATIONS

An Angel Reminder: When "bad" things happen, the true meaning of life will settle into our souls, and we will be able to laugh at ourselves and not take the illusions so seriously.

A popular book a few years back explored "why bad things happen to good people." Humans love to explain things, and the mystery of misfortune is one of the most popular candidates. Too often, religious leaders jump out and speak for God on such matters. Some examples are "AIDS is a punishment for immoral sex," and "Earthquakes happen in Los Angeles because it is a pit of vipers." The main problem with proclamations like these is that at their root is the belief that death is a punishment. "Death will infiltrate the cults of secret sinners," some say. This is just not the case. A lot of "secret sinners" lead very long lives, and many innocent children die. God acts in ways that are much larger than we as humans can perceive. And many of those acts involve humor—not the humor of slapstick or sitcoms, but the humor of the trickster, who works in the world through mysterious means.

We project all kinds of meanings onto life. Think about some recent misfortune that you or another experienced. Did you trust that the divine trickster was working in mysterious ways, or did you try to decide exactly why the situation occurred and what it meant? Life can be full of paradoxes. Just when we have it all figured out, in come the angels to remind us there are things we may never know and that not knowing can be very creative.

An Angelic Reflection: I am aware that God's questions have a multitude of answers.

UPROOTED

An Angel Reminder: "Meditation is not an escape from society. Meditation is to equip oneself to reintegrate into society, in order for the leaf to nourish the tree."

Thich Nhat Hanh

The Buddhist monk Thich Nhat Hanh often uses his favorite occupation, gardening, as a metaphor for life. "I have been gardening in our community for many years," he reflects in his essay "Being Peace." "I know that sometimes it is difficult to transplant cuttings. Some plants do not transplant easily, so we use a kind of vegetable hormone to help them be rooted in the soil more easily. I wonder whether there is a kind of powder ... that can help people who are uprooted be rooted again in society." This powder would be akin to meditation, which is not withdrawing from the world but a grounding in the soil that keeps us connected to our true roots. When we go deep enough into meditation, we move out of the physical body and into the realm of the soul, which, because it dwells in the homeland of God, can never be uprooted.

Have you ever been uprooted from anything, say a job or a home, a relationship, or even a country? Has anyone close to you died, making you feel suddenly rootless? Often it is this sense of rootlessness that can point us in the direction of our own true home—God. When we use meditation as a centering tool, we become anchored to those eternal truths whose roots can never be pulled up because they are planted not in the shifting sands of material reality but in the bedrock of divine consciousness.

An Angelic Reflection: I know that I can never be rootless as long as the angels are by my side.

DIFFERENCES

An Angel Reminder: **Not wrong, not right, simply different.**

It is okay to be different. We are all different, but some of us are uncomfortable with the differences. A difference is measured by degrees. For example, an apple is different from an orange, but they are both fruit. An apple is different from a piece of fried chicken, but they are both food. An apple is different from a tree, but it grows on a tree. In our human relationships we *feel* the degrees of difference. This can lead to a great exploration in which each party is fueled by the differences to learn about themselves. Or the degrees of differences may be too much and result in constant conflict. The point is, when we encounter differences, that it is not a matter of right way, wrong way, good way, bad way; it is just something different.

When we encounter differences, it is up to us to decide how far we can go in accepting them. Can the degrees of distance be shortened? Or will we grow farther apart from the other person through frustrated conflict? Ask the angels to help you know the answers from within.

An Angelic Reflection: **My differences from others are not so great, and my sameness is not so similar.**

DRUGS

***An Angel Reminder:* Just say "know."**

Are you on drugs? You don't have to be hooked on the hard stuff to answer yes. Food, sex, relationships, TV, shopping, exercise—just about anything can and does perform the function of a drug in our lives. The trouble is that we don't often know when we are under the influence. A relationship can be a drug if we're obsessed with the person and it is impairing our ability to function at our best. Anger can be a drug; we might have a pattern of getting ourselves into frustrating situations that keep us enraged, which in turn gives us a sort of energy we're lacking. The angels know that it takes courage to recognize when we're using a substance, activity, or relationship as a drug and even more courage to put a halt to our using. They also know that we've got the courage and that once we put it into action we stand a good chance of finding the satisfaction that our drugs never seem to deliver.

What's your drug of choice? It's interesting just to observe when we're using activities, relationships, or substances to avoid certain problems or feelings. Sometimes we might be amazed at the things we never thought performed the function of a drug. If you discover that you have a drug of choice, watch the effect it has. Even though it may make you feel great temporarily and might even seem like it's good for you, you may want to examine how it helps you avoid certain issues.

***An Angelic Reflection:* I find completeness in awareness, not avoidance.**

REFLECTION OF THE WORLD

An Angel Reminder: "We cannot discover ourselves
without first discovering the universe, the earth,
and the imperatives of our own being."
Thomas Berry

Our psyches reflect what is happening globally in a personal way. Think about the planet, the globe, as a central psyche to which we are linked. When new information is fed into it, we are affected. So when there is a leap in technology, it is reflected in our psyche. When a war breaks out over conflicting beliefs and land rights, we are all affected by the hatred and violence. We can bring the picture in a little closer and find that we reflect what is going on in our city, neighborhood, family, and home. Each of us reflects the *anima*, the world soul, in different ways; some of us respond with artwork; some find images of world situations in our dreams. Thomas Berry says that to know ourselves, we need to be aware of our world also.

What do we do if the images of the world overwhelm us with their violence or misfortune? We seek a sense of balance in our own psyche, so that the negative does not gain control. We keep our energy as healthy as possible by looking to divine providence. This way we will have a healing imprint on the anima mundi, the world's soul.

An Angelic Reflection: **My healing brings healing to the world around me.**

LOWERED RESISTANCE

An Angel Reminder: **The path of least resistance is often the road to enlightenment.**

We all go through "down" periods, when our bodies and psyches seem more susceptible to depression and disease and more vulnerable than usual to stress. These periods are often referred to as times of lowered resistance. During times of lowered resistance, the angels suggest that we tune in to what's going on in our lives in general. What are we trying to "resist"? What obstacles might we be facing or creating that are taking too much of our energy and leaving us worn out and more open to physical and mental turmoil? When our lives are out of balance, our bodies often take over and force us to rest, allowing us to get sick so that we can really get well. A lowered resistance is a signal to slow down and reflect. If we listen to our bodies, we might actually have a good experience. It's when we turn off the daily grinder and concentrate on resting and healing that we are more likely to receive spiritual insights and brilliant ideas that have the potential to turn our life in a new direction.

Is your resistance low in any area of your life? If so, what are some ways you can strengthen it? Write down the things you want to be doing that you aren't, the things that make you happy, and different ways that you can take care of yourself so that you can boost your resistance. Take a ten- or fifteen-minute break to rest, relax, and listen—to your body and to anything else that might have a message for you.

An Angelic Reflection: **I take time to nurture my body and feed my soul.**

COSMIC PARENT

An Angel Reminder: "A child will not become an adult until it breaks the addiction to harmony, chooses the one precious thing, and enters into joyful participation in the tensions of the world."
Robert Bly

If we are going to treat God like a cosmic parent who better give us what we want or we will cause a tantrum, then we may be treated in turn like children who don't know any better. If you had a child to whom you kept giving beautiful jewels, and your child wanted friends and power so much that he or she gave the jewels to people who hung around waiting to collect them so they could buy their own power or pleasure, leaving your child with nothing, would you continue to give this child jewels? Probably not. How would you feel if you were a parent who had put beautiful food on the table every night, but the child kept going to the neighbor's for crumbs because she or he had an extreme fascination with the neighbor and so was willing to settle for crumbs? And if this same child then turned around and blamed you for starving? This is how we treat God—expecting much but enjoying little of the blessings God is sending our way. Maybe we're treating God like a cosmic parent instead of like the highest divine force of love.

God loves us and wants us to enjoy all the blessings we are given. When we have a heart full of love, we can share it with others whose hearts also are full of love. In doing so we know and honor the original source of that love.

An Angelic Reflection: I will learn to appreciate God's gifts so I will be entrusted with God's abundance.

BETRAYAL

An Angel Reminder: "For we must be clear that to live or love only where one can trust, where there is security and containment, where one cannot be hurt or let down, where what is pledged in words is forever binding, means really to be out of harm's way and so to be out of real life."
James Hillman

When life—people, places, and things—betray us, we have a choice to close down so no further pain can reach us or to open up and stay present in the betrayal until the chemistry changes and we are ready for love again. We can learn a lot from betrayal if we look closely at those situations where we feel continually betrayed. Have we set up expectations that others must reach in order for us not to feel betrayed? Why do we expect them to live up to our expectations? We know that it isn't easy to live up to expectations that others have for us, so perhaps we are setting ourselves up for disappointment if we set expectations for others.

If you feel that you have been betrayed, ask the angels to help you understand why it has happened. Explore any expectations you have, and allow yourself to let go of them. When you are ready, as the angels to help you forgive, let go, and stay open for love.

An Angelic Reflection: **The angels will never betray me; they are always loyal to God.**

No Longer Useful

An Angel Reminder: **Spiritual yard sale up ahead.**

What do we do when we no longer need something? Unless we're pack rats, we usually give it away, sell it at a yard sale, or throw it out. But while we take it for granted that things that are worn out, broken down, or outdated need to be replaced, we are less conscious about habits and behaviors that have outlived their usefulness in our lives. Perhaps we have outgrown certain people. Perhaps our job is no longer satisfying. Perhaps we're holding on to emotions that are no longer relevant. The angels suggest that we go through our psychic quarters and make an inventory of those things that do not meet our current needs. Then we can decide what we want to do with them and what things we might replace them with that would better serve our growth.

What are some of the habits and behaviors that have outlived their usefulness in your life? Do you ever stop to question why you act in certain ways or associate with individuals who aren't keeping pace with your emotional and spiritual growth? What would happen if you got rid of the things that are holding you back in your life? What and who would you replace them with?

An Angelic Reflection: **I am not afraid of growth and change.**

ILLUSIONS OF JOB SECURITY

An Angel Reminder: "The illusion holds power over you when you are not able to remember that you are a powerful spirit that has taken on the physical experience for the purpose of learning."
Gary Zukav, *The Seat of the Soul*

What happens when we find out that the life we have recently been living is an illusion, that everything we had been basing our reality on has suddenly been swept away and we are left with the shock of reinventing ourselves? One such illusion is job security. If you have based your identity on what you do for a living, then losing your job will be devastating. But perhaps there is a vision of light on the horizon, maybe a chance to do something you have always wanted to do. The key is not to feel mocked by life. The word *illusion* comes from the Latin word *illudere,* meaning "to mock and make fun of." We can adjust to a new reality if we are willing to humble ourselves and realize that we are all subject to the winds of change.

When you are ready to begin reinventing yourself, remember the first rule of the angels: this isn't as serious as is seems. If you feel mocked by the universe, have a good laugh at yourself, and you will disarm unkind forces. The angels will join you, and you will start to see life through the eyes of humility. This will give your life a new sense of meaning based not on the illusions of security, but on your true job in the big picture. Be yourself, not your job. Get to know who you are without all the trappings, and you will rise again.

An Angelic Reflection: I shall not be mocked by illusion. I will listen to the angels, incorporate humility, and remember that I am here to learn.

HAUNTINGS

An Angel Reminder: **It's when we mistake memory for life that we get into trouble.**

All of us live, to some extent, in haunted houses populated by the noisy ghosts of memory. Voices of parents, grandparents, old lovers may haunt us. Regrets for things done or left undone may dog us, filling us with guilt and freezing us in our tracks every time we try to get on with our lives. Unfortunately, the goblins and demons of the past often shriek and moan so loudly that we can't hear the present. And so, without even realizing it, we live according to old patterns that are no longer useful, mistaking memory for reality and letting past mistakes destroy present possibilities. When we're being haunted, it's helpful to remember that our ghosts are just as stuck as we are. They, too, would like to get a life, but they are compelled to repeat their tiresome patterns because they just don't know any better. Psychics say the way to end a haunting is to talk to the ghost, set it on the right track, and give it a boot in the behind, right into the light. The next time you find yourself haunted by a painful memory, you might try doing the same thing.

Are you being haunted? If so, by what or whom? Are there regrets or past actions that you haven't resolved, or people from the past who still hold you in their grip? How is this affecting your present life? Have you ever looked these ghosts straight in the eye? When we examine our ghosts, we realize that they really have no power over us, for we can see right through them.

An Angelic Reflection: **I make the distinction between past and present reality.**

TOO MUCH NOISE

An Angel Reminder: **Silence is not deafness.**

We live in a noisy world. Long ago, before cars and beepers and phones and TVs and boom boxes ruled the Earth, things were noisy, too. But it was a different kind of noise. The chirping of crickets or the rushing of a river can be loud, but they are nature's voices and so are not disturbing to the delicate balance of the ecosystem. In today's age, however, mechanical noise has drowned out natural noise, alienating us from our natural environment and, even more significantly, from our own inner voice. The angels urge us to carve quiet spaces out of our noisy days, into which we can retreat for rest, contemplation, or the opportunity to listen to the wise and important inner voices that might be trying to reach us. Even a half hour of silent time, be it on a mountaintop or in the bedroom, can have an extraordinarily beneficial effect on body, psyche, and spirit.

If you are running from silence, avoiding inner work, or fearing aloneness or abandonment, the angels assure you that a good dose of restful silence, taken on a regular basis, can do more than anything else to help you feel connected to the world. As we grow more comfortable in solitude and more attuned to the wisdom of our own souls, our spirit is rekindled and others are drawn to the serenity and quiet strength we naturally begin to exude.

An Angelic Reflection: **I know that it is in times of quiet that my soul speaks and my spirit is refreshed.**

FAMILY DUTIES

An Angel Reminder: **The seeds that are sown
at home are reaped in the world.**

Everyone in a family has, or should have, their duties. But in this case, duties are not synonymous with chores. Real family duties involve nurturing one another through a system of mutual support that covers every dimension of life, from the practical and economic to the psychological and spiritual. If it is true that the family is not only a microcosm of society at large, but the place where society either begins or ends, what could be more important to our survival as a civilization than developing and practicing values that promote self-esteem, compassion, integrity, love, and joy among family members? Family duties have been tragically neglected in today's society. But being eternal optimists, the angels believe that it's never to late to take up our family duties—that today, now, each and every one of us can begin to explore ways in which we can be more sensitive, more positive, and more cherishing of our children, husbands, wives, parents, and anyone who makes up that amazing place we call home.

What is your relationship to your family? Try holding a family council in which all the members of your family can reflect upon this meditation and discuss some of the issues it brings up. Then think of ways in which all of you can be more positive and uplifting toward one another.

An Angelic Reflection: I honor and respect the members of my family, both immediate and global.

LOSS AND THE DARK NIGHT OF THE SOUL

An Angel Reminder: "For whoever is bent on saving his [temporal] life [his comfort and security here] shall lose [eternal life]; and whoever loses his life [his comfort and security here] for My sake, shall find [life everlasting]."
Matthew 16:25 AMPLIFIED BIBLE

When we find ourselves in a "dark night of the soul" brought on by loss, we meet up with mortality and death. A dark night of the soul is a mystical experience, for it brings mystery in many forms. During the pain we may begin to think that our own death can save us from all this painful loss, but then a voice from the depths of our soul says no, death will not save us; it is time to get up and fight for life. Time to get up and stand in the fire, allowing your life force to lead the way. The angels will be there as midwives, not to remove you from the pain of new birth, but to assist in the birth, allowing you to go through the labor until you awaken in the new light of sacred consciousness that will mark your soul with strength.

Write down what God would tell you in a moment of pain and loss. Write until you feel the truth dancing its way out of you. Write until the sacred sound from your beating heart is in tune with the highest choir of singing angels. Be with yourself and your pain until your soul is floating in the water of life. God blesses your failures and your losses; look what they have brought you.

An Angelic Reflection: I will remember that dark nights always turn to day.

THE WRONG PRIORITIES

An Angel Reminder: **A bank balance is not nearly
as important as a life in balance.**

Being human, we don't always have the foresight and discipline we'd like
when it comes to aligning our priorities. How many people do you
know—yourself included—who don't watch their diets or put off going
to the dentist or doctor because they're "just too busy" or "don't have
insurance"? How many of us have let our marriages, partnerships, or
family relationships suffer while we work too long and hard to spend
time with those we love, rationalizing that we have to get ahead in order
to support them, and we'll put in quality time when "things settle down"?
How many of us don't relax or meditate because we "don't have the
time," only to find our bodies breaking down and forcing us to find the
time to rest as a result of our high-stress lives? All this is about as sensible as making plans to drive across America in a car with no gas. After all,
what good is a new car or a fat bank account when you're too stressed out
to enjoy it or, worse, six feet under because you never took the time to
make your physical, emotional, and spiritual health your first priority?

*Take some time now to check your priority list. If you've been neglecting your health or
taking it for granted, think about what would happen to your priority list if you were to
break down in any way. Now list some ways that you could incorporate health-promoting
activities into your schedule.*

An Angelic Reflection: **I put my health first.**

HIDING IN THE SHADOWS

An Angel Reminder: "When you avoid knowing things in yourself, you avoid knowing those things in others. And when you avoid mastering something, it masters you. Be the ultimate Master. Master yourself with a loving touch and the world will come to you, because you will be ready to receive it. Master yourself and become an angel."

Kim Conrad

A shadow is formed when we stand in the light. We can't deny or think that the shadow disappears when we find the angels; we are still in a human body, which will always cast a shadow. Avoiding the shadow because it has so much negatively charged power means we are missing great avenues of insight. Just as the beautiful night sky shows us the stars, planets, and other wonders that we cannot see in the day, our shadow allows us to see what we miss if we are only acknowledging and seeking the comfortable, ordered, clean, or sterile aspects of life. Shadows gather around the opposites of the ideals held by the ego. The ego, which is our persona or the mask we show the world, needs to incorporate both our ideals and our shadow.

Think of your ego as a boat. Do you load your boat with only pleasant, happy, spiritual, light? Or do you allow the shadow on board, too? Is the shadow just "down below," where it can cause trouble, or do you allow it up on deck so it can work together with the light? If we forget to place the contents equally, our shadow stuff eventually will sink the boat. Don't fear your shadow, ask the angels to help you load your boat carefully, and you can navigate the dark waters of the soul.

An Angelic Reflection: **My shadow and I work together with the angels.**

WATER

An Angel Reminder: "Our thoughts and feelings flow like
a river. . . . We must be aware of every little stream that
joins it . . . of all the thoughts, feelings and sensations that
arise in us—of their birth, duration and disappearance."
Thich Nhat Hanh

The ceremony of baptism was originally a near-death experience in which
the person being baptized was held underwater until he or she drowned
and then was revived. The idea of rebirth thus became more than an
abstract concept. It was an actual event that had powerful repercussions
on the psyche. The fact that the baptismal font was described as a womb
reinforces the idea of being born again, to the soul rather than the body.
In psychology, water represents the unconscious, the inner depths, the
realm of the soul. This is the world of feelings, intuition, spiritual life,
the real location of the mythological wellsprings of youth and immortal-
ity. Listening to our feelings and respecting our intuition keeps us truly
vital, ever young. Water is thus a symbol of cleansing, renewal, and inner
wisdom.

*What images of water speak most strongly to you? Does water stand still in a pool or
pond, reflecting something important in your life? Is it a stream, inviting you to think
about a pressing issue in stream-of-consciousness fashion? Does it take the form of a well,
signifying a well of knowledge or perhaps a wishing well, the answer to a specific need or
prayer? Take a moment to free-associate on the idea of water, and write down whatever
images or insights pop into your head.*

An Angelic Reflection: I plunge into the depths of life without fear.

REJECTION AND ABANDONMENT

An Angel Reminder: **The original meaning of the word *reject* is "to throw back." If you are ever rejected by a fellow human, think about it as being thrown back to God and the angels.**

Often when a personal relationship has ended, causing us great sadness and grief, well-meaning friends tell us that we must deal with our abandonment issues or we will never heal. The real truth is that we all have abandonment issues and a deep feeling of rejection, most likely resulting from the moment we entered the Earth plane and took our first painful breath. How dare God cast us out of this safe womb, where we were still able to play with the angels and feel true unconditional love? No matter how close we feel to another person, it will not heal our deep fear of abandonment. Our true home is love, and love comes from God, so if you can always remember whence you came, you will always be at home when love is in your heart.

In the care of the angels, you may come face-to-face with the painful feelings of being cast off, discarded, deserted, left alone, and never accepted for who you are. If you have been abandoned, then abandon your defense mechanism and surrender to the feelings that arise. Know that the angels are guiding you through this painful process.

An Angelic Reflection: **Regardless how painful rejection can be, my comfort comes in the truth that the angels never abandon me.**

TRAGEDY AND DESTINY

An Angel Reminder: **Within tragedy lie the seeds of our destiny.**

Have you ever thought that tragedy and destiny might go hand in hand? It may be destiny that we experience loss when we do. We don't know why; it's part of the grand surprise package that God has sent us. Through tragedy we may discover our destiny, our real purpose. In the words of the Tibetan teacher Sogyal Rinpoche, "Bereavement can force you to look at your life directly, compelling you to find a purpose in it where there may not have been one before." Tragedy connects us to deeper values; when we have suffered a big loss our little grievances seem insignificant by comparison and things that once seemed so important lose their power over us. We may finally understand how precious the days are and may begin to put them to real use instead of waiting for tomorrow. It helps, when confronted with tragedy, to remember that even the most horrendous atrocities have repeatedly failed to extinguish the flame of the human spirit. It is only when we allow that flame to go out—when we ourselves extinguish it—that the angels weep for the pain we were unable to transform, the light that we were unable to see, the destiny that was almost ours.

Have there been any tragedies in your life that have opened the door to your destiny? The people who are able to rise above tragedy are those who are able to view their difficult experience as a test of courage, will, and commitment to life. If you are faced with a tragedy, know that you have the courage to face it as long as you are committed to life.

An Angelic Reflection: **I know that tragedy can be life's most powerful agent of transformation.**

GETTING EVEN

**An Angel Reminder: We only need to get
on an even footing with ourselves.**

Getting even with someone is an odd concept. It comes from feeling wronged or slighted, which in turn stems from feeling helpless, powerless, victimized. What usually happens is this: we allow someone to hurt us in some way, and then, rather than confronting the situation honestly, we retreat in a rage, nursing our wounds with the comforting balm of revenge fantasy. Getting even might serve a useful purpose if it gets us off our duffs; anger is often a powerful creative fuel, and plenty of success stories can be traced to a burning desire to prove oneself in the face of criticism or condescension. But the bottom line is that getting even gives the object of our rage a disproportionate amount of power. We expend way too much mental effort on people who don't deserve our time and energy and probably will not learn anything from being one-upped. The angels suggest that when we're tempted to use our valuable energy to get even with someone, we channel it instead into giving ourselves some extra love and attention. Then we can calm down enough to ask ourselves why we're angry and what purpose that anger serves. If we are really angry with ourselves for not living up to our full potential, we can begin to reverse that trend—not to get even but to get happy.

Is there anybody you'd like to get even with? Why? How do you think you could accomplish this? Would it matter to that person? Or, if you made that person suffer or "pay up," would that really improve your life? Aren't peace of mind and self-satisfaction your ultimate goals?

An Angelic Reflection: If I am happy with myself and my life, I don't need to get even with anyone.

AUTONOMY, NOT AUTOMATONS

An Angel Reminder: "If everyone is thinking
alike then somebody isn't thinking."
George S. Patton

An automaton is what we call a person who acts mechanically or auto-matically and without thinking autonomously. An autonomous person is self-governing, self-ruling, independent, and self-contained. For an auto-maton, life is an endless assembly line of rules and regulations followed blindly. An autonomous person respects rules yet understands that often they have nothing to do with the actual laws of nature and God. Culti-vate autonomy; this way you can play creatively with the angels.

Which would you rather be, an automaton or an autonomous person? Which kind of per-son would you want loving you? Think of any situations in your life that may foster automatic behavior. Think of situations that foster autonomy. Ask the angels to give you a reminder when the autopilot starts to take over, and get back in the driver's seat.

An Angelic Reflection: I am autonomous; my life is not on automatic.

VETERANS

An Angel Reminder: "You furnish the pictures
and I'll furnish the war."
William Randolph Hearst,
to Frederic Remington

We are all veterans of life. A veteran by definition is someone who is sea-
soned, skilled, experienced, or a former member of the military. Each of
us in our own way ranks as a veteran. Life has its battles and can be an
ongoing war. In the battle of life, some are awarded a medal if they
merely stub their toe or happen to be in the right place at the right time;
they are not asked to face the trenches and real combat. Those who put
their lives on the line in the real battlefield may never even get a mention.
God knows the real soldiers, because the angels go into battle with us;
they know when a real serviceman or servicewoman is in their presence.

*Think about your status as a veteran. Do you feel good about it? Have you ever gotten
acclaim when you didn't think you deserved it? How would the angels rank you in the service of your country and God's providence?*

An Angelic Reflection: I am happy being a veteran of life.

TRAPS

An Angel Reminder: **When you take the bait you're hooked.**

Life is full of traps that are just waiting to spring. And like little mice, we are lured into them by the scent of good cheese. There are many enticements that act as the bait in our lives. We may be seduced by the promise of wealth, fame, love. We may be so hungry for attention that we search for it in all the wrong places. We may get into the trap of conspicuous consumption, believing that the more we can prove we own, the more important we will be in the eyes of others. The biggest trap of all, of course, is the illusion that the answer to our prayers lies outside us rather than inside us. The angels caution us to make choices based on wisdom, not desperation. They remind us that it is not the cheese but our own illusions and delusions that have trapped us and that will hold us prisoner until we see them for what they are and look beyond them for happiness.

What traps can you recall falling into, either in the past or lately? What propelled you toward them? What delusions or illusions keep you in them? There is always a way out of a trap, and it simply involves being willing to change the belief or behavior that got you in it in the first place. When we start to become aware and awake, the traps in which we've been stuck automatically open, and we find that we have reclaimed our freedom.

An Angelic Reflection: **I am not seduced by the siren song of illusion.**

MYTHIC SENSITIVITY

An Angel Reminder: **"Called or not, the gods are present."**
C. G. Jung

To what extent does mythology affect us each day? That depends on our level of mythic sensitivity. Many of the ancient and archetypal symbols are present in our everyday lives, but we rarely notice them. Take, for instance, the days of the week. The name of a god or goddess lies behind each of the days of week. Monday, the official start of our business week, refers to the moon, the watery feminine influence. Think about that next time you just can't get in a business moon on a Monday. Take a moment to reflect upon the moon and what it represents. Sunday is of course ruled by the sun. Tuesday: Mars/Aries, Wednesday: Mercury/Hermes, Thursday: Jupiter/Zeus, Friday: Venus/Aphrodite, and Saturday is Saturn's day.

Tune in to the god or goddess representing this particular day. Pay attention to subtle influences, and think of a way you could honor the divinity who rules the day. Start to notice other ways in which the gods and goddesses interact with our lives. Notice when you come across statues representing them or companies named after a god. Pay attention if one particular god or goddess shows up more than once.

An Angelic Reflection: **I will develop my mythic sensitivity as a gift of awareness.**

PURIFICATION

An Angel Reminder: **It's never too late to come clean.**

The idea of purity can be downright intimidating. Who but the Holy Virgin could be free of impurity? But the angels would rather we take a different view of purity, regarding it not as a hopeless ideal beyond human reach but as a form of spiritual cleansing. We know it's a good idea to bathe frequently; why not accord our souls the same courtesy and care? There are all sorts of ways we can purify our lives that have nothing to do with whether or not we are virgins or saints. We can do service for others. We can spread joy and hope. We can refrain from judgment and practice understanding. Pure actions, which are those taken in the spirit of love and concern, not only cleanse our souls, they also uplift the energy around us and gladden the angels' hearts.

What does purity mean to you? Retaining your virtue? Not having impure thoughts? Or taking a proactive role in making the world a better place? List some ways in which you could purify your life from the standpoint of your spiritual self and its effect on others. One definition of pure is "complete and thorough." What things could you do to make yourself more complete, more thoroughly part of God?

An Angelic Reflection: **As I uplift my environment, so I help to purify it.**

SEPARATION

An Angel Reminder: "Coming together is a beginning; keeping together is progress; working together is success."

Henry Ford

Whenever we separate ourselves from the truth that all creatures—humans, other animals, all nature—are important to God, we are leaving room for evil to enter. The word *devil* comes from the Greek *diabolos*, meaning "slanderer," which in turn comes from *dia*, "across," and *ballein*, "to throw." To "throw across" or to separate, and to slander or tell a lie—these are the original meanings of evil. The lie of separation is what brings us most of our problems here on Mother Earth. Racism is a product of separation. When we separate ourselves from nature, thinking it is not really alive or is not as important as the welfare of humans, we create an evil imbalance. All of the things we try to separate ourselves from will return to haunt us. The people we have cast off have the same frailties and need for love that we do.

The angels want us to have reverence for life. If we separate ourselves from any aspect of life, then we are diluting our reverence. What do I try to separate from? Certain people? Certain pieces of the world? Ask the angels to heal the separations in your life and to bring your reverence to wholeness.

An Angelic Reflection: I will ask the angels for guidance next time I separate myself from the whole picture of life.

STUPID PEOPLE

An Angel Reminder: "Listening to all who come to us,
regardless of their intellectual level, is a human duty."
Paulo Freire

It's a great feeling to be smarter than everyone else. It means you know just what to do at all times and that you understand the reasons and motivations behind everything. Why, you could be God's partner in running the universe! The problem is, even God doesn't control everything. Humans are always doing surprising things that divine power doesn't control. And even God learns from the most simpleminded among us. It's true that really stupid people do exist—and worse, that they're often in positions of power. This is frustrating to the more brilliant among us. But in general, stupidity comes in all forms, and the smartest people can do and say the dumbest things, while the dumbest people might have insights we'd never expect. The angels caution us not to gloat over our own seemingly superior intellectual abilities but rather to concentrate on being as smart as we can be at all times. This will keep us so busy that we're guaranteed not to have even one spare moment to devote to scrutinizing someone else's intelligence or lack of it.

Are there people whom you think are particularly stupid? Why? Does it make you feel good that you're smarter than they are? Do they have any redeeming qualities? What are some of the stupid things that you've done in your life? How would you feel if you knew that other people were labeling you stupid instead of seeing you as a complete, and perhaps complex, human being?

An Angelic Reflection: I realize that human beings have many selves, and I try not to reduce people to one aspect of their being.

CORRUPTION

An Angel Reminder: **"Cowards can never be moral."**
Mahatma Gandhi

The definition of *corruption* is "dishonest, accepting bribes, immoral, wicked, and decaying." Someone who corrupts others taints them, often by persuading them to take a bribe. When we take a bribe we accept something with the understanding that we must behave dishonestly in order to give the person's wishes our first priority. We hear about corruption in many facets of public life. It comes about when people are jockeying for power. But what about our personal lives? Doesn't each of us maneuver to gain advantage over life and others? What about the little bribes we accept, such as agreeing not to be completely honest with ourselves in order to fulfill someone else's wishes? Children know when they are being bribed, and they also find out how easy it is to bribe others. What connections might there be between small-scale bids for personal power and corruption in high places?

It is important to look at how we try to gain power, and then ask ourselves if we are corrupting or being corrupted in any way. Are we disregarding our own truth in order to play the game? When corruption sets in, decay will follow. A corrupt structure will eventually come crashing down. In what ways am I setting myself up for a hard fall?

An Angelic Reflection: **I will step beyond the realm of corruption and keep the beauty of love in my heart.**

THINKING STRAIGHT

An Angel Reminder: **If you can't think straight, think crooked.**

We all know how frustrating it is not to be able to think straight. Our mind goes in circles, and it seems like a big wind is sweeping through our brains, scattering thoughts like leaves. When we can't think straight, the angels say it's okay to think crooked—to let our thoughts race and scurry in whatever zigzag direction they want while we merely observe them. This is the first thing one learns in meditation—to let thoughts come and go without judging or trying to resist them. Eventually—once we are no longer attached to our thoughts—the mind quiets down, and clarity comes. At first it isn't easy to let go of our thoughts, even when we can't catch them. We let them frighten, irritate, and confuse us. But gradually, if we have the courage just to take a deep breath, sit back, and let them run where they will, the unhelpful ones will tend to disappear, while the useful ones will return to us calmer and more focused after their little bit of exercise.

If you feel confused about something, sit with the confusion. Close your eyes, and let your thoughts roam free. Don't attach yourself to any of them; just let them come and go. Keep breathing and relaxing. Pretend that your thoughts are children in the playground and you're their nanny, sitting on a bench and watching them. Note how, as you begin to practice meditation and become detached from your thoughts, your mind begins to clear.

An Angelic Reflection: **When I can't think straight, I take a break from thinking.**

ASSUMPTIONS AND INTERPRETATIONS

An Angel Reminder: "We make assumptions about what others are doing or thinking—we take it personally—then we blame them and react by sending emotional poison with our word."

Don Miguel Ruiz

We are little satellites of assumptions and interpretations, each of us in our own little orbit of truth. When was the last time you listened to someone without reading something into what that person was saying? When was the last time you were able to be around someone and not interpret that person's actions and behavior? It takes practice to be able to just let people be without projecting our assumptions onto what they are doing and saying. It is frustrating when our behavior is assumed to be something other than it is or when what we are saying is mistakenly interpreted. So we need to take the initiative in letting go of conjecture. The angels will be there with us to teach us to listen to life, without throwing our own veil over everything.

Next time someone tells you something, take it as it is. If someone compliments you, don't assume ulterior motives. If someone is telling you a story out of their own experience, don't question it in any way. When you feel the urge to finish someone's sentence, thinking you know what the person is going to say, stop yourself and let them finish. Examine your own discomfort. It could be you want others to think you are smart or in control, or maybe you don't want the intimacy that comes from truly listening. Ask the angels to help you make this a continuous practice, and your life will change.

An Angelic Reflection: I will no longer assume; I will simply listen.

THE BRIGHT SIDE

An Angel Reminder: **The bright side is the right side.**

The expression "look on the bright side" is not just a platitudinous crumb thrown to the suffering by the nauseatingly cheerful. It is, in fact, one of our most powerful survival tools. Dr. Peter Lodewick, an M.D. who wrote a great book called *A Doctor Looks at Diabetes: His and Yours,* makes a wonderful observation that applies not just to diabetics but to all people. He said that while many diabetics resent having to take insulin, he has always regarded it as a blessing. "Were it not for the discovery of insulin in 1921, my chances of survival would have been slim," reflects Dr. Lodewick. "I am both amazed and thankful, viewing insulin as a miracle drug that gives me strength and vigor." No other comment could stand as better proof of the fact that in life it is always possible to look on the bright side—and that when we do, we stand a better chance of living better and longer. Statistics prove that it's the diabetics who regard insulin as a curse and a curtailment of basic freedom who have the most trouble controlling their disease. But Dr. Lodewick leads an active, happy, and exceedingly productive life, particularly in his efforts to help others do the same. We have the choice as to how circumstances will affect us. We can either curse our insulin or use it to our advantage. But the bottom line is, if we'd be dead without it, it must be a blessing in some form.

Think of some things that you view as restrictions in your life. Now turn them over and see if they have a bright side. How do you think your attitude determines the degree to which you are either restricted or liberated?

An Angelic Reflection: **When I look at the bright side I see the light.**

A DIRECT CONSULTATION

An Angel Reminder: "Better to create prophecy
than to live prediction."
Caroline W. Casey

Many people in recent years have consulted spirits from the other side when they needed information about their lives or the world. But if we want to grow and mature in our spiritual lives, we need to consult the more mature voices for advice. Instead of listening to spirits from afar, why not listen to our own spirit? Why not talk to the Great Creator directly? Instead of being wowed by life after death, let's start creating a beautiful, heart-centered experience of life *before* death!

Many fears come to the surface when we know it is time to stand on our own, next to the angels, and make decisions in which we must search our own heart and psyche for the true information we need. Next time you have the urge to go to a psychic or channeler for information, remember that the information you receive may reflect your own fears. Practice consulting directly with the Divine in your heart.

An Angelic Reflection: I will listen to my heart, soul, and spirit for the details of my destiny.

KEEPING TRACK

An Angel Reminder: "It's really difficult to become a contented person if you're keeping score of all you do."
Richard Carlson

If we keep close score of all we do, then we will interpret what others do for us with strict conditions. We might even make up little rules in our mind for others to follow yet neglect to let others know about the rules. Some people put restrictions on a friendship by keeping track of how much time the person has given them. If a friend is going through a hard time and they have been there for the friend as a supportive ally, then the friend owes them. Owes them what? How could a friendship be a true friendship if debts are being recorded? There are certainly situations where keeping track of something can prevent future resentments, such as in the arena of money. But little that we do for others can be assigned a monetary value, so we better get over this notion of owing in the realm of our friendships.

Keeping track usually leads to resentment. Generosity freely shared leads to love without conditions. Start keeping track of yourself rather than others. If you don't have something to give, don't give it. Think about what would happen if the angels started keeping track of all they do for us.

An Angelic Reflection: I have no need to track love.

PASSIVE-AGGRESSIVE

An Angel Reminder: **There are certain situations in which we just can't win, so it is better not to enter the contest.**

One of the clearest examples of a no-win situation is when we bear the brunt of someone's passive aggression. We are tried, found guilty, and punished, and we never even realized that a case had been brought against us. Passive-aggressive behavior is a trap for both parties involved and is a true form of dishonesty. We all have the tendency to be passive-aggressive at times; we are passive-aggressive when we put obstacles in someone's path instead of telling them we were hurt by their behavior. We are passive-aggressive when we let others make decisions for us, then resent them for controlling us. Dealing with situations in which we feel powerless takes honesty and courage, and a continuous IV drip of wisdom from the angels. The angels will always steer us away from being passive-aggressive by asking us to be honest about what we are doing, then get over it and have some fun.

When you are the target of somebody's sneak attack of negative energy, the best thing to do is to get clarity by noticing what is happening. A passive-aggressive person really just wants to be heard but is going about it by backhanded, sometimes destructive, means. If the situation is important enough to confront, bring the angels with you, and ask the person if they have a problem with you. Then stay clear in your own truth, because dishonesty in the air can be picked up like a airborne virus. Sometimes it is best to get some distance when passive aggression is in the air.

An Angelic Reflection: **I will not let the sticky dishonesty of passive aggression insult me; the angels show me I have more important things to do.**

POWER OUTAGE

An Angel Reminder: **Sometimes we are forced
to do our work by natural light.**

You know what a power outage is like. Suddenly, nothing works. Every daily convenience that we've taken for granted unexpectedly goes on strike. This tends to throw us into complete chaos. What will we do without lights, phone, hot water, microwave, TV, computer, fax? During a power outage we are jolted into realizing how dependent we are upon external objects and how alienated we've become from our natural environment. At the same time we are given the opportunity to find inner sources of strength and ingenuity of which we may not have been aware. The effect is similar when we suffer an emotional power outage. When we are confused, frustrated, and despairing, all the energy sources that we've relied upon to get us through the day seem to give way, and we are left in the dark, fumbling our way around. The thing to remember during a power outage is that sooner or later the light will come back on. In the meantime we can sit quietly without the usual distractions and get to know ourselves, our families, our neighbors. We can figure out alternative sources of energy. And we can always draw new strength from the angels' generator, a power source guaranteed never to fail.

Have you suffered any emotional power outages recently? If so, what did you rely on for an alternative energy source? Did you learn anything meaningful from being in the dark? How long did it take for the lights to come back on? The next time you have a power outage, take a moment to think about what's draining the energy from your power source, and work at getting it out of your life.

An Angelic Reflection: **I have a personal power source within me that is always available.**

TAKING FOR GRANTED

An Angel Reminder: "Don't it always seem to go /
that you don't know what you've got 'til it's gone."
Joni Mitchell, "Big Yellow Taxi"

If we really consider everything we fail to appreciate as a gift and not an entitlement, the list can be surprising. Opening our eyes in the morning and being able to see what's around us. Getting out of bed by ourselves, washing and dressing unaided. Breathing without difficulty. Walking, running, dancing. These are just some of the basic functions that we don't even notice until, through illness, accident, or aging, they are taken from us. And for those of us who are physically disabled, there are still enjoyments to be savored. In the short story "Little Herr Friedemann," Thomas Mann describes the ecstasy his main character, a physically disabled man, experiences as he trains himself to be grateful for what life still has to offer. "He learned to understand," writes Mann, "that to everything belongs its own enjoyment, and that it is absurd to distinguish between an experience which is 'happy' and one which is not. With a right good will he accepted each emotion as it came . . . whether sad or gay . . . how tenderly he loved the mild flow of his life . . . full of a tranquil and quiet happiness which was his own creation."

Reflect upon all the abilities that you usually take for granted. How about being able to feed yourself or drive or remember things or cut your own toenails? Try practicing the presence of God in every task that you do throughout the day, giving thanks for the abilities you have.

An Angelic Reflection: I do not take the gift of life lightly.

NUMBERED

An Angel Reminder: "We are mortal, vulnerable, and fallible; our days are numbered, often filled with sorrow, pain, and humiliation. Some people think that this is a good reason to avoid the here-and-now. I think that this is a good reason to drink deep of the here-and-now."

Timothy Miller

In the recesses of our psyche is the belief that our days are numbered, that we have a certain amount of time to get everything accomplished before our number is up. But this belief can numb us to the essence of life. We can number anything—our minutes, our money, our children, our lovers, and ourselves. In centuries past, people even tried numbering the angels by arguing about how many of them can dance on the head of a pin. Numbers are useful tools, but the angels urge us not to be numbered by them. Let's take a look at life beyond numbers.

Think about numbers for a minute. You may have a favorite number, or you may be superstitious about certain numbers. Ask yourself if any of your beliefs about numbers make you numb to the here and now. Numbers are an intellectual concept to help us understand certain things. The mystery is found right here and now. When we are awake, we can step out of the human concepts that numb us to the mystery..

An Angelic Reflection: I am counted for without being numbered.

DRAMA QUEENS

An Angel Reminder: You ought to be on the stage;
it leaves in ten minutes.

We're all familiar with the drama queen. In fact, there's probably one in your life right this minute, driving you to distraction. Drama queens either do wild and crazy things that keep them on the edge of perpetual disaster, or they just scale up every little thing that happens to them. Whatever they do, they make sure that all the world's their stage and no one else's. These human magnifying glasses blow up the most trivial events into scenarios of critical proportions. They can't understand why their latest love crisis isn't on the AP wire or why their ingrown toenail didn't make the cover of *Time*. They particularly can't figure out why friends don't stay in their lives for very long. The angels know that down deep, drama queens are full of spirit and yearning for passionate connection to life. If we ourselves happen to have a little of the drama queen in us (and let's be honest—who doesn't?), we can ask the angels to suggest ways in which we might make a real contribution to the world. By listening more to others and less to ourselves, we might discover that true excitement comes from observing, not manufacturing, the continuing drama—and comedy—of life.

Some people are closet drama queens, who live vicariously through romance novels, movies, the soaps, or Jerry Springer. Others fall into the more active category of drama queen. If drama is your fix, ask yourself why crisis, instability, or extremes of joy and pain are appealing to you. If you want to be a little less crazy, ask the angels to help you find positive ways of connecting to your creative spirit.

An Angelic Reflection: I have healthy ways of making my life exciting and meaningful.

THE WORLD IS A PROJECTION SCREEN

An Angel Reminder: "You are not only *who* it is that you're looking for, you are also *what* it is that you're looking *at!*"

Charles A. Hillig

It may be hard to believe, but most of what we notice in the world and in other people resides inside of us in a profound way. That is why we "know-tice" it. Quite often the things we are upset about are things that we use to upset ourselves and others. If we are brave enough to look at life this way, great healing of the mind and consciousness can take place. We *are* the center of a universe, the universe of our mind. It takes great courage to begin to notice our projections on the screen of the world and to begin trying to see the world as it is instead of as we would like it to be.

If you feel strongly about a wrong that was done to you, write it down in detail. Then ask the angels to let you know how and when you may have done something similar. If you are willing to look at it, then you will know why you were so upset. The angels then will guide you into having a good laugh at how complex, yet simple, we are at times.

An Angelic Reflection: **Projections will lead me to look closer at what is.**

PETTY

***An Angel Reminder:* Petty isn't pretty.**

Pettiness is a distinctly human trait, one that other species wouldn't bother to indulge in. Pettiness means to be overly concerned with the trivial, a pastime that the angels must find incredibly boring. It also has a couple of even less savory definitions, like "of an unbelievably narrow mind" and "spiteful and mean." Too often we get caught up in pettiness without even realizing it. We squabble over insignificant things and let our little grievances ruin our day. We discount the importance of others' feelings as we concentrate solely on our own. Pettiness usually centers around the issue of debt; a petty person goes around with a scorecard, tabulating who owes them what and never forgetting a single cent or a single favor they did for someone, probably grudgingly, that they insist must be repaid. The angels would like us to be able to make the distinction between what's really important and what's merely a figment of our egos. Pettiness is not a winning trait, and those who indulge in it are the losers. In keeping score, they may think they are the victors in this silly battle of their own making, but in truth they have lost the respect of everyone around them and the chance to enjoy genuine and fulfilling relationships.

Do you know any petty people? Do you want to be around them? Are there any problems in your life that might be the result of a petty perspective? What are some petty grievances that drive you up a wall? When you are tempted to engage in pettiness, take a cue from the angels and chill out. Try moving out of the confines of your narrow mind, into the wide open space of consciousness.

***An Angelic Reflection:* I keep the lens of my heart and mind at the widest aperture.**

COMMON COLD

An Angel Reminder: "At any given time, an estimated five percent of all Americans have a cold. That's at least twelve million miserable people. It also means that there's a one-in-twenty chance you have a cold right now."
Joan and Lydia Wilen

Nothing will make you feel more common than when you are in the midst of a common head cold. A common cold is really a group of minor illnesses spread by one of almost two hundred different viruses. A cold usually infects the nose and throat, but it can also infect your larynx and lungs. Everyone gets an occasional cold, and once it starts, it has to run its course. Medical studies have shown that getting a cold does not come from getting cold; exposure to cold or drafts or going out with wet hair will not give you a cold, since colds come from viruses, not from cold temperatures. There is always some mystery in who gets sick and why, and the angels ask us to honor the mystery by honoring what is happening to us.

If we have a common cold, maybe it is good to be humbled by the fact that we are as fragile as everybody else. Or maybe it is time to be cold and distant from things in our life for a short while—to isolate ourselves from others so we don't subject them to our cold. When we have a cold our main sensory apparatus has been compromised; we cannot smell, hear, or even see as well as usual, so we feel more removed from everyday life. It is also clear that our body is cleansing. So, next time you get a cold, consider getting away from it all so that you can recover.

An Angelic Reflection: I am not afraid to distance myself and let my body cleanse.

FENG SHUI

An Angel Reminder: Our environment is nothing more
and nothing less than an extension of ourselves.

The ancient Chinese practice of feng shui, or the art of placement is
based on the concept that everything has an energy field, and that correct
placement of homes and objects within them will create harmony. Feng
shui is very specific, to the point of being superstitious. For instance, the
Chinese believe that since kitchens represent wealth and bathrooms are
places where water escapes, a bathroom that faces the kitchen is bad luck
because the family fortune might wash away. There is a logic to feng shui
and a reverence for space and aesthetics from which we can learn much.
But we don't have to create an environment based on superstition. If you
lose money, it is unlikely that it is because your bathroom faced your
kitchen; it's more probable that you made a bad investment or have
money issues that need your attention. The angels caution us not to put
too much emphasis on superstitious beliefs, which put our environment
in control of us rather than the other way around.

*Another feng shui notion is that the fortunes of the former occupants of a home will deter-
mine the fortunes of the new occupants, meaning that your life will take the direction of the
people who lived in your home before you. It is true that dwellings have energy fields and
that negative energy may become trapped in a space. It is also true that if we are conscious
of our own energy, and if we surround ourselves with light, love, and angelic forces, any
home we move into will acquire our good vibrations and will attract good energy.*

An Angelic Reflection: I respect the energies of my environment, but I
know that my attitudes are the primary predictor of my fortune.

OUR ONLY ANSWER

An Angel Reminder: **Expect the unexpected miracle.**

When we are stuck in a dilemma we naturally stop and try to figure out how to solve the dilemma. Sometimes our thinking moves toward negative scenarios, and we scare ourselves into believing that there's no way out. Other times we return to a solution that seems to be "our only answer," such as a good love relationship, a windfall of money, or some new possession that would assure us a way out. How often do you get stuck and then ask for a miracle? A miracle comes from God; it is not under human control. We position ourselves for a miracle when we ask for one and then let go of our attachments to the usual answers and worn-out methods. Letting go opens the way for the miraculous to enter. Expecting miracles means we cannot define the outcome, we cannot expect our situation to turn out a certain way. In fact, our miracle may be the very opposite of what we would ever expect.

When a solution comes into your mind, entertain it and then let go and ask God for a miracle. Sometimes miracles can be subtle, so pay attention to the mystery in order to recognize the miraculous.

An Angelic Reflection: **I trust that God knows best.**

DECEMBER 3

JUST MY LUCK

An Angel Reminder: If you subscribe to luck, then you have given over your wondrous gift of human choice to the merciless master of superstition and the random beneficence of luck or fate.

Have you ever said, "With my luck . . . ," and then followed it with something negative? "With my luck it will rain Sunday and ruin my dress." "With my luck an asteroid will come through my ceiling." Think about what we are saying when we make comments about our bad luck. First, we are assuming that there is a force called luck, and, second, we are admitting something truly depressing: we are feeling a lack of grace in our lives. Have you ever entered a contest and then said, "Oh, I never win anything," meaning, "I am such a victim of the mean ol' god of fate"? The angels want us to stop limiting our experience of life with labels of good or bad luck and instead embrace the idea that we are blessed. No matter what life brings at any moment, it is all a blessing.

Today, throw out your concept of luck, and let yourself be blessed. To be blessed means we have gratitude; gratitude means we know whence we came and will trust God in every situation. Buddhists look to the quality of equanimity, the ability to accept all events, happy or not, without judgment, as perfect parts of the whole. It takes time to shake the shackles of superstition and embrace being blessed. The angels will always be on hand to show you the humor of your ways, anytime the word luck comes into your mind. With your luck. . .

An Angelic Reflection: I am blessed with no luck.

INAPPROPRIATE

An Angel Reminder: "His socks compelled one's attention without losing one's respect."
Saki, *Ministers of Grace*

In the days of the Monica Lewinsky scandal, there was a lot of discussion about "inappropriate" behavior. President Bill Clinton admitted to having an "inappropriate" relationship with Ms. Lewinsky; the Starr Report was considered by many to be an inappropriate disclosure of salacious material; the videotape of Clinton's grand jury testimony was released on what many felt was an inappropriate day—Rosh Hashanah, the beginning of the Jewish High Holy Days. In fact, inappropriate behavior seemed to rule the day. People often disagree about what is appropriate. But the angels offer a handy definition that we can always turn to when in doubt: appropriate behavior is any action taken in the spirit of decency, which Webster defines as "propriety of conduct and speech; proper observance of the requirements of modesty." When we have to make a behavioral choice, if we can truly say that we are acting with modesty and integrity—with the purpose of upholding truth and justice—then our actions are appropriate, however uncomfortable they might make others. Then we can compel people's attention without losing their respect.

Write your own definition of what inappropriate means to you and see if you act with consistent appropriateness in your own life.

An Angelic Reflection: If I have a statement to make, I make it with modesty, integrity, and decency.

Due Yesterday

An Angel Reminder: **It's time to give time to God.**

So often we get into trouble trying to fit life into a crazy schedule. Just think about the phrase "due yesterday," which has become so popular in our technocracy. When something is due yesterday, we are doomed before we've even begun. The deadline is past, and we didn't even know it. Our only recourse then is to turn our lives into a game of catch-up, in which we're always going to be behind. What we don't seem to understand is that humans can only manage time, not control it. The angels look with loving amusement on our futile race to overtake time. They wait for us to stop for breath so that they can remind us that this highly mercurial commodity belongs not to us but to God. When we allow ourselves to give time to God, not just in prayer but in trust, we begin to discover that things have a mysterious way of getting done and working out on time, no matter what the human deadline is or was.

Do you have projects that are due yesterday? If so, how are you handling them? Are you going bonkers? Pushing yourself and others past reasonable limits? Living in terror of failure? Some people thrive on crazy deadlines, meaning that they need an adrenaline rush to get them going. Others find themselves in untenable positions at their jobs, with too much work piled on them and not enough time to do it. Whatever the case, the angels have the solution. Just hand time over to God. If you like, write your project and deadline on a piece of paper, put it in an envelope, address it to God, and imagine it going out in the mail. You don't even have to overnight it; God will get it on time. Meanwhile, sit back, relax, work at a reasonable pace, and let yourself be surprised.

An Angelic Reflection: **When I punch in to the divine time clock, my workday acquires a new dimension.**

LONGING

An Angel Reminder: **Longings are like guideposts, pointing the way to the soul.**

A longing is a deep desire for something that will in some way fulfill us. We long for the freedom to do the things we'd like to do. We long for the home that will bring us peace and security. We long for the work that will excite our passion. We long for the love that will fill the aching emptiness in our hearts. It is good to have a longing, for then we will always have a dream. But when our longings prevent us from appreciating and making the most of the here and now, we will be unhappy rather than inspired to work toward a happier life. The angels say, let your longings speak to you, and know that you can make changes in your life that will bring you more security, freedom, and satisfaction. You can attract love by opening your heart to others. Your longings are a call to uplift your life, and the best way to begin that process is to give thanks for that life as it is. When we generate gratefulness, we always receive abundance.

What are some of your longings? How do they affect your life? Do they make you restless and dissatisfied? Do they inspire you to satisfy them? Longings often connect us to the deeper needs within us. What are your longings telling you about what your soul requires? Ask the angels to inspire you with ideas and send you opportunities that will help you to fulfill your soul requirements.

An Angelic Reflection: **I am grateful for my life and grateful for the longings that connect me to my soul.**

VAMPIRES

An Angel Reminder: "See the spider, spinning
the web for the unwary fly."

Dracula

Not all vampires have fangs, roam the Earth from sundown to sunrise, and ooze the European charm of Bela Lugosi. We meet plenty of vampires in our everyday lives, people who seem to be able to live only by draining energy from others. How many of us have had to suffer with the narcissistic friend, neighbor, co-worker, or relative who calls us only to complain about their troubles and smother us with their neediness? How many times have we offered up fervent hosannas for the invention of the answering machine, when we hear the familiar whiny voice on our messages? Curiously enough, even though they act like the ultimate victim, we become their victims, the unwary flies heading straight for their manipulative web. If you have a vampire in your life, who's been draining you of valuable energy in terms of time, effort, and the resulting expenditure of anger and resentment, here's a suggestion. The next time your vampire calls, give him or her the number of the Red Cross, and tell them they'll never go hungry again. Then hang up and start living *your* life.

If you would like to be rid of vampires but have difficulty confronting them, put one of your angels on the job. Ask this angel to give you the courage to be more honest with this person and to help you set limits with others.

An Angelic Reflection: **I do not allow others to drain me of precious energy.**

SORCERY

An Angel Reminder: "A sorcerer is a person who attempts by some special art to divert the forces of nature to his own personal ends. The true purpose of metaphysics is to perfect the inner self in wisdom, virtue, and understanding. All forced growth is sorcery."

Manly P. Hall

Manly Hall suggests that it is better to engage in metaphysics than in sorcery. To be involved in metaphysics with integrity is to grow in our understanding and wisdom. To use metaphysics to serve our own ego's needs and to force the world to do our bidding is the dark side, sorcery. Those who curse others or put spells on them so that they will be punished are acting out of the dark side, and their sorcery will act like a boomerang coming back to the person who threw it. What you wish or send out is what you get back, and the negative will come back in a form you cannot predict. We often hear about "white" and "black" magic, or magic that is done for positive goals and magic that is done to harm people. The problem is that in both of them we are trying to control destiny and other people. The angels prefer that we pray for the highest outcome instead of trying to force God's hand.

Forget about sorcery and magic. Keenly examine your life to make sure you are not using it. Sorcery works against angel consciousness; it is no better when, in our need for magic, we try to use the angels to do our bidding. If you ever get the feeling that someone is trying magic on you, tell the angels and ask Archangel Michael to help transmute and transform the directed force field for the highest good of all concerned.

An Angelic Reflection: I am not a sorcerer; I am a spiritual being here to create love.

CHECKOUT STAND

An Angel Reminder: **What if the person next to you is really an angel?**

All of us know what it's like to wait in the grocery store checkout line. We stand there waiting to purchase our food, surrounded by candy, gum, good healthy foods, bad greasy foods, "self-doubt women's magazines," tabloids, and temptations to buy things we probably don't need. And then there are the other people waiting in line—people who are sad, people who are happy, many of us stressed, parents with small children, loners, old, young. Most of us also know what it's like to watch someone ahead of us in line holding everyone else up because they are haggling over a price or a coupon or the ability to pay by check. But we also have met the kind people who flash a smile at us. Do you remember how instantly you were reminded through a smile that you really weren't in that big of a hurry? The power of kindness overcomes small-mindedness, and an angel is present whenever we accept the invitation to slow down and cherish a moment of connection with another.

Next time you find yourself in the checkout line, take a look around and then check in with yourself. Do you feel connected to the people around you or isolated from them? Imagine each person loved and protected by an angel. Do you see them differently now?

An Angelic Reflection: **When I am in line, I relax and practice seeing others through the eyes of divine love.**

THE GOOD LIFE

An Angel Reminder: "Just do your best—in any circumstance in your life. It doesn't matter if you are sick or tired, if you always do your best there is no way you can judge yourself."
Don Miguel Ruiz

How often have you gone through the day talking about all the doom and gloom in our world, using it as small talk or as a way to start a conversation with others? Our friend Mick Laugs helped us realize how much precious time we waste talking about negative things instead of focusing on what is good in our lives. Mick uses conversation time wisely, letting you know about his goals and dreams and the positive things that are happening in relationship to them. He talks about his progress and spiritual growth, and I always learn something positive by talking with him. By focusing on what's good in life, Mick also receives in return helpful information from others. It is possible to have a good life in this world, and we start on the path to finding it when we focus on what is good in our lives rather than on what's wrong with the world.

The angels want us to know that all around us are people living a good life. Try noticing the great examples around you of people who are actually enjoying life. Why not focus on what is working properly instead of what is breaking down? Next time someone you are sharing with heads toward the negative, gently change the subject.

An Angelic Reflection: I will share and accentuate the positive in my everyday conversations.

FIND YOUR "ECCENTER"

An Angel Reminder: **It's okay to be eccentric.**

People who are on a quest for perfection will never be able to relax into themselves. Eccentric people, however, can always do this well. The word *eccentric* means, literally, "out of the center," and it has been used to describe people with unconventional appearance or behavior. Those who have studied eccentrics find that such people are actually much happier and contented with their lot in life, and that from an early age they knew and accepted that they were not like others. When we find our own center, strengthen it by our own spiritual practices, then enjoy ourselves, we will be happier. In other words, we all have the capacity to be eccentric, and that is why we need to "eccenter" ourselves—find our sacred center and keep it strong. The best thing about eccentering ourselves is that it is not boring; it is creative, satisfying, and meaningful—and something the angels can take direct part in.

Sometimes the consensus reality is so different from the way eccentrics see and experience life that their sanity is challenged if they don't have a strong spiritual center. There are many assaults on our centeredness in today's world, and the angels can help us to understand these and help us counteract the uncentering forces. Only you can find your own sacred eccenter, but remember you are not alone. The angels love to help with this special quest.

An Angelic Reflection: **My center is only a prayer away.**

TOUGH LOVE

An Angel Reminder: **Love is patient, love is kind, love is tough.
With apologies to the apostle Paul**

Tough love is something of a redundancy. By its very nature, true love is tough, meaning honest. When we really love someone, we not only tell it like it is, we do what's best for them, even when it means not bailing them out when they seem to need it the most. It is not easy to give the boot to your twenty-five-year-old kid who hasn't found a job and is still living off of you. It is not easy to refuse to loan your friend money when they're broke because they've spent their last dime on drugs. It is not easy to let somebody you care about make their own mistakes and live with the consequences, instead of giving in to the temptation to rescue them and make it all better. By the same token, it's not easy to confront a friend or loved one when they've hurt you or overstepped their boundaries and say, "These are my limits, and you've gone beyond them." Yes, love is tough, and sometimes it's tough to love correctly. But the angels know that we've all got the courage to love, which means the courage to set our own boundaries and help those we love to respect them and set their own in the process. Tough love doesn't mean withdrawing our support. We can always be there for others, as a sounding board, an empathetic presence. We can always be there to help them help themselves.

Is there anybody in your life who could use a little tough love? Is it hard for you to give it to them? Do you have difficulty establishing or respecting boundaries—yours and those of others? If so, examine the function and purpose of boundaries in your life, and ask the angels to help you defend them.

An Angelic Reflection: **I know that rescuing is not necessarily love.**

RUDE AWAKENINGS

An Angel Reminder: **God isn't always polite.**

Nobody likes rudeness. Being ill mannered and unrefined goes against the grain of a civilized society. But sometimes rudeness has its place, like when it jolts us out of unconsciousness and into stark reality. A rude awakening isn't a kindly tap on the shoulder, a polite suggestion, a gentle hint. It's a boulder falling on our heads, a swift kick in our behinds, a cosmic scolding that doesn't mince words. When we have a rude awakening, it's usually a signal that God has finally managed to get through to us. Instead of being upset, we should be grateful that our divine helpers cared enough about us to shake us into awareness, even if the way they went about it wasn't exactly according to Miss Manners. Rude awakenings are generally painful, for they force us to confront our own blindness and folly. But the angels are there to give us the courage to evaluate our predicaments honestly so that we can make the kind of choices that help us to be awake instead of asleep.

Have you been asleep when you should have been awake? Did a rude awakening come your way as a result? Think about some of the rude awakenings you've had and how they changed your life. Is there anything that you are in denial about at the current time, any situations that demand more of your honest attention? If so, ask yourself what part of the picture you're not seeing and what might happen if you listen to your intuition regarding this issue.

An Angelic Reflection: **I choose to face rather than deny uncomfortable realities.**

PATIENT

An Angel Reminder: **The angels have many patients in their care.**

Someone who is patient bears affliction with calmness. Being patient often is a battle, since in most of us there is something stirring to be impulsive, to act out. The word *patient* comes from the Latin *pati,* which means "to suffer," and is also the origin of the words *passion* and *passive.* Someone who is a patient is someone who is suffering. St. Teresa said, "Patience obtains all things." What she meant is that in time you have everything you need and will learn to want what you have. To make patience a divine experience, we need to be comfortable with giving up our need for control, and have the faith that there is a divine force of wisdom that can sort things out for us in beautiful ways we had not thought of. The magic behind patience is that when we back off from trying to control a situation—when we let go and let God—we allow time to do us a favor.

Are you feeling impatient about something? If you have tried to let go of control but find yourself suffering instead, as the word patient *connotes, then are you really winning? Often we try to be patient, and we fail, because we are trying, not doing; we are not paying attention to the messages the angels are sending us. What is your impatience wanting to tell you? Is there some action you need to take? When it comes to sorting out the time to be patient and the time to take action, wisdom is our only tool.*

An Angelic Reflection: **I will let the angels bring wisdom to my patience, and I will know when to act.**

ENTITLEMENT FANTASIES

An Angel Reminder: **A free ride is always taken at someone's expense.**

Have you ever met somebody who thinks the world "owes them a living"? These are generally not the nicest people to be around. Either they are always complaining about how deprived they are, or they are always expecting other people to do things for them, or they spend their lives looking for "something for nothing." Of course, most of us feel entitled to a degree of happiness and fulfillment, and we should. The angels will always affirm the fact that we deserve love and joy. It's when we start believing that we don't have to give in order to receive that things get screwy. We are entitled to happiness, but we are not entitled to a free ride. The angels caution us that whatever we take from the universe without returning in some form will be waiting for us on our final tab. Keeping our entitlement fantasies under control assures us that we won't be hit with a bill we can't pay when it comes time to check out of Hotel Earth.

What do you think you're entitled to? Are you willing to pay for it with the currency of effort, commitment, and persistence? Do you ever take without giving back? Are there people who do that to you? What are the things you'd like to have now in your life? What are you willing to give in order to receive them?

An Angelic Reflection: **I work willingly for what I receive, both materially and spiritually.**

PLEASE GOD

An Angel Reminder: **Thank you, God.**

Considering how challenging life has become in this fast-paced world, one can imagine that the words *please, God* are rising at all hours, in all languages, from all kinds of people. We usually beg God to change our environment or the people around us. But the truth is, when we ask God to please bring us a change, we are in fact asking God to change us. Since we are the ones sending the prayer, God can best answer that prayer by initiating changes in us. Sure, it would be great if God could get rid of all the mean people messing things up, but that will happen only when individuals truly reach a change in their own consciousness—when each person takes responsibility for changes in the world by being, themselves, willing to change. The angels are here to help us change, and then change some more.

Next time you have the urge to send out a "please, God," think about sending out a "thank you, God, for giving me the strength and courage to change." You will begin to see with new eyes the things you can change in your own life and your own perception that will bring more peace. At the heart of each cry to God is a simple intention to bring peace to our hearts and souls. When we are truly peaceful, we have no need to beg God for anything; we have it all.

An Angelic Reflection: **I will let the angels intercept my pleas and usher in a real change of heart and consciousness.**

TAKING OUT THE TRASH

An Angel Reminder: **If life stinks, it's time to take out the trash.**

Taking out the trash is nobody's favorite job. But it's one of those things that just has to be done. Imagine what would happen if we didn't take out the trash—if we let it pile up for days, weeks, months, years. Well, don't imagine! Yet this is often what we do in our personal lives. We all have inner as well as outer trash that needs to be cleared out on a regular basis. Just because it doesn't turn into a public eyesore or nosesore doesn't mean it's not a health threat. Anger that has built up, responsibilities that we've neglected—sooner or later their unsavory odor begins to permeate our life and the lives of those around us. The angels know that it takes courage to take out the trash—to clean out our lives and discard the outmoded or destructive beliefs and behaviors that impede our personal growth and happiness. They also know that it can't be done in a day. But they encourage us to check in, notice the things we do or think that hold us back or contribute to our problems, and make a periodic effort to leave them out for the angel sanitation engineers, who will be more than happy to pick them up.

Do you have trash in your life that you haven't been dealing with? If you like, draw a picture of your psychic garbage can, and fill it with all the appropriate items you can think of. These could include relationships that are no longer serving you, habits that you want to get rid of, fears that are preventing you from living life more fully. Then put the can out for the angel sanitation engineers' next pickup.

An Angelic Reflection: **I put regular effort into keeping my life healthy and balanced.**

WHAT'S THE HURRY?

An Angel Reminder: **Slow down.**

In the movie *The Bishop's Wife*, the two main characters are taking a taxi drive, and they ask the driver to take the back roads to their destination so they can enjoy the snow-covered scenery. The taxi driver says how refreshing it is to meet two people who know where they are going and don't mind taking their time to get there, unlike the many people he meets who have no idea where they are really going but are in a great hurry. Think about the word *hurry*. Doesn't the sound of it alone make us nervous? Why do we ever have to be in a hurry? Even when we are late, if we ask the angels to smooth the path and then proceed at a natural pace, we will find that we get there just at the right time.

When we are in a hurry, we do not notice our surroundings. This causes a separation in us, for as long as we're hurrying, we're separated from the things around us. It is good to know where we are, where we are going, and why we are going there. So today, slow down, take a break from hurry, and notice life along your way. Ask the angels to help you take it all lightly.

An Angelic Reflection: **I'm in no hurry.**

UNNATURAL VICE

An Angel Reminder: **Do not mess with the angels' vice squad.**

A vice is an evil or immoral practice or habit. The original meaning of the word *vice* is "wickedness." We sometimes make light of a vice, saying of a bad habit, "Well, it is my only vice." It is time to look at vices and see them for what they are. Any habit that causes us or others pain or ill health or in any way diminishes the quality of life on this planet can be called a vice. Many people think of smoking as a vice, but do we also consider burning fossil fuels in our cars and homes a vice? Yet burning oil damages the environment of the planet as a whole, just as smoking damages the environment of our lungs.

Get out of any vice grip you may be in, regardless of how innocent you think it may be.

An Angelic Reflection: **When the angels fill my consciousness, vice is kept far away.**

WHENCE WE CAME

An Angel Reminder: "The journey is life:
the destination was left behind."
Ella Patterson

Our destination is the same as our origin, since life is a journey back to our source. But it is not just a ride around the same old block. We came here to fulfill a contract, one that is hidden from us now. As we ventured through the dark night of the birth canal, many things were forgotten. All we are left with are questions, such as: What or who do we take with us on the journey? What are we looking for? What is truth? and Does our life really mean anything in the big scheme of things?

Ask the angels to help you remember whence you came. Tonight as you prepare for sleep, ask the angels to come into your dreams and guide you deeper into the journey of life. Keep it up, and each night your dreams will give you clues.

An Angelic Reflection: I know my journey with the angels will never end.

SUN

An Angel Reminder: **The sun rises, the sun sets, the sun rises again.**

The sun is the ultimate source of energy for our planet. It is illumination, not only a source of light but also a metaphor for truth, knowledge, and divine wisdom. For this reason the sun is often used in art and mythology to represent God, the supreme being of light, and the angelic realm; the angels' halos, for instance, are a sort of sun, a circular disk or ring that emits rays of light symbolizing spiritual enlightenment. When we have gray days, when sadness seems to rain down upon us, it helps to remember that the sun is always there, even when it is obscured by clouds. When the sun seems to be setting on an aspect of our lives, the angels remind us that it will inevitably rise in the morning, illuminating a new path. This is the natural cycle, and when we move with it instead of trying to fight it, our way will always be lit, even though we may not always know where we are going.

Where is the sun in your life right now? Is it rising, just beginning to shed light on a problem or mystery? Is it shining with the force of the noonday rays, giving you creative energy and enthusiasm? Is it setting, abandoning you to the darkness of the unknown? If you are experiencing frustration and a lack of clarity in any area of your life, remember that the sun never runs out of energy, and illumination is always on the horizon, as long as you are patient and expectant.

An Angelic Reflection: **Remaining aware of the natural cycle of things, I am not afraid of the darkness, for I know that it is a prelude to the dawn.**

THE ETERNAL FLAME

An Angel Reminder: "There is a slumbering fire in nature which never goes out, and which no cold can chill."
Henry David Thoreau, "A Winter Walk"

The fire that Thoreau refers to in the above quote resides in the human heart, the wellspring of "virtue," to use one of Thoreau's favorite words. It is the goodness that creates summer even in the midst of winter. This fire is like an eternal flame, for it is the breath of the spirit, the creative force that keeps all things alive. Thoreau had the ability to see nature not as an adversary but as a constant friend; to him, winter was merely summer under a "thicker covering," and the sun was a perennial source of light and life on the coldest as well as the warmest days. The angels remind us that like the sun, our inner flame—our spirit—is always there to warm us, even in times of greatest emptiness and sorrow. When we connect with the gifts of the spirit—creativity, passion, imagination— we are capable of melting the deepest snowbank of despair and uncovering the resilient life that is not dead but merely lying in wait for spring.

How deeply are you in contact with your spirit? How effectively are you using the gifts of the spirit in your life? If something is repressing or killing your spirit, can you identify it? Remember that the angels are always on hand to rekindle a slumbering inner fire and help it to burst into the blazing flame that will burn away sadness and fear and radiate energy, passion, and creative action.

An Angelic Reflection: I warm myself by the radiant energy of my eternal inner flame.

PSYCHIC REFUSE

An Angel Reminder: "The currents of the Universal Being circulate through me; I am part and parcel of God."
Ralph Waldo Emerson

We are a part of the collective psyche, whether or not we are conscious of what we are contributing to it. Perhaps it's time to look at what we're adding to the collective. Many of us are finding ways to heal society, but some of us are searching for more conspiracy theories, criminals to punish, and fear-born causes to pull us down. Such spiritual refuse will contribute stress and fear to life instead of easing the burden for all. Just because we have found our spiritual path doesn't mean all our energy is going into making the world a better place. Perhaps we're still playing the judgment game, contributing psychic refuse to the spiritual landfill instead of recycling our judgmental attitudes with the help of the angels.

Even if we stay isolated all day, we are affecting the collective psyche. Take today and observe what you are giving to the collective. What psychic refuse are you sending out to the big spiritual dump? Can it be recycled? Is it trash that someone else may find treasures in? Our first step is awareness. Start to create an awareness of your own behavior, thoughts, and stirrings. Bring in the angels for the higher view, and you will know what to do.

An Angelic Reflection: I am part and parcel of God.

RISKY BUSINESS

An Angel Reminder: **'Tis better to have risked
and lost than never risked at all.**

When we hear the phrase "risky business," our first impulse is usually to run in the other direction. The warning that "stocks are a risky business," for instance, has deterred many people who prefer to remain safe from playing the market. But it hasn't prevented others from becoming millionaires. So what are the consequences of avoiding risks? Well, we may not lose anything in the way of money or illusions of security, but we sure haven't gained anything either, in the way of dreams coming true. The truth of the matter is that those who are willing to risk—not unwisely but boldly—are those who generally end up living life to the fullest. The angels know that by its very nature, life is a continual risk, because it never remains the same. Life is change, and risk is adaptation to change. Of course, risk is not synonymous with taking foolish chances. On the other hand, other than daredevil racing or putting all your money into that swamp in the Everglades, who's to say what's foolish? Changing careers, running off with a penniless poet, screwing up the courage to tell someone you love them—all sorts of risks might look unwise but may be just what the doctor ordered. When we have the courage to follow our hearts, we have never failed, no matter what the outcome.

Are there risks you are afraid to take? Risks you wish you had? If you're unsure about taking a risk, stop for a moment, ask the angels what to do, and listen to your heart, intuition, or inner voice. Know that if you decide to take this risk, the angels will be on hand to guide you, no matter what the result.

An Angelic Reflection: **I know that to risk is to live.**

IN THE NAME OF JESUS

An Angel Reminder: "Holy and awesome is His name."
Psalm 111:9

Most Christians are taught to end their prayers by saying "in the name of Jesus, Amen." For a Christian, the name of Jesus is the most sacred word connecting people with God. Jesus represented Christ consciousness, the highest state of light available. No matter what your religious tradition, if you read the words of Jesus in the New Testament gospels, you will find it difficult to argue with any of his teachings. Check out the gospels if you need some tried-and-true inspiration.

If life suddenly becomes frightening and you need to find inner balance with lightening speed, say in your mind and heart, "in the name of Christ Jesus," and then see what happens. Regardless of what religion you were born into, the highest light is called forth when you ask for something in the name of Christ Jesus. Repeat it until you feel balance being restored. Remember Jesus is for each of us.

An Angelic Reflection: I know nothing can alter my faith in the Christ.

HOLIDAY BLUES

**An Angel Reminder: It is in giving the gift of
ourselves that we receive the gift of our divine self.**

Holidays are supposed to be "holy" days, during which we rejoice in God's love for us, take time to reflect upon our lives, and celebrate the great gift of being alive. Yet who else but humans could make the holidays into nightmares of stress and chaos? Our holy days have been turned into excuses for greed and unrestrained materialism, which in turn lead to tension, dissatisfaction, and inner hollowness. We honor God by fighting over who got the better gifts and who gave the cheapest ones, by overeating, and by running ourselves ragged. And that's if we're lucky enough to have a family to share the holidays with. Those who don't often find the holidays unbearable reminders of their loneliness. The angels ask us to return to the real meaning of the holidays—to use them as times of thanksgiving and opportunities to extend angelic love and service to others. Then the holidays become not trials to endure but blessed moments of contact with our divine selves.

Take a moment to reflect upon what the holidays mean to you. If they mean extra stress or depression for you, the angels have some antidotes. Do volunteer work during this time— serve up a holiday dinner at your local mission, visit the sick and lonely, collect toys for underprivileged kids. Or, have yourself a merry little Christmas handing out gifts of true love—answering the special personal needs of friends or family in ways that might be unexpected and truly appreciated.

An Angelic Reflection: I welcome the holidays as a chance to expand and extend my spiritual consciousness.

ON THE TREADMILL

An Angel Reminder: It's better to be on the
track than on the treadmill.

Treadmills are useful items. They tell us what kind of shape our heart's in. They're great for exercise. But there's one thing for certain; we weren't meant to be on them twenty-four hours a day, seven days a week. Treadmills were designed to be health aids, not health threats. Yet too many of us find ourselves on a daily treadmill that we can't seem to dismount and that's taking us nowhere fast. Job duties pile up, along with bills, debts, and worries. We work harder and harder just to stay in place. As a result, we become worn out and susceptible to all manner of distress. We might get sick more often. Our relationships tend to suffer. Our mental and spiritual health takes a nosedive. Nobody in their right mind would go to the gym, get on the treadmill, and never get off. The result would surely be cardiac arrest. Similarly, when our lives become a treadmill, that's when we're most likely to suffer a heart attack or some other serious trauma that will force us to come to a halt.

If you're on the treadmill, it's time to get off and get yourself a personalized angel trainer instead, who can design the proper spiritual fitness plan that's just for you. This could involve shifting priorities, making more time for the things that are really important, enlisting people's help in sorting out your difficulties or sharing your duties, giving up some work in order to rest and regroup. You might have to make big decisions, like changing careers, moving, extricating yourself from an unhealthy relationship, declaring bankruptcy. Whatever your situation, know that there is an answer and that you can get off the treadmill if you really want to.

An Angelic Reflection: I will take the time to reduce the stress in my life.

THE END OF THE SPIRITUAL SEARCH

An Angel Reminder: "But if the self collapses, if the walls come down, is it fear that remains, or is it freedom?"

Steven Harrison

If we are searching for the spiritual, what happens at the end of the search? What may very well happen is that we will find nothing, just emptiness, at the end of our search, and this will feel more right than anything. We will be emptied of our soap opera stories, which have been following us. We will be freed of our gurus, our methods, our meditations, our practices, our belief systems, and we will be free of knowing. If we ever get to the end of our spiritual hunting, we will have suffered the collapse of the self we identified with, we will have met the demons in the dark night of the soul, and we will see that all our traveling to create a deep meaningful experience will be meaningless. So why would we want to come to this point? The reason is true freedom and true angelhood.

To become like the angels is to become a healing force wherever we go. The possibility lies in each of us; the path is clearer than we might think. When you reach the state beyond the self, you don't need to identify with good and bad anymore, there is nothing left but the expression of freedom.

An Angelic Reflection: I am not afraid to go beyond my self and dance to the expression of freedom.

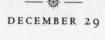

DECEMBER 29

BARREN

An Angel Reminder: **A life without the angelic spirit is sad and barren.**

What comes to mind when you think of a broken spirit, lost soul, dark heart, comfortless body? All these images call up feelings of sadness and hopelessness. If we have experienced any of these, we know that at such times life seems barren, void of beauty and divinity. A lost soul is sad, while a found and well-founded soul is a treasure chest of riches. What could be worse than a dark heart, with its urge for revenge? A comfortless, restless body is like an empty house that used to be a home, with a once-happy family residing within its walls. The angels have the antidotes for each of our ills. They want to help us turn every barren place inside us into a bountiful, loving refuge.

If you are feeling barren and cheerless, call in the angels quick, and ask them to help restore your bounty. Your body can be in partnership with your spirit, soul, mind, and heart. The angels guide us into full partnership with the bountiful selves we are.

An Angelic Reflection: **My soul and spirit are filled with angelic light.**

HITTING THE WALL

An Angel Reminder: Hitting the wall hurts!

Have you ever hit the wall? If so, you probably broke your hand. Walls are pretty formidable adversaries, and when we hit them we should be prepared for the consequences. The expression "hitting the wall" means that we've come to the end of our rope. Nothing's working out, our juices have run dry, we've given all we've got, and we just can't go a step further. Unless we're Casper the Friendly Ghost, we can't pass through walls, so our only alternatives are to cut a door through them or stand there and stay blocked. If we're in a frustrating situation and we're headed toward the wall, the most sensible solution is to screech to a stop before we hit it and reflect on how we got here. If we're working too hard, how can we pull back? If we're dealing with impossible people, how can we get them out of our lives, or at least not let them push our buttons? If we're deadlocked on a project, what alternatives can we explore that will give us a fresh start? If we're in a relationship that isn't working out, what issues do we need to face that we've been avoiding? The angels remind us that there's usually a reason we've allowed ourselves to get to such an extreme point as hitting the wall. They also invite us to ask their help in regrouping, refocusing, and moving ahead.

Have you hit the wall lately? If so, what were the factors involved that led to the impasse? Try to envision your difficulty as a wall with a graffiti message scribbled across it. What does the message say? Write it down, and think about how it relates to the problem. Now, imagine yourself gaining advantage over the wall. Can you break it down? With what? Can you climb it? Fly over it? Visualize yourself successfully getting passage over or through the wall of your problem.

An Angelic Reflection: I confront difficulties before they become walls.

WHERE TO FIND ANGELS

An Angel Reminder: **Angelic timelessness can be ours**
if we are willing to sit with ourselves awhile.

You don't have to go anywhere to find the angels; they are always in the still space that surrounds you, in the wondrous void that we call nothingness. Going on a quest to find angels is like going on a journey to find happiness; you can go all over the world looking, and then you realize it was inside you all along. The angels respond to us when we respond to life with angelic consciousness. When we are in angelic consciousness, we remember to say thank you, we stop to think about how other people are affected by our actions and words, and we are honest about our pain, not trying to hide it.

Next time you are looking for the angels, feeling that they are far away, take some time to just sit. Sit alone with the intention of some new information or image coming to you that will link you back up with the timeless consciousness of the angels. All you need to do is sit and let go of the need to define the outcome.

An Angelic Reflection: **I know where the angels are.**

INDEX OF TITLES

IF YOU ENJOYED *Angel Courage,*

DON'T MISS

Terry Lynn Taylor and Mary Beth Crain's

Angel Wisdom

365 Meditations and Insights from the Heavens

Daily reflections, reminders, and exercises bring the grace,
serenity, and joy of the angels down to earth and easy to reach.

— ✦ —

Published by

📖 HarperSanFrancisco

Available at your local bookstore.